Tales out of School

The early misdeeds of the famous

Tales out of School

The early misdeeds of the famous

Collectors' Books Limited
Kemble
Gloucestershire

ISBN 0 946604 00 2

© Copyright: Collectors' Books Limited 1983.

Published to advance the work of

Help the aged

The stories in this book
were generously donated
by their famous contributors
to support the work of
Help the Aged to whom all
royalties will be given.

This book was published by
Collectors' Books Limited, Bradley Lodge,
Kemble, Cirencester, Gloucestershire.
Illustrations by Brian Blake, design
and artwork by Admark Advertising Cirencester.
Printed by Christian Brann Limited.

First published 1983.

Introduction

"Tales Out of School", compiled by Mary Rose and Christian Brann with Clare Scarlett is designed to assist the work of Help the Aged. In 1961 a group of businessmen who were seeking to carry out the Christian injunctions to feed the hungry, clothe the naked and heal the sick felt compelled to turn their attention to what they believed to be a major but largely ignored problem facing the world – the huge number of old people, many of whom were in desperate need. So, Help the Aged was born.

Following a Service in Westminster Abbey in 1974 Help the Aged became a truly international organisation, including training people in some Third World countries to raise funds for their own needy elderly.

Throughout the years Help the Aged has strived to provide a more abundant life for old people. In the Third World is has provided food, shelter, clothing, medical supplies and self-help schemes for those who were destitute. In the U.K. it has been a stimulating and creative centre for the study and practice of matters which affect the welfare of old people. In housing, medicine, education, pensions and many other fields it has made particular contributions. It has been a powerful advocate in getting rid of an attitude of mind which has existed for a very long time and which is nowadays known as "ageism" – the assumption that old people are inferior citizens fit only for geriatric homes and hospitals.

In the future, Help the Aged is determined to continue its efforts to ensure that old people remain in the main body of society, are treated as citizens with rights and capabilities of their own, and recognised for the unique contributions they have to offer.

"Tales out of School" will not only provide the reader with many hours of enjoyment but will give him the pleasure of knowing that he is, at the same time, assisting a very worthwhile cause.

Hugh Faulkner OBE, Help the Aged

*The stories in this book are published after
the names of their distinguished contributors
in alphabetic order.*

R. B. Adams.
Chief Executive, P & O Steam Navigation Company, 1981–1983.

At the age of five I was attending a Dame's School at Richmond where we lived. One of the other pupils, a young lady who was incidentally a doctor's daughter, celebrated her birthday with a tea party to which the whole school was invited. It was noted at the time that I was the only guest who greeted our hostess with a staid handshake instead of a kiss, whether through shyness or a sense of foreboding I cannot remember. Next day she came out with a splendid rash of measles spots and shortly afterwards everyone in the school but myself went down with measles. The school closed and I was dispatched to spend a heavenly June in the country staying with an aunt. I am not sure what the moral is!

Sir Campbell Adamson.
Former Director-General, Confederation of British Industry.
Chairman, Abbey National Building Society.

My sister and I, after the departure of a much loved Governess, found her replacement so strict as to be unbearable and we planned a series of sharp lessons on an increasing scale to force her resignation. We rather hoped that murder would prove unnecessary!

Our first effort was to be comparatively mild. When she came into the nursery I was to jump on her from behind the door while my sister would be inside a wardrobe and was to jump out of it to follow up the original shock.

The moment arrived, but didn't quite go as planned. I jumped from my position behind the door, but my sister (inside the wardrobe) failed to open its door and the whole wardrobe came crashing down. It struck the unfortunate Governess on the head necessitating removal to hospital and a few stitches. Her resignation reached my parents next day.

8

Peter Adamson.
T.V. Actor.

Our teacher, Miss Nairn, who must have been at least a hundred and fifty, kept a large orange cat on her wall with strict instructions that, if any of us were naughty, the great evil monster would inform her and we in turn would be severely punished. It was only a cardboard cutout but at the age of five, we believed her and were consequently terrified of it. Our Friday afternoon pursuit was mainly devoted to modelling in Plasticine and it occurred to me one day that I might curry favour with Miss Nairn (and the monster) if I were to make a model of it so I duly rolled out an enormous portion of that sickly-smelling stuff and proceeded to carve out what I thought was a lifelike image of the cat. After a few sorry attempts, it became obvious that sculpting was not going to be my forté and I was rather hurt at the reaction of my fellow boys and girls. Typical of my colouring, I became very angry and tearful, so out of red-headed perversity I consumed the entire model, tail and all and then sat there in stoic defiance until Miss Nairn returned. Now, whether Miss Nairn was looking through the window or not, I have no way of knowing, but on her return she asked Marmalade (the cat monster) if we had all been good. She then peered at me over her pince-nez.

I have died a few times since, but at that moment there developed in me a fear that would stay with me until my late teens.

Miss Nairn, with a delightful smile on her face (Margot Bryant – Minnie Caldwell – always reminded me of Miss Nairn), advanced on me, clasped her hands together in front of her and said sweetly, "Where is it?" Before I could answer, my fellow criminals piped up shrieking "He's eaten it, he's eaten it."

I hated my friends and have been suspicious of most people ever since.

At the age of seven, when I left infant school to go into the "big boys" I wondered if Miss Nairn had remembered the incident. In my childish way, I asked her. It was an innocent attempt at an apology. She secretly drew me to one side and said, "I don't know whatever happened to your model that day, but Marmalade knows, and perhaps he'll tell me."

You weren't allowed to hug people in those days but that is just what I should like to have done.

Sir Godfrey Agnew, K.C.V.O., C.B.
Clerk of the Privy Council, 1953–1974 and Vice Chairman of the Sun Life Assurance Society.

I was six and we were living in Kenya. I must have overheard my father and mother discussing a friend who was coming to lunch. When the day came, half way through the meal, my mother rebuked me for staring at the friend, at which I defended myself by saying "but Mummy, he doesn't drink like a fish at all".

John Alderson, C.B.E., Q.P.M.
Chief Constable of Devon & Cornwall, 1973–1983.

Justice operates in many differing ways. I well remember how it caught up with me. When I was around the age of ten and on a country walk with equally mischievous companions, we came across a clutch of eggs in what are now known as 'free range' conditions, close to a farm. Unable to resist the temptation which old Satan had placed in our way, we shared them between us, and put them into our pockets. I was wearing my brand new Sunday-best blazer.

The ensuing chase by the farmer put our ill-gotten gains at risk and breathless after our escape (we were fleet of foot) I gingerly put my hands into my pockets only to find something resembling old scrambled eggs. The damage to my best blazer became obvious as the liquid oozed through the cloth.

Although I escaped the retribution of either the farmer or the majesty of the law, I fell to the scourging of the stick which my father maintained for such wild excesses. Justice was done.

Sir Geoffrey Aldington, K.B.E., C.M.G.
H.M. Ambassador to Luxembourg, 1961–1966.

I was staying in the country with an uncle and aunt, at the end of whose garden was a stream with an unfortunate tendency to flood in any prolonged spell of wet weather. To deal with this, my uncle, at some considerable expense, had had a drain installed, and this ended in an iron grating set in the paved area outside the house.

During my stay, the flood water rose with a vengeance and eventually reached a depth of a foot or more over the paved area. I watched my uncle (a delightful but choleric man, whose liver had been permanently impaired as a result of service in the Indian Army) descend the steps from the house, uttering imprecations against the plumbers responsible for the obviously ineffective drain, and wade into the flood with the purpose of pulling up the iron grating – now invisible beneath the muddy waters – and so improving the drainage. He groped about and finally found it, grasped its bars with both hands and heaved! Again and again he heaved without success; and I perceived, as he had not, that he was endeavouring to lift up a grating on which he was himself standing. At the age of ten this appeared to me to be extremely amusing and I burst into fits of happy laughter. My uncle, now purple in the face from his exertions and my unseemly mirth, demanded to know what the devil I was laughing at: I was by now almost incapable of speech, but eventually managed to get out "You're – ho, ho, ho, – s-s-standing on it!"

It took him days to forgive me: at the time I felt that his sense of humour was decidedly deficient, but I now realise what an appalling little brat I must have seemed to him.

The Marchioness of Anglesey, C.B.E.
Chairman, National Federation of Women's Institutes, 1966–1969 and of the Welsh Arts Council, 1975–1981.

Miss Morison was a splendid but formidable headmistress. She dominated school prayers from the high platform of the Assembly Hall. I was seven; the girl in the row behind had early but rather minor religious doubts. We decided *not* to bow the knee in the Creed; we giggled from nerves at our conspicuous daring. We were reported. I was told any future failure to conform and I, and I alone, would kneel on that platform beside Miss Morison before 300 senior girls throughout our daily prayers. I became an instant "trimmer".

The Marquess of Anglesey, D.L., F.S.A., F.R.Hist.S., Hon.F.R.I.B.A. F.R.S.L.
Military historian and conservationist.

In the nursery of our ancestral home, Plas Newydd, at the age of six, I threw a full-sized hammer at my nurse's head. It only just missed both her and a window. Out of that window at that moment I saw, passing along the Menai Strait, a steamer carrying slates from the great Caernarvonshire quarries. I shall never forget that sight, nor the awful sense of guilt for ever after associated with it.

I was punished for many succeeding weeks by being laid on the floor at tea time, the nursery maid's knee on my chest while I was force-fed with the congealed remains of the sago pudding which I consistently refused at lunch time. This torture entailed the squeezing of my nose so as to open my mouth. I've never thrown a hammer at anyone since.

Dom Raphael Appleby.
Headmaster, Downside School, 1975–1980, Novice master, Downside Abbey.

Sunday afternoons at boarding school very many years ago were not the most exciting periods of the week: for those of us who generally played games they were particularly uneventful. On one such Sunday while walking rather aimlessly up a nearby road a few of us came across an unusual object: a large beer barrel, slightly leaking, lying in the side of the road. It must have fallen from a lorry. A quick look both ways, and then a sweaty struggle to drag and push the barrel through the hedge and into an overgrown little copse. Then what to do? We remembered that one of our friends lived and worked in an hotel – he would know how to tap the cask and make the beer available. And so he did. Thus the next few Sundays became days to look forward to and whether it rained or shone there were we to be found in our little club in the copse. As the weeks went by, more and more people got to hear about the find and the numbers lining up to sample the barrel increased, until on the last day there must have been fifty hopefuls grasping tooth mugs, anxious at least to taste the precious nectar. Most were disappointed and so were we when the normal Sunday routine of aimless walks had to be resumed – but at least there was always the hope that, well, who knows, it happened once, could it not happen again? Authority never found out.

Sir John Arbuthnot, Bart., M.B.E., T.D.
M.P. for Dover, 1950–1964 and a Church Commissioner, 1962–77.

One of our Classics Masters had spent many years in China on which he was an expert. We boys knew that if we could once get him going on China any thought of Latin Construe could be forgotten. On this particular occasion we had all collected quantities of orange-peel which we had rolled up in the map of China above his desk. We then encouraged him to dilate upon his Eastern travels. Once he had been hooked, novels came out from under our desks, knowing that he was good for the rest of the hour, when in walked Dr Alington, the Headmaster, and sat down under the fateful map. We back-pedalled like mad to try to get Latin Construe re-instated, but to no avail. The division-master felt that he was on safer ground with China than he was with Latin Construe. Down came the map and down came the orange-peel all over the Headmaster. We finished up with having to write a Georgic apiece, and the hapless division-master was heard of no more.

John Arlott.
Writer and broadcaster.

Looking back, Miss Tregarthen must have been quite good-looking – seen by adult standards. She was a red-head from Cornwall, probably in her early twenties. It is difficult to believe that she really liked little boys, certainly she did not like this particular six-year-old, who reciprocated by finding her "ratty".

One summer morning *the men* who were cutting the grass outside the house found a grass snake and, with the 'generosity' of countrymen, gave it to a delighted small boy. It went to school in his pocket and in the first lesson – taken by Miss Tregarthen – he decided to show it to Ted Jones who sat next to him. As they joined in mutual admiration of the beautiful beast, Miss Tregarthen interrupted them. "What have you got there, Arlott, what are you playing with?" The grass snake was hurriedly pushed back into the trousers pocket. "Give it to me" she said. "Give it to me, give it to me at once; give me what you were playing with or I will send you to the headmaster to be caned – at once now".

What else was there to do but obey? No sooner did she have the poor, inoffensive grass snake in her hand than she screamed, threw it in the air and said "Go out to the headmaster at once – go out to the headmaster and tell him you are to be caned for disgusting behaviour."

That was the first recognition of the injustice of adults. Caned for obeying the instruction of a person in authority. The lesson sank deep. Mischief? Or the malice of authority?

Major-General Geoffrey Armitage, C.B.E.
Director, Royal Armoured Corps, 1968–1970.

As a child one often got into trouble quite unwittingly. It was at home in the south of Ireland one summer holidays over fifty years ago when I was about eight years old that I went fishing for perch in one of the loughs near the house. My companion and instructor was a young farm hand, who was as keen as I was.

Every time he got a fish on his line, he shouted "Cum op, ye bogger!" and slipped the net under his capture. A few days later, my grandmother was presiding over a bridge party in the drawing room. Three tables of elegantly attired ladies were absorbed in their games, as I entered.

"Geoffrey, please do something about the wasps on the window," called Granny as she played a card. Just my form, and I advanced with enthusiasm to exterminate the creatures. "Cum op, ye bogger!" I commented as I scored my first and only success.

Consternation! Up rose my elderly relative. "Go to your room, at once!" she called in acid tones, while those around her continued to shake their heads in disapproval. I slunk out, tail figuratively between my legs, none the wiser. Not even the young farm hand could enlighten me next day.

I was reminded recently of this occasion by my three-year-old granddaughter Harriet, who emerged from her first plunge in somebody's private swimming pool. "Bloody cold, isn't it!" She commented. Her father was blamed.

Sir Thomas Armstrong, M.A., D.Mus., F.R.C.M., Hon.F.R.C.O., Hon.R.A.M.
Principal, Royal Academy of Music, 1955–68 and Organist of Christ Church, Oxford, 1933–55.

Early in the first war, because so many young men had already joined up, I found myself, whilst still a schoolboy, appointed assistant to the famous Dr Haydn Keeton, organist of Peterborough Cathedral, where, as Head Verger at that time, there was a morose and sardonic character called Harry Plowman, who regarded all musicians as his natural enemies and myself as a particularly conceited and tiresome upstart.

There came a Sunday morning when, in the absence of Dr Keeton, I was left with the responsibility of playing Matins and was feeling rather important. Plowman didn't fail to notice the fact, and as I came down from the organ-loft after a rather elaborate voluntary, he met me with:

"There was a gentleman in the congregation this morning who was very much interested in your playing. He said he was an organist himself and a friend of Dr Keeton's".

I took the bait. "Did he make any comment?" I enquired.

"Well, no" was the answer, "he just asked, was that Dr Keeton playing?"

"So you had to tell him it wasn't", I said: and then I was stupid enough to persist – "and did he add anything further?"

"Not really", Plowman concluded, "he just said: 'My God! I should hope not.'"

John Arnatt.
Actor.

This is really a rather sad story about a misdeed that never was. I must have been about nine or so at the time and the family were on holiday in Brittany. Staying at the hotel was a little girl – perhaps a year or two older; I can see her now – very dark, very pretty, half French.

We used to play together on the beach and I often thought it would be jolly nice to kiss her – but I never got around to it, because I thought she might think it was silly. Then, one day, she said to me: "Would you like me to come and sleep in your room tonight?"

Now, I had only just won a battle to get a room to myself, instead of having to share with my elder sister or my brother, and whilst I didn't like to refuse, I remember saying to my mother what an extraordinary little girl she must be, wanting to share a room, when she was lucky enough to have a perfectly good room to herself – particularly as my room only had one bed. I forget what my mother said – she probably agreed.

Anyway, about four o'clock the next morning, the little girl came into my room and got into bed. Fortunately it was quite a large bed, so there was plenty of room, so long as I kept right over to my side. It did occur to me that this might be a good opportunity to try to kiss her – but I didn't because I still thought she might think it was silly: and at about seven o'clock she got out and went back to her own room.

And it wasn't until about ten years later that I realised that there are some opportunities in life which, if not grasped at the time, never come again.

The Very Reverend John Arnold.
Dean of Rochester.

I had just been appointed Secretary of one
of the Boards of the General Synod, and was
attending the rather pretentiously named
'Church Leaders' Conference' organised by the
British Council of Churches in Birmingham.
My wife fell ill and I had
to return home suddenly.
In my haste I forgot to pack
my pyjamas, which were
folded up out of sight under
the pillow. They were
retrieved by the conference
centre staff and handed to one
of the B.C.C. secretaries, who took them back to London.

Once settled in my office, I sent her a quick business-like note which
went, if I remember correctly: "Dear Elizabeth, Please may I have my
pyjamas back as soon as possible? Yours ever, John".

At the time I did not know that additional copies were made of all
correspondence and placed in a file at the end of the week for circulation
throughout the department. My new colleagues thought that this was an
auspicious start to my career as an ecclesiastical bureaucrat.

The Earl Attlee.
Public Relations Consultant; Author.

Some time before the war, we were having Sunday lunch at Heywood,
our home in Stanmore. I was a normal, hungry boy and the pudding was
one of my favourites. I watched my mother serving up a helping, which I
thought was for my maternal grandmother who had come to lunch.

"All that for Grandma?" I asked my mother.

"No dear, for you." My mother replied.

"What a little bit!" I am alleged to have replied. Which only goes to
show that, at least in the eyes of a greedy child, sauce for the goose is
certainly not sauce for the gander!

Gillian Avery.
Novelist and Historian of children's books.

I set down the most dreadful event of my childhood with the idea of illustrating the timidity of my generation and the ferocious discipline of girls' schools in the 1930's. I was educated, if you can call it that, from seven to seventeen in a private school in the Home Counties. At this time anybody with a little capital could buy a house, install a few desks, put up a brass plate, and parents who believed passionately in the middle class caste system would come flocking to the gate. Orwell has described the sort of place in *A Clergyman's Daughter.* Mine was rather grander. It had begun just like this, but within seven or eight years it had moved, via various humbler premises, to a splendid Victorian-Palladian mansion, set in beautiful grounds with a formal garden, spreading lawns, woodlands and rhododendron glades.

This was the greatest point in its favour. There was little to be said for it otherwise. We were monotonously reminded of our privileged position in life, our superiority to the wretched products of grammar schools, and were crammed with enough facts to get through what was then known as School Certificate. English literature was reduced to a parrot knowledge of figures of speech and the anachronisms in Shakespeare, science to writing down experiments we could not perform because there were no laboratories. And the emphasis on the minutiae of school rules kept us in a perpetual state of anxiety. There was no way that a pupil, however well-intentioned, could be certain of evading the wrath of authority. You might not know that the edict had gone forth that morning that hats should be worn in the garden. Or galoshes. Or not galoshes. You might be late for a lesson because the games mistress hadn't given you enough time to race from the netball field, tear off your royal blue tunic and scramble into the immensely elaborate day uniform (20 girls struggling with blouses and ties, the royal blue overalls with their infinity of buttons and fasteners, in a little cell where the knives, or the boots, had been cleaned in palmier days). And then present yourself in good order in your classroom for the next lesson.

We feared the headmistress with her sharp tongue and hot temper. But mercifully she didn't teach very much after the junior forms when she had beaten our hands with the sharp edge of a ruler if we didn't form our pothooks satisfactorily in our daily handwriting lesson. Most of all we feared the mistress who taught us both geography and scripture. (To this day I wake on Wednesday mornings with a profound feeling of thankfulness that now it doesn't mean double geography.) She was lame, which perhaps was responsible for her savage and unpredictable temper. Some of the higher-minded and more earnest girls said so (and we were in general a high-minded and earnest lot), and held that it was a privilege to be in contact with her – an early preparation for purgatory was what they said in effect, though they wouldn't ever have heard of purgatory. The rest of us were daunted by this moralizing, and so we did not say as much about our detestation of her as we might have done.

At the time of which I am writing the middle school had its classrooms over the old coach-houses. They had probably been where the coachman and his family lived. Our room was approached by a passage. We would listen apprehensively to the slow footsteps up the stairs, and then the thump, thump, thump (an extra thump for her stick) as she limped down that passage. The monitor would spring to the door, the rest of us would rise to our feet and try by the correctness of our posture to avert some of the wrath that would be slung at our heads together with our corrected, inevitably inadequate, homework. No doubt everybody, as I did, tried to tell from those doom-laden footsteps just what sort of a mood she would be in. Not that she would be amiable, we knew better than to expect that; but would she be especially savage?

That day she was white with fury. She threw down the exercise books she had been carrying and we wondered whether there had been some extraordinary deficiency in the way we had done last week's homework. There had been that time, for instance, when Joan Campbell had cried so much over her map of China that she had rubbed a hole in the paper. But it was not anything to do with our work, it was about apples. Our minds were so conditioned to being dragged down the railway line of school that they were not agile. We were thrown off our balance, totally mystified. What could apples possibly have to do with our present state? All those who had eaten apples at break were asked to put up their hands. This let out the boarders, who were given glasses of milk at 11 o'clock. About ten hands went up. And the owners of the hands were one by one catechised; what did you do with your apple core?

It would be impossible to convey to a child of today the awe that the children of my generation felt for those in authority, whose behaviour, in reaction to ours, seemed always inexplicable, capricious, arbitrary. Or to convey the terror with which we waited for our turn to be cross-examined. Due to the chance position of my desk in the room, my turn was to be last. And I knew that I had not put my apple core tidily in the litter basket by the cloakroom door, but had tossed it lightheartedly into a rhododendron thicket. (Where of course it would never more be seen but would rot away among the dead leaves.) Even then I thought it the best place for an apple core, but it was unthinkable that I should say so. I was crying so much when my turn came that my answer must have been nearly inaudible. But she grasped the essence of it. "I suppose you're the sort of person who leaves sandwich papers blowing around whenever you picnic." That was all, but it kept me in tears for the rest of the lesson, because she had put me, in public, on a level with the common herd, the people from whom we were always being urged to distinguish ourselves, the people who did not know how to behave.

What was perhaps interesting was that none of us dreamed of lying, we were too frightened; she seemed to have God's all-seeing eye and was only asking us because she knew the answers. In fact she had tripped on an apple core in the courtyard on her way to our classroom, but none of us happened to be responsible so we never knew the reason for this interlude until later; it just seemed part of the mysterious way in which our mentors moved. But never again while I was at that school did I dare throw an apple core anywhere else but in the bin; I carried them around, soggy and smelling, in my blazer pocket. And when many years later I got a letter from a contemporary (one of those high-minded girls who had thought contact with this monstrous woman was character-building) asking for a contribution towards a retirement present, I got out my pen and my cheque book, and then remembered this particular humiliation and put them away again.

The Lord Baker, O.B.E., F.R.S., F.Eng.
For 25 years Professor of Mechanical Sciences, Head of Engineering Department, University of Cambridge. Designer of Morrison air-raid shelter 1940.

Nothing worth recording ever happened to me but my friends were a constant joy. I shared a study with F. Pollitt, a charming but pampered boy who came to school in 1915 equipped with every gadget, including a large fountain pen and an even larger penknife. He was put into the first form (Form Master 'Cabby' Marsh, whose score of 185-not-out stood as a record in the Varsity Match for about 75 years). The first form was housed in the new Modern School, Marsh's pride and joy. During the first day, Marsh in his perambulations came to Pollitt's corner.

"What's this?" said he, pointing to a crescent of ink blots on the beautiful green wall.

"Oh" said Pollitt "it must be my new pen, it sticks", giving it a flick which produced a new crop of blots on the wall.

"You're a bit of a fool, aren't you" said 'Cabby', "that will cost you five shillings".

Next day when Marsh reached Pollitt's desk, it was to find the virgin oak top inscribed with the letters 'F.P', three inches high and a quarter of an inch deep.

"I knew you were a fool" said 'Cabby' "I didn't realise you were a *damned* fool. That will cost you ten shillings".

Another 13-year-old friend, F. L. Armstrong, sat next to Pollitt. One day, Marsh said "Armstrong, are you reading a book under the desk? Bring it here".

This Armstrong did – it was the Book of Form. Surprising for 'Cabby', but it would not have been, could he have foreseen that 'F.L.' was to become 'Sammy' Armstrong, the famous Newmarket trainer who died early in 1983.

Carroll Baker.
Film star ('Baby Doll', 1957) and writer.

When I was six years old a Creature came to live with us! I absolutely hated that Creature, so I refused to give it a name.

I gave everybody else names, even myself. I called myself Shirley.

I knew, of course, that my real name was Carroll. But in my inner world, I was Shirley Temple; daughter of Virginia (who was Dorothy Lamour), and William Baker (who was Spencer Tracy).

My Daddy was a travelling salesman and he had a very good sales record. I think this was because he resembled – you know who. He must have been irresistible to his customers!

I wonder if Mother ever wished for one of those washing machines that my father sold. I can't remember her ever asking for one, or complaining about scrubbing our laundry over a washboard in the kitchen sink. Washing clothes demanded a great deal of energy – Mother put her back into it – but she was young and strong. I wonder if she ever minded?

Doing the laundry meant that she was in one place for an hour or so, and I never missed an opportunity to present a movie story for us to act out. I was either a sweet little girl struggling against a cruel fate, or an extremely wealthy child who made people happy by giving them my money. Mother accepted any part I assigned her. She would play the Fairy Godmother or the Wicked Witch with equal conviction. If I suddenly decided to turn our play into a musical, Mother made the transition smoothly and without hesitation.

Our hair was very important to us. Mother had dark naturally curly hair that reached her waist. She brushed it faithfully two hundred strokes a night, no matter how tired she felt.

Mother set my straight blond hair in rags, and made me twenty-five or so long corkscrew curls by brushing them around a broom handle. Mother would spend half an hour every morning making my curls, and as soon as I entered school, the Nuns would pin my hair back. The Nuns said that it was vain to have curls and that vanity was a sin, but Mother didn't care. She was beautiful and she wanted me to be beautiful, too.

It wasn't just our hair, Mother and I did everything together. You see, my father was away a lot because of his work. Together we did the cooking, the grocery shopping, and the housework. We took the bus together to and from my school and together we did my homework.

Togetherness was wonderful. Then it changed and I didn't like it one little bit. It changed ever so slowly but I noticed. First Mother asked me to do my homework by myself, then she taught me to take the bus by myself, then we stopped shopping together because she had the groceries delivered. The final blow came the morning she announced that she was going to sleep in for another half an hour. She stopped making my curls!

My mother was sick. She never told me why. It was her stomach. Her stomach blew up like a balloon. She tired easily, and would hardly ever act out movie scenes with me, the way she used to do before her malaise. I never complained. I was also very careful not to ask either her or my father about the nature of my mother's illness. Anyway, I knew. I knew her death was close at hand. I never cried, not even when I was alone — and believe me, I felt like crying. You see, I knew that a good little girl never asked questions or upset her parents by crying. However, I did begin wetting the bed, but I couldn't help that because in my dreams I imagined that I was sitting on my potty.

I woke up one morning in a puddle, as usual, to find that my mother was gone. My father simply said that she was in the hospital, nothing else. Naturally, I didn't question him. I spent the next few days stealing flowers for her funeral.

I prayed that my mother wouldn't die. I prayed that she would get well and come home from the hospital so that I could hand her all those lovely flowers that I had stolen. My prayers were answered. Mother didn't die. All the same, what did happen was not what I would call a happy ending.

Imagine this movie scenario:

> That perfect couple, my parents, were blessed with the perfect child, me: a singing, dancing, blond curls bouncing, six-year-old; dimples ever present in my rosy cheeks, making the best of every hardship in life, taking every disappointment on the chin, never allowing my parents to feel inadequate; understanding, forgiving, wise beyond my years — in other words, I was Shirley Temple. What parents could ask for anything more? Shouldn't they have been quite content to have me and me alone?

My relief at seeing Mother alive and well instantly turned to shock at the sight of the Creature. It was wrapped in a blanket, and thoroughly enjoying itself in my mother's arms. I called the Creature "No Name." (She was certainly no Screen Goddess, and didn't deserve to be called after a Movie Star.) Imagine my horror when my parents called the No Name Creature "Boopie," and "Woopie," and "Poopie."

I didn't recognize my parents any longer. They had turned into blind, gurgling idiots. This creature shattered our lives, and nobody saw that but me. My poor Mother was always exhausted. She hardly ever brushed her beautiful hair or put on lipstick. No one played with me or took me to the movies, and when I did something cute – and believe me, I knew ever so many ways to be cute, and I was always inventing new ones in front of the bathroom mirror – well, all my efforts went totally unnoticed, as did my accomplishments.

No Name always needed something. I took to staying in my room after school, because if I dared show my face, I was asked to help, and I didn't want to go anywhere near Boopie, Woopie, Poopie. She smelled bad. She did disgusting things like throwing up, and making poo-poo in her panties. She cried all the time – Mother and Father had to keep getting out of bed in the middle of the night – and our house was a mess, too. The bathroom was full of dirty diapers, and a clothes line dripping with wet laundry; the kitchen was full of bottles, and sterilizers, and cans, and jars, and baby lotion, and baby soap, and baby oil, and a clothes line dripping with wet laundry. It was unbearable. My only hope was that No Name would not stay long. After all, any actress who had a baby in one film had the good sense not to show up with that baby in the next film.

This baby stayed on, and on, and on. I began to lose hope of ever being rid of her. I thought a lot about murder. She grew bigger, she sat up in her crib, she attempted to speak, she started to crawl, she grew bigger. Action had to be taken and soon. My parents were obviously not going to do anything. It was up to me, but I didn't know how to kill.

The baby was christened 'Virginia,' after my mother, but the name 'Boopie' stuck. Everybody called her Boopie – now do you wonder I was so upset? It was Boopie, Boopie, Boopie – "Isn't Boopie cute," "Did you see Boopie try to stand," "Did you hear Boopie say 'Da-Da'" – I had been doing all those things for years! Boopie, Boopie, Boopie – did you ever hear of such a silly name? *I began to think of her as Boopie* – things were getting out of hand.

Yep, once I thought of her as having a name, I was hooked on the baby, too. Oh, well, it was not in my Character, after all, to be wicked. Shirley Temple was never wicked. So I began to like Boopie – I even began to sort of love her – I guess it was only No Name that I had hated.

Tony Ball.
Chief Executive Henlys, former World Sales Chief BL Cars. The man who launched the Mini and the Metro.

The war was on when I was at school. Times were tough and I earned pocket money in various ways, including delivering newspapers, doing impersonations of Winston Churchill at the Baptist Chapel concerts, and even holding the cap out for a one armed busker at Bridgwater Fair.

One enterprising venture was with a friend, selling bundles of firewood around the back streets. I can see it now, two small boys and a wheelbarrow, offering firewood at fourpence a bundle. It was good value because firewood was sixpence a bundle in the shops. My father thought it was marvellous too. Until he found out I was actually making the firewood from his garage doors!

I left home at 16 to start as an Engineering Apprentice at the Austin Motor Company. I shall never forget my very first day. Pitchforked, straight from school, into the foundry at Longbridge. It was like walking into the devil's kitchen. Enormous furnaces, belching out smoke and fire. Everything was noise, heat and rivers of molten metal. Everywhere were sweating men, stripped to the waist, covered with black sand, muscles bulging, and eyes covered from the light. In the lunch break, after the Foreman had shown me around, I noticed a group of dirty faced apprentices huddled round, having a small wager. The stakes were five shillings each, on who would possibly dare go over to a beautiful looking girl, who was making sand moulds on the foundry assembly line – and ask her for a kiss. The 'pool' for the bet was standing at the princely sum of four pounds and I was only earning £1.0s.8d. a week at the time, rarely having seen four one pound notes actually together before. The temptation was too great. I put my five shillings down and said I'd do it – on the condition that I could just whisper something romantic in the girl's ear first. I went across to where this lovely girl was surrounded by six huge and threatening foundry men. Each one looking like Goliath and clearly reckoning they had first refusal on her. Summoning up all my courage I intruded into this formidable group and whispered very gently in her ear. She gave me the most wonderfully spine tingling kiss I have ever had in my entire life. I can still taste the black sand now. I won the bet. And to this day none of them ever knew what magical romantic words I had whispered to her. Which was just as well. Because what I actually said was "I'm only doing this for a four pound bet luv – And there's two quid in it for you!".

The Ven. A. J. Balmforth, M.A.
The Archdeacon of Bristol.

My father was the Vicar of a down-town parish. I was about seven years old. The Dean of the ancient Cathedral was coming to preach and have Lunch at the Vicarage afterwards. There was some panic. The fatted calf was killed – for in those days, Deans were Deans! The service ended and the Dean arrived for Lunch. He asked to 'wash his hands' for no one 'went to the lavatory'. It was an old Victorian lavatory with a bolt inside the door and an ordinary lock worked with a key from both inside

and outside. I had carefully transferred the key to the outside. When the
Dean was safely bolted inside, I crept up to the door and turned the key.
In the dining-room all was ready, the joint hot and the vegetables
steaming – but no Dean. Five minutes, ten minutes, a quarter of an hour
passed. Of course, the Dean was far too gentlemanly to bang the door. My
parents too embarrassed to shout. My father went upstairs to investigate
and noticed that key! Now it was his turn to creep up to the door and
turn the key. Moments later the Dean was in the dining-room. Not a
word was said, that is until after the Dean had left. I had some explaining
to do and needless to say, I found it painful to sit down for a week!

A. L. Barker.
Writer, winner of Atlantic Award in Literature, 1946,
Somerset Maugham Award, 1947.

At five years old, though fond of poking about on my own, I was an
unenterprising and fairly docile child. I was taken by my mother, who
had business of her own to transact, to a largish house of the kind which
nowadays has mostly been converted into flats. At that time, such houses
were occupied by the still existing middle classes, a single family to each,
and a couple of maid-servants in the attics.

This particular house, set back behind laurel hedges with a driveway of
sea-pebbles, was inhabited by a solitary old lady who employed a
resident nurse, a housemaid and cook to look after her. These three
women, and the old gardener, had things much their own way in their
separate spheres because the old lady was bedridden and never came
downstairs.

The house was beautifully kept, dusted and polished, vases of crimson
peonies everywhere, and dishes of peaches, stately chiming clocks, and
from the basement the smell of coffee and roast potatoes. Cook, Annie
and the nurse liked things nice.

My mother took me to the kitchen. It was a bitterly cold winter's day
and my bones fairly blossomed at sight of the great red-hot fire in the
kitchen range. The range itself was burnished bright, as were the copper
dish-covers hanging on the wall and the beautiful pink–tiled floor. I
thought that floor beautiful, I thought it was being kept for the feet of
the old lady, the mistress of the house, and that the flowers, the peaches,

the glittering copper and the splendid plates arranged on the dresser were all reserved for the moment, any moment, when she might wish to smell the flowers, eat the fruit and walk upon her floor. I was properly awed, because to have so much waiting, so much prepared in case – just in case – she felt like getting up, seemed to me the epitome of power. I sat meekly where I was told to sit, seen but not heard.

The moment came when Cook and Annie and my mother went out of the kitchen together and I was left alone. I jumped up, my plans already made, and ran to the kitchen range. In the middle of the oven door was a totally unexpected and marvellously irrelevant object. A brass tap. Like the ones in our sink at home. But what would, or could, come out of a tap in the middle of a fire? Smoke? Flames? A genie! I had to know, and I turned it on.

Water came out, hot water. At first I was disenchanted. The ordinary stuff hissed and steamed as it reached the steel fender. But when it reached the tiled floor it too became a thing of beauty. Rose-coloured and pure, it crept in an ever-growing tide across the kitchen.

I watched it flow under the rug, brim round the legs of the table and chairs until it reached my shoes. It was so gentle and loving. I felt my feet wet and as warm as when I had paddled on the sands at Margate on a summer's day.

The door opened, I looked up with all my pleasure in my face, and got a resounding box on the ears.

Keith Baxter.
Actor.

Since I was a very little boy I was determined to be an actor, and I have always been very pleased that nothing ever deflected me from that ambition. Of course all actors have bumpy times as well as good ones – but I cannot imagine any other life would have afforded me as much happiness. However, there was an incident in my teens that has made me squirm with embarrassment whenever I have thought of it – and for that reason I have thought about it as infrequently as possible. I have certainly never confessed my guilt until now, and perhaps confession will exorcise the demons that over the years have teased me.

When I was about fourteen I had a small part in a production of DEAR OCTOPUS with The Barry Players at St. Nicholas Church Hall in Barry, Glamorgan. I had a lot of time to hang around backstage during the performances (four) and I used to get very bored. One evening – during a particularly tense scene – I was idling behind the scenery waiting to make my entrance, and wishing that the actors onstage would hurry up so that it would be My Turn. I saw a cord wound round a small hook. With my mind elsewhere, I began to unwind it. Suddenly there was a very loud crash. Followed by a brief but terrible silence. Followed by a great shout of laughter that went on and on for ages. In the middle of the scene, when the drama was rising to its climactic moments, every picture on the set had crashed to the floor. They had all been tied to the one hook backstage and I had released them. No-one ever knew how such a thing could have happened and no-one ever explained because no-one but I knew the secret. It taught me a lesson I've never forgotten: 'The Devil finds work for idle hands.'

Raymond Baxter, F.R.S.A.
Broadcaster of State Occasions, motor sport and technology: wartime RAF Spitfire pilot.

Second only to my parents, cars and aeroplanes were the first love of my life. My father built me my first car with his own hands. I suppose I was about four at the time. It was in the mid '20s, long before mass-produced cars for children crowded every toy-shop.

My car had a wooden frame, metal coachwork, a wooden steering wheel, and was chain driven to the rear wheels by rotating pedals – much more efficient than the 'to and fro' pedals of the shop-bought models of today. It went like the wind, and it taught me a lot. I drove it as fast as I could at all times, particularly round corners, to see if it would turn over. Thanks to my father's skill as a designer, it never did.

But disaster was, sooner or later, inevitable. Hurling my car round a familiar blind corner on the pavement near our respectable suburban home one day, my vision was instantly and totally obscured by the towering bulk of a very large gentleman taking his morning constitutional. I hit him very hard, from behind, just below the knees.

Down he came like a felled oak, depositing his vast posterior squarely onto the bonnet of my little car. Such was the momentum of my arrival that I carried him thus for several feet – his legs stuck out on either side, umbrella firmly clutched, the contents of his shopping bag flying in all directions.

Now in those days the mere idea of having one's name and address taken – as by Ernest the Policeman in Toytown, my constant delight on radio's 'Children's Hour' – was simply too horrific to contemplate.

Quick as a flash, I jerked my car backwards from under its unwanted load, depositing my victim in an inelegant, if stable, sitting posture in mid pavement. And terrified of pursuit, I pedalled off home even faster than I had arrived. Only then did I burst into tears. That man had dented my bonnet!

More than 50 years later I can see every horrific moment of that accident as in a slow motion replay on television.

It was a full 48 hours before I dared take that corner flat out again.

Stanley Baxter.
West End and television actor.

The Empire Exhibition in Glasgow was held in 1938 at Bellahouston Park. My aunt Jeannie gave me a junior season ticket and never have I loved or utilised a birthday gift so much. Although the park was at the other end of Glasgow from where I lived, the long school holidays meant I could go almost every day to marvel at the delights of the innumerable pavilions representing the different countries of the then British Empire. There were Sengalese dancers, giraffe-necked women, Henry Hall at the concert hall and a food hall where free samples saw me through lunch. A sliver of Canadian cheese on a cracker at one stall followed by a tea-spoonful of beef curry on a miniature chupatty at another and for a penny a huge glass of Cremola Foam as dessert. When I tell you that the centre-piece of the Exhibition was an art-deco tower and the entrance to it sported an ice-cream machine which disgorged double-cream cornets at the lift of a lever of impressive high-tech design, you can see that Disney-land was anticipated in Glasgow's south-side park.

It was a wonderful summer for me and if I'd kept out of the fairground my humiliation could have been averted. The rides cost money, and I'd little enough. On a day of infant profligacy I overdid it and ended up with one large brown penny bearing George V's head. It cost tuppence to get home by tramcar and a roll-a-penny stall suggested the chance of winning the fare home – it was a heart-pounding, desperate gamble. I sent His Majesty rolling down the wooden slat and on to the numbered squares. It ran and ran and lurched back towards me and fell on a dividing line. The showman had his back to me. Trembling eight-year-old fingers slid beneath the mesh to grasp the coin and make a wild second bid for solvency.

The thwack of the penny-croupier's stick on my thieving fingers brought my sole flirtation with theft and gambling to an end in one scarlet-faced moment.

It was a long walk home and I had time to wonder anxiously if I might

be arrested at the Cremola stall on a future visit. Dillinger coming out of the picture house . . . Cagney dragged screaming to the hot seat . . . They all haunted me before I fell into a guilty sleep. Just before I dropped off I remember feeling I'd somehow made the King an accessory after the fact.

Tufton Beamish (now Lord Chelwood).
Soldier, politician, music lover and would-be naturalist.

I was out of bed like a shot when my raucous alarm rudely awoke me. It was the summer hols. I was fifteen and a half, staying with my father in a small hotel on the west coast of Sutherland for my first ever salmon fishing on the Kirkaig and Inver. Both rivers were so dead low that after five blank days we had given up. Even our eternally optimistic gillie, Roddy Macleod, had admitted defeat.

His mad-keen son Angus, just my age, promised to take me up for my last day to a 'wee lochan' for some Brownies. "Have fun" said my very strict father, "and remember, no poaching. As an MP who helps make the law, I can't have my son breaking it".

After a rough, uphill climb of some seven miles we arrived just before dawn at the little loch near the foot of Suilven, the sugarloaf peak like a mini-Matterhorn. Angus' rod, which we were to share fish for fish, was up in a jiffy with a butcher on the tail and a pennel (my favourite fly) on the dropper of the 4X gut cast. The orange rim of the sun nosed over the horizon on what was promising to be a sparkling autumn day with just the steady, stiff breeze we wanted. As I made my first cast I asked my friend why his reel had not got a ratchet in it.

"So we won't be heard, of course. You can't be too careful when you're poaching. The keeper's a devil, and I don't want to get caught again".

My heart gave a flutter just as my line tightened. Only my second cast, and I was into a fat trout which took out half my backing.

I handed Angus the rod, and he netted another good fish, assuring me that the keeper would not be along until 9 o'clock at the earliest. He also apologised for not telling me that we would be poaching as he knew my father would have objected.

The next three hours flew by. Spied only by a pair of high soaring eagles, some chuckling grouse and a blue hare or two, we just couldn't stop catching fish. They were all about the same size, the largest just over two pounds. In all we landed twenty-one fish weighing twenty-six pounds, as well as hooking but losing a dozen or so. What a thrill!

"Let's go" said Angus, who was as excited as I was. "If we meet Mr Macdonald on the way down, just do what I tell you".

Halfway down we heard the clatter of ponies' hooves coming up the stony track.

"Quick" whispered Angus. "Follow me".

We plunged into the tall bracken and lay down 25 yards away. My heart felt to me like a tom-tom, and I was sure I could hear his thumping too. The tough-looking keeper and another man ("his lordship" muttered Angus) rode past on two eel-striped dun Highland ponies, luckily without a dog which would surely have scented us.

Walking back through the village, the trout hidden in our rucksacks, we looked as innocent as possible as we passed the constable who said to Angus, in quite a friendly way, "Poaching again, I suppose? I'll catch you one day".

Back at the hotel we downed huge helpings of porridge, kippers, black pudding, scrambled egg and bacon, rounding it all off with two or three baps and marmalade. Finding my father, who had broken his duck with a seven pound cannibal trout in Loch Assynt, I proudly showed him our catch and he photographed us beside it with half a crown and a box of matches to show the size of the fish.

"A day to remember all your life" he said. "You weren't poaching, were you?"

"I'm afraid we were" I said sheepishly. "But nobody saw us except a few people in the village".

"You both deserve a good hiding. If you get copped, don't cry on my shoulder".

I felt this was fair enough.

At supper that evening we were relishing the fresh trout cooked in oatmeal when the same burly bobby in uniform clumped into the dining room and spoke to the waitress. My heart sank as I just caught my name,

"Beamish". He strode over to our table looking straight at me. My father looked at me too, and so did everyone else in the room as I managed a wan smile.

"Your car is obstructing the highway" the constable said to my father in a loud voice, "and you forgot to put your sidelights on. I'm afraid I'll have to report it, Admiral".

I bit my lip.

The Reverend Vicars Bell, M.B.E.
Headmaster, priest, author.

It was nearly the end of the Summer Term. Exams were over. The remaining three weeks before we 'broke-up' stretched interminably before the three of us. We decided that next Thursday we should go on an exploration. But where should we go? The Downs? The Common?

And there was the River. Not, like the Common, close at hand, but six or seven miles away, stealing furtively along the edge of the Weald. There came a time when I regarded a twelve-mile walk as a thing of negligible account; but then at the age of nine or so, I might as well have been fifty miles away for all the chance I had of getting there.

Bicycles, of course. But then I had no bicycle. That was a luxury which didn't come the way of our family. I was able, however, to borrow (without permission) a length of clothes-line. I wound it round and round my waist and chest and hoped my jacket might conceal it from the paternal eye. Perhaps my father's whole attention was focused on the short piece of board which I was carrying on the lee side.

"What are you doing with yon bit of wood?"

I brought it fully into view, with the frank air of one who has nothing to conceal.

"This bit?"

"Yes."

"Oh, George and Leslie and I are going to make a kind of seat out of it."

"Well, mind and bring it back. And see you don't get up to any mischief."

At the edge of the Common I met my confederates. We cut the line in two, and setting the bicycles about three feet apart, we adjusted the

board to rest on the crossbars, and lashed it into place.

We made a few preliminary trials. The original idea had been that I should sit on the board with an arm embracing the shoulders of each of my companions, and so travel in a dignified triumph, but we soon abandoned this idea for another which entailed less work for the pedallers and a shorter distance to fall for the passenger. I rested my chest and elbows on the board and dangled my feet earthward, taking an occasional striding kick to assist our progress. It was an uncomfortable, exciting, and erratic mode of travel. The policeman whom we met three miles from home seemed to feel, indeed, that it was dangerous. Moreover he stood by while, silently protesting, we demolished our handiwork.

I rode the rest of the way 'on the step', and arrived at last with numbed and aching feet at the edge of a spinney. Here the bicycles were hidden and it was as a man and an equal that I climbed with the other two over the fence into the meadow.

The sun glared down on the heavy green of the grass. To the right there was a blaze of kingcups, noblest of all the flowers of early summer. A few willow trees hung outward over the hidden river, grotesque and menacing like Arthur Rackham drawings.

George said, "Come on. There's no one about," and took a step forward.

Leslie said, "Half a mo. Do you reckon those are bulls?"

He pointed over to the left where elm trees stood in a cluster. Under them, with restless tails, quivering sides, stamping feet, and (worst of all) tossing heads, we saw a bunch of cattle.

There was no question about them, as far as I was concerned. They were all bulls, and all in state of raging fury. You could see that, I said, at a glance. They were lashing their tails, and tossing their horns.

George said, "I bet they're cows. Anyway they're a long way off. I bet you I dare walk right up to them. Come on."

It was all very well for him. In later life he rode from Cape to Cairo on a motor-bike, and did aerobatics, and other incredible things. But neither Leslie nor I were to be shamed into mock courage. We climbed back into the wood and skirted the outside of the field. We reconnoitred the next. It was tranquil enough. Again the border of kingcups, again the contorted willows. But this time the only living occupant was a large placid-looking cow, knee deep in the rich grass, and grazing contentedly on the meadow's farthest edge.

"I suppose," George said, in tones of heavy scorn, "I suppose you think that's a bull."

No, we conceded. This time it was all right. This time it was a cow.

Silently we trekked for the banks. The grass was different. There was no scuffling through it with the bents sliding their polished shanks from our thrusting boots. We had to lift our feet, and force our way as though through a jungle. It was hot, and it seemed sometimes as though we should never traverse the heavy stillness which lay between us and our goal. But suddenly we were there. The grass became thinner, reeds appeared, and the kingcups, and a black oozy mud into which our feet sank with a squish, and from which they rose with a succulent squelch.

We gazed in delight at the Mole. This was a real river. No miserable brook. It must have been at least eight yards across. A water vole plopped into the flood at our feet. The tell-tale wake vanished, reappearing again half-way across, and then disappeared once more. Then he scurried into a hole at the far bank. We said it was an otter, and pretended to believe ourselves. A new smell was in our nostrils. The smell of river mud. And though I have never become at home on rivers, it is a smell 'unforgettable, unforgotten'.

We wandered on by the verge, stopping to dabble our fingers, pressing our now bare feet into the warm mud. Presently we came upon a smooth river-bank, where there were no shallows, but where precipitous under-cut baulks of short turf hung steeply to the water.

Half-way to the next tree we were disturbed by a loud bellow in our rear. We turned our heads. Incredible. Awful. The cow, showing unmistakable signs of masculinity, was bearing down upon us at a heavy shambling run. His tail (it was no good blinking the fact, she was he), held vertically behind him, seemed to carry a menace which each of us felt to be directed solely, and personally at himself.

George said, "Gosh! The tree. Quick."

It was no proud spirit of emulation which brought me first to that desired haven. I had hold of the lowest branch and had a bare foot on the gnarled trunk a split second before George. But it was he who, by means of a quick shove, took my place as the first to ascend to safety. Leslie and I, with anxious little groans and whimpers, managed to leave the bank just in time for it to become the undisputed territory of the bull. He arrived as we gained safety among the long whippy branches, and just rapidly enough to make little skid marks as he came to a stop a few yards away.

He raised a ringed nose in a glare of astonishment at our temerity. We watched in terrified silence as he pawed the ground and tossed his head. Then he lowered the horns which we had so recently experienced in vicarious proximity, and began to crop his way silently and quietly back to the far corner.

George said, in a subdued whisper:

"He's a dangerous bull. Look, he's got brass knobs on the ends of his horns. I bet he could kill a man."

I remarked with a lamentable lack of tact, "I thought you weren't afraid of bulls."

"Well, I'm not. Not when they're standing still."

"You took jolly good care to get out of the way," I said. "I was here first."

George said, "Well, I wanted to get up because I'm the best climber, and I thought I could help you up." He eyed me hopefully, and added, as a kind of make-weight, "Of course *you* can run best. I bet you could beat any chap in the school. Except the big chaps, like Gilbert and Jennings."

It was long before we dared to descend, and when we did so it was with silent humility and discretion. We had no eyes for voles, otters, or any other wild-fowl living. We stole, without speaking, from one tree to another. As we left the safety of each, we walked reluctantly and slowly, with many a backward glance. But as we gained the midway point between one refuge and the next our steps broke into a furtive trot.

When at last we were over the fence we burst into howls of laughter. We shouted ribald and ferocious mockery at the unresponsive end of our late adversary. He remained unmoved. But I believe that even then, with a good stout fence between us, it would have needed only one brief bellow from under the copper ring, to have sent us scuttling like rabbits for the safety of the Brighton road.

The journey homeward is not a thing of blessed memories. The road wound uphill all the way, and as third man I was hardly popular. And in two breasts, at least, there lurked an unresolved misunderstanding. Of the three of us, I am, strangely, the last survivor. Each of the others travelled widely over the world's face. Leslie died young and long ago in Singapore. George was a sailor, a stunt-merchant, a company promoter, a pilot, and a dozen other things in turn. His final tragic descent to earth was a sudden and violent one. They saw, both of them, strange sights and lovely that I shall never know, and now they 'wear the turning globe'.

John Bennett.
Actor of stage, screen and radio.

When I was thirteen I was taken away from our local council school and sent as a boarder to a posh 'prepper' in Berkshire. This was during the war. With my fairly ripe Stamford Hill accent I was quickly labelled by the other boys as 'The Oik', which proved that class-distinction was alive and well in 1942. Many of the other boys had nick-names hardly less offensive but they were usually crude distortions of their own names. Hence Donald Carter was known as 'The Farter' and Lesley Bhoem was simply 'Smelly Bum'. My own name was fairly uncompromising and I thought I had got away with it fairly lightly. But my would-be tormentors were simply giving 'the beastly new boy' time to settle in before visiting upon me the full force of their wit.

At first I was very nervous and apprehensive in this totally strange environment. This has always had a physical effect on me. My mother said it 'binded' me. At any rate it must have been three or four days before internal pressures forced me to un-bind and I paid my first visit to the row of dismal, hissing, puddle-floored water-closets next to the changing-rooms on the ground floor. There on the lavatory-pan, in clear

38

blue print, was not 'Armitage Ware' nor the infamous 'Thomas Crapper & Sons' but 'John Bennett & Co. Ltd., Sanitary Engineers, Reading, Berks.' I soon discovered that every loo in the school had emblazoned upon it that same cruel, compromising epithet. As I cringed through classroom and dormitory during the ensuing weeks the vile, anal insults rang in my ears. I did survive the ordeal. It was I think, in the best prep-school tradition, a character-forming experience.

Peter Bennett.
Actor of stage and screen.

My Great Aunt Bertha Lowe was Music Mistress at St. Edmund's School, Hindhead, the Preparatory School that my brother Robin (who was alas killed in action in the Battle of Britain) and I attended in the early 1930s. She was known in the School as 'Buffalo' – or 'Buffa' for short – and was a very remarkable lady, wrongly believed by the schoolboys to be Beethoven's illegitimate daughter, a belief fostered by her sadly increasing deafness and the fact that she prominently displayed a black and white drawing of the great composer in her drawing room. This rumour was encouraged by a mischievous young schoolmaster who evidently had scant regard for historical accuracy because Beethoven died in 1827, forty years before the birth of my aunt.

Aunt Bertha tried unsuccessfully to teach W. H. Auden to play the piano when he was a pupil at the school and years later was even less successful in attempting to teach me. She appeared to us boys to be incredibly ancient but at the time she was actually no more than in her early sixties. A lady of great energy and variegated activities, which included keeping chickens in her garden. She would sometimes seize hold of an unfortunate bird and, while subjecting it to a vigorous shaking, would cry out in stentorian tones "You damned hen, you have gone broody again!". She was very definitely 'a character' and I was extremely fond of her. She died in 1950 at a ripe old age and gave me much encouragement during the early part of my theatrical career.

Bertha Lowe's house was adjacent to the school where my brother and I were boarders. We were boisterous energetic lads and our games were sometimes quite inventive. Bilberry shrubs grew profusely in the locality, and indeed in my aunt's garden. They produced small dark blue or purplish berries which could be eaten raw or cooked. We thought that it would be a good idea to make some bilberry wine and painstakingly pressed enough of the berries into liquid to fill three or four glass bottles, and, believing that our wine would be improved by keeping, we buried the bottles in aunt Bertha's garden. This interment had a startling effect on the 'wine'. Some weeks later when aunt B. was pottering in her garden there was an alarming explosion. The wine was fermenting and the purple liquid spurted in cascades from the ground causing a fair amount of havoc. To say the least the aunt was rather cross but I believe she thought that the 'misdeed' was not altogether unenterprising. Anyway that particular experiment was not repeated.

Francis Bennion.
Barrister, Oxford University lecturer, author on legal and professional subjects.

The year was 1929. Aged six, I had a morning off from Miss Steele's Infant Academy at Harrow. There, a week or two before, I had first encountered the joys of the Sand Tray. You could make any country or landscape you liked in that, loose sand being so versatile. I have never since felt such power.

Although well supplied with pocket money, I must have convinced myself that I needed cash. We lived in a small terrace house in Butler Road. A narrow, rarely-used alley ran alongside the house to the pavement. You get cash by selling things, but I had nothing to sell. Not put off by that, I decided to sell whatever was lying about the house and portable.

We owned a rickety folding card table with a green baize top. Father, who worked in the Exchequer and Audit Department, had won this table by saving an enormous number of coupons from Player's Navy Cut cigarette packets. I dragged the table along our narrow alley, and set it up by the pavement. On it I deposited a tray laden with such trinkets as I had been able to lay my hands on. A ring of my mother's in a white ivory box. A silver-plated button hook. An empty photograph frame. Our crystal set (to which I was not allowed to listen). And so on.

Feeling I should contribute something of my own, I carefully cut several used envelopes into strips. These I offered for making shopping lists, at a penny each. It took me an hour to write out a label conveying this information.

Throughout its commercial existence, the stall had one paying customer only – a gracious lady who bought a shopping list, and smilingly handed over one of those old heavy copper pennies. I was overjoyed. Shortly afterwards my mother arrived on the scene. Failing to understand her rage, I was enraged myself when she confiscated my hard-earned penny.

That afternoon mother took me shopping in Harrow. For years I could not understand why her anger broke out again, was indeed redoubled, when, as we passed a sweet-shop, I righteously demanded that an ice cream cornet be purchased with *my* money. Her refusal has rankled ever since. By my labour I converted a worthless used envelope into something exchangeable for value, and sold it on the market. Isn't that what economics is about?

Martin Benson.
Actor, Screenwriter, Film Director.

Imagine an Orthodox Jewish house in the East End in the early 1920's. Think of Mother being a Queen, Grandmother being an even more authoritative Queen, and myself at Junior School age subject to the whims of the Elders.

It was Passover. An important and, to a youngster, a burdensome occasion which involved going to the Synagogue, lots of Hebrew prayers which I barely understood at that tender age, old men with beards patting me on my head, and, at home, the flurry of getting the house ready for Passover. The ritual of this festival involves a total upheaval. In culinary terms, the house must be cleansed, for no food normally eaten, no pots, pans, cutlery, crockery normally used can be used during this week.

At that time, every Orthodox household kept a special set of everything which was used only in that one week. This was treasured and, for 51 weeks of the year, wrapped and carefully put away. Wasteful but traditional!

It was also an occasion for best clothes. Father wore his bowler hat to the synagogue, mother and grandmother sort out tenderly closeted gloves and silken clothing.

My father kept a grocer's shop which, for the most part, served non-Jewish customers. And both mother and grandmother worked in the shop. So it was something of a rush to prepare the house for Passover.

I volunteered to help. The only task with which they would entrust me was putting out the soup bowls for the 'Seder' – the Passover supper. They disappeared upstairs to change, while I took the task in hand with enormous enthusiasm. After all, it was an important job!

But there was a problem; too few soup bowls for the number of people attending the dinner that night. Loathe to let the side down, I felt a little breaking of the rules would be in order.

When the family came down, the table was resplendent with candlesticks, bright silver, and every place setting with a soup bowl. One of these, however, had a slightly different appearance from the remainder. Mother went around the table in one direction, checking; grandmother went in the opposite direction, also checking. They both arrived at the same offending place setting at the same moment. There, instead of the Crown Derby or the Royal Doulton, was a large bowl which announced its ownership with lettering on the side. It said 'CAT'!

Bill Benyon.
Member of Parliament for Milton Keynes

Aged 7, I fell off my bicycle and cut my chin very badly. My mother was taking me to stay with my grandmother but as the wound had to be stitched this was impossible, so she sent a telegram.

"Bill cut chin. Off bicycle. Alright."

Unfortunately the stops were put in the wrong place so the telegram read on arrival:

"Bill cut chin off. Bicycle alright."

The girl on the telephone exchange is reputed to have remarked: "What a dreadful thing to happen but I'm glad the bicycle is alright."

Nicholas Bethell.
Writer and Member of European Parliament.

As an 18-year-old on my first visit to Paris, I was invited by a French couple, friends of my family, to a glittering dance. I knew no one there, but my host, everyone's ideal of a sophisticated Frenchman, kindly asked if there was anyone that I would like to meet. I pointed to the most beautiful girl I could see, he brought her over and I asked her to dance.

An hour later at the bar he asked me how I had got on with the lovely

French lady. Very proud of myself, I told him that we had got on famously. We were going to have dinner the following evening and she had suggested the possibility of a night-club afterwards.

"I knew she'd like you," said my cynical host. "She's the biggest gold-digger in Paris and I told her that you were an English multi-millionaire."

John Bickersteth.
Bishop of Bath & Wells; a countryman, married to a pianist, and father of four.

My tale is partly in and partly out of school. I was thirteen, and in the top form at my prep school. It was a few days before the end of the Easter term 1935 when three or four of us planned and executed a daring and reprehensible deed. We broke out after the boys we were in charge of were asleep in their dormitories, and went for a midnight walk.

The passing of time makes for fishermen's tales, and I doubt if it was much later than 10.30 p.m. when we miscreants dressed quickly, went downstairs to a classroom, and climbed out of a window, dropping quietly on to the flower beds (the building was a high one and I am sure none of us made ropes out of sheets!). We walked up the road to the village a mile away. It was certainly dark because I have a distinct recollection of nipping smartly into the ditch when what seemed likely to be a master's car swept out of the school drive and we did not like the look of the headlights. Outside the pub we put money in a slot machine and extracted bars of chocolate, which we took back to prove we had been there. In an hour we were in bed again, with a great sense of achievement and no one the wiser.

Alas the bars of chocolate, much-admired proof to our peers next morning of the night's escapade, also proved our undoing. 'Matron', that redoubtable character in any prep school, spotted them in our lockers, and the whole dreadful truth had gradually to come tumbling

out. Parents were informed of their sons' dire activities, and the punishment was meted out – gating for four days of the Easter holidays. We were kept back, tearfully, as our friends sped home by car, or taxi to the train.

Our headmaster – for whom it must have been such a nuisance to have a group of wretched boys spoiling the start of his holiday – was a big man. Once the others had all gone, the school was horribly empty, and the main impact of our punishment had been very definitely felt, the mood changed entirely; and after now nearly 50 years, as if it was yesterday, while I can feel again the shame of doing wrong as a senior boy mingling with a certain pride in the successful doing of it, my chief recollection is of the kindness of the headmaster and his wife who made up marvellously for the loss of precious days at home by special meals, daytime expeditions, and hilarious games round the drawing room fire at night.

Major General (retd.) Sir Alec Bishop, K.C.M.G., C.B., C.V.O., O.B.E. O.M. (Ger.), C.St. J. of Jerusalem.
Formerly Commissioner, North Rhine, Westphalia 1948–50.
Deputy High Commissioner, India 1957–62.
British High Commissioner, Cyprus 1964–5.

During the second World War the Dorset Regt. was serving in Mesopotamia, now called Iraq. The Regiment was brigaded with Regiments of Sikhs, Gurkhas, and Mahrattas. Naturally the men of all these Regiments were anxious to obtain sanction to visit India on leave and to see their families. This was not easy to achieve because of transportation difficulties. However, a soldier of the 105th Mahrattas solved the problem for himself and some of his friends by the exercise of ingenuity. He found the body of a dead jackal, severed its head and removed the skin and flesh from the skull of the animal. This enabled him to hinge together the upper and lower jaws. He used these to make tooth marks on his posterior. He showed these to the Regimental Medical Officer, who made immediate arrangements for him to be transported for treatment of the fell disease of rabies at the special anti-rabic hospital in Wellington, South India.

A few days later two other soldiers from the same Regiment reported to the Medical Officer with similar symptoms. Careful enquiry revealed

that this service was rendered by the owner of the jackal skull for the modest fee of four annas. This brought to an end this way of gaining home leave.

In the days before Independence, the posts of Governor General and Viceroy of India and the Governors of the Presidencies into which the sub-continent was divided, were held by British officials of distinction who were appointed by the British Government. In 1920 the Governor of the Madras Presidency was Lord Willingdon. The summer headquarters of the Madras Government was at Ootacamund, in the Nilghiri Hills. This was also the headquarters of the Ootacamund Hunt, which hunted jackal over the Ootacamund Downs, there being no foxes. Lord Willingdon was Master of this Hunt. His A.D.C. and I, who was serving on the staff of the military commander, acted as whippers in. One day we brought the hounds to a popular meeting spot known as 'staircase'. Lady Willingdon cantered up to the meet and told the A.D.C. and me to "get on with it". We moved the hounds off reluctantly and slowly because Lord Willingdon had not yet appeared on the scene. When he did appear a few minutes later he enquired why we were moving off before he had arrived. "Because I told them to," announced Lady Willingdon. Her husband's reply was, "My dear, you may be the Governor of the Madras Presidency, but you are not the Master of this Hunt, and it will *not* move off in future until I have arrived!"

Sir Winston himself had a great sense of humour. He was once chairing a meeting of a group of defence experts who were trying to decide which of several foreign generals we should support in their struggle against communism. One of these generals was called General Plastiras. After a long discussion Sir Winston summed up with this splendid sentence, "It seems to me, gentleman, that we should give our support to General Plaster-arse, and hope that he does not turn out to have feet of clay.''

In 1938 when I was holding the appointment of Principal Staff Officer to the Secretary of State for the Colonies, I was required to write letters to certain individuals to inform them of the appointments they would be required to take over in the event of war breaking out. One of these was a retired naval officer who was living in Kenya. I wrote to tell him that his post on mobilisation would be that of Beach Master at Mombasa, and that he was to ensure that military personnel and stores would have priority of passage through that important port. The typist, perhaps because she had been reading a series of articles published in a London newspaper over the signature 'Beach Comber', typed those words in the letter in place of 'Beach Master'. I unfortunately did not notice what had occurred, and signed the letter and sent it off. I received a very cross reply from the recipient, telling me in no uncertain terms that if I thought my letter was funny, he did not, and would like to remind me that he had served in the Senior Service. After consulting some of my colleagues in the office, I wrote to him a letter of apology, expressing the hope that he would overlook this most unfortunate error. I then put the correspondence in a separate file and sent it to the Central Registry endorsed on the minute sheet, 'Put by, at once.' Unfortunately, however, the file did come to the notice of a senior member of the office staff, who circulated it around the office with the following minute pinned to the cover:

"To all young gentlemen who may be required to issue letters in the name of the Secretary of State, I invite your attention to the correspondence contained in this file. It is hardly necessary for me to add that grievous occurrences such as this are gravely detrimental to the Dignity of the Department.''

I was, however, not the only one in the office to make mistakes. We were at that time in discussions with the War Office on the further development of the Survey Grid in what is now the Federal Republic of Nigeria, with a view to improving the available maps of that area. The

Colonial Office representative was the Head of the West Africa Department, Mr. John Sidebotham, and by a queer coincidence the Head of the Survey Department in the War Office was Colonel Winterbottom. The negotiations were not going too well, Colonel Winterbottom complaining that the Colonial Office did not know how to spell his name correctly. Mr. J. R. A. Bottomley, an Assistant Secretary serving in the Colonial Office, who was trying to smooth out the different views of the two Ministries, wrote the following minute on the Colonial Office file, 'Mr. Sidebotham should be the first to realise that we fundamentalists are very particular about how our names are spelt.'

The Army and the Civil Service are not, of course, the only organisations in which humour appears. It sometimes breaks out even in Press circles as it did some years ago after the completion of a new bridge over the River Thames in the London area. It was decided to invite a very distinguished lady to carry out the opening ceremony. The report on this event in a London newspaper concluded with the following sentence, 'After cutting the traditional ribbon which was spanning the entrance, the distinguished lady passed over the bridge and proceeded to her home.' Unfortunately, the compositor who was setting out the type was on notice of dismissal for some misdemeanour. He decided to substitute the letter 'i' for the letter 'a' in the word 'passed'. When the effect of this came to notice in the Editorial Office, every available member of the editorial staff was sent post-haste to every stationer's shop that could be reached, with instructions to take possession of, and to destroy every copy of the day's issue of the newspaper that they could lay their hands on.

Isla Blair.
Actress, films and T.V.

When I was a child, my parents lived in India and, as was the custom in those days, my elder sister and I were sent to boarding school in Scotland. She was 9 years old and I was 5.

One day I was feeling a bit off colour and was told to stay in bed (there was no sick bay). Our dormitory had eight beds in it with a bed in a special position for a senior girl who, as a prefect, was expected to keep

order. Gwen Kelly was our prefect and we teased her unmercifully. She was a plump girl from Paisley with flawless skin, but an appalling speech impediment. This vulnerability made her stricter than was always necessary.

She kept a treasured collection of glass animals on a shelf beside her bed which we 'babies' were not allowed near. Feeling better after an hour of silence and counting the cracks on the ceiling – the day stretched emptily ahead and boredom (the devil's ambassador) awoke my curiosity which, in turn, pulled my pyjamaed legs out of bed in the direction of the forbidden glass animals.

They were so beautiful. Little blue sea horses, black and white penguins, opaque sheep with yellow eyes, ginger horses with curling tails. To my horror, I dropped a striped cat onto the rest of these delicate treasures, which fell smashed to the floor. I scurried back to bed – red with shame, heart a-thump waiting for Gwen Kelly to discover my crime.

For some reason, I couldn't own up and express my sincerely felt anguish at my action. Instead, I found myself saying that a huge gust of wind had swept the beautiful little creatures to the floor – "It was like a tornado and blew all the clothes off my bed. I was so scared – it blew everything round the room". My eyes met those of the other girls, Gwen Kelly's and, by now, the Matron's. After their eyes had looked over the ordered room, teddy bears in place on beds, dressing gowns neatly on pegs – only the splintered glass on the floor – hot tears of humiliation and shame filled my throat and flowed down my cheeks.

My punishment was to stand in the corner without my trouser bottoms. I think the idea was to humiliate. No punishment was more severe than the disappointment I felt in myself for the act of cowardice that had urged me to lie, instead of admitting my clumsiness and asking forgiveness!

Rt. Hon. David Bleakley, M.A.
Chief Executive, Irish Council of Churches;
former Minister of Community Relations, Government of Northern Ireland.

'Finishing school' for me was the Belfast Shipyard of Harland & Wolff, where I enrolled as an apprentice at fourteen. It was a tough but egalitarian academy of life – a sort of industrial Gordonstoun – where the fledgelings were on the receiving end of a host of initiatory tests. We all learned what it was to be sent on most improbable errands (a bucket of 'blue steam' or the 'left-handed' screwdriver) or to suffer a surreptitious painting of one's heels with white paint, which on the way home raised the cry of 'heel-ball'.

But sometimes the worms turned – I recall a memorable 'turning'.

Chief targets for retribution were the foremen, into whose corrective hands we fell in the first year of apprenticeship – shipyard RSM's, their aim in life was to knock us into shape for the industrial trials to come. These foremen were known as 'hats' because of their wearing of splendid black bowlers presented to them on promotion to management.

The big chance for repayment came when one day six of our 'hats' had to preside at the launching ceremony of a notable ship. We, the apprentices, were on hand to conduct distinguished guests to their seats and to present floral tributes. Above all, we were at the beck and call of the foremen and, in particular, had to receive and return their special occasion bowler hats at the beginning and conclusion of the ceremony.

The drill was simple: we presented each foreman with a brand new hat which he raised in 'Three cheers for the guests' and then donned as he joined in leading the platform party from the reviewing stand through the long parade of spectators.

Revenge is sweet! The bowler hats were collected from the foremen, then duly redistributed at the critical moment when cameras were clicking. But a swift switch had been made – those with heads designed by nature for a modest size were presented with the largest possible edition, while those in need of a more generous version had to do with minute ones.

The donning of the hats caused social chaos, as a bewildered sextet marched off – some with precariously balanced bowlers and the remainder with hats settling down on embarrassed ears. Efforts to effect an exchange completed the farce, with guests and spectators erupting in laughter and derisory cheers.

Fortunately our foremen were a forgiving crowd and we survived to tell the tale. But to this day when I receive a bowler I check it for size!

Edward Blishen.
Writer, editor, & teacher.

I was about nine, I suppose, when I decided to give certain gracious awards to my best friends. Books, in fact. The trouble was that they weren't my books to give.

At Byng Road School, Barnet, c. 1929, friendship was a positive industry. We'd list our friends in our pocket diaries in order of merit: and they'd be shifted up or down daily according to the way one felt about them. It was something we did in the playground, and I have the most vivid memory of being one of a small group at playtime busily sending Friend No 1 toppling down to tenth place, and elevating Friend No 20, who'd offered a bull's-eye under the desk, to a position somewhere near the top. There was a frightful romantic warmth about it all. You longed not only to have a better range of friends than other boys, but to be known yourself as having some outstanding quality in this field. A friend in a thousand. Best Friend in the World, 1929. Something like that.

Marking your feelings for a friend by giving him a bull's-eye or a gobstopper was well enough. But I had ambitions beyond that. And I suddenly saw what I could do. It was a matter of the books that were to be found here and there at home in boxes and in cupboards. My parents weren't bookish, and I was never sure how this motley collection had been assembled. Some had my grandmother's name in them; which puzzled me greatly. She read, I knew, *The News of the World*, and an occasional tract: but I could not imagine her reading Macaulay's *Essays*, or Carlyle's *The French Revolution*, or *The Christian-Man's Calling, or a Treatise of Making Religion One's Bufineſs, wherein Chriſtians are directed how to perform it In the Relations of Parents, Children,*

*Husbands, Wives, Mafters, Servants, and in the Conditions of
Profperity and Adverfity: The Second Part,* by George Swinnock, M.A.,
published in 1663. Mostly these were books of some seriousness, if not
solemnity, and might have come from the library of a slightly dotty
scholar. I suspect that many working-class Victorian households had
such a collection, picked up perhaps on penny stalls, and regarded not as
literature but as items of furniture.

It was, anyway, to these that I turned when the grand idea dawned of
making what might have been called the Blishen Award for Outstanding
Services to Friendship. I guess my own character, as one doomed to
bookishness, showed only too clearly in this somewhat grotesque
enterprise. What at this distance astonishes me is that the books I
smuggled out of the house were accepted by their small recipients with
total gravity. Roy Rogers (who was later to become my best enemy when
he had the insensitiveness to fall in love with Joan Rankin, who was well-
known to belong to me and Bernard Gray) made no fuss about the gift of
Macaulay's *Essays*: Freddie Spriggs was happy enough with a mid-19th
century study of working class dwellings: and Jackie King didn't turn a
hair when made the possessor of Mill's *On Liberty*. I don't remember
that they carried themselves thereafter with obvious pride, or even that
they treated me with more respect than before: but I was happy with my
dizzy awareness of the existence of a growing number of Blishen Prize-
winners.

It could have come to an end in several ways, I guess. One or two of
my laureates said their parents had expressed unease about the origins of
these unlikely tomes. Someone would certainly before long have come to

school to have a word with Mrs Gibson, my classteacher, who already had reservations about my character based on a tendency to giggle in not obviously amusing lessons like Arithmetic and Dictation. But in fact it was my mother who brought the scheme crashing to the ground. I was leaving the house one day in the rapid and evasive manner made necessary if you had a large square book tucked under your jersey. My mother remembered noticing a smut on my cheek and came after me to remove it with a lick and a scrub of the hanky. In no time she had in her hand the book that was to have been presented in a modest playground ceremony to an entirely new friend, Jimmy Brewer, who'd given me (with no strings attached, so to speak) half a dozen old golf balls.

As it happens, fifty or so years later I have that book still on my shelves. What Jimmy missed was the first volume of *England As It Is, Political, Social, and Industrial, in the Middle of the Nineteenth Century*, by William Johnston, Esq., Barrister-at-Law. I notice that the preface (over which Jimmy was never to run an eye) begins: 'The Essays contained in these volumes had their origin in a design of writing letters to a friend on the Continent, in order to make him acquainted with the present state of England.'

A *friend*! I wonder what position he occupied in William Johnston, Esq's listing?

Michael Bond.
Author, creator of Paddington bear.

One of the most irritating things for a small child is to be introduced to others as a paragon of virtue, second to none in the list of all that is innocent and good; especially if it isn't true.

I often wonder how many seeds of rebellion are sown by proud and well-meaning parents in this way. It is not that one necessarily *wants* to be thought of as bad; it's simply that being labelled 'good' so early on in life does seem an incredibly dull start. One always slightly envies the wicked.

From an early age such moments invariably induced in me a desire to prove how bad I could be, and it was probably some such remark made at a family gathering one day that caused me to throw my feeding bottle across the dining-room when we were taking tea with my Auntie Ethel. It may not sound much, but if you'd known my Auntie Ethel you would know what a family crisis that little event caused. The shock tremors which rose as the bottle hit the sideboard and burst amongst the ornaments echoed round the room for days afterwards. We weren't invited back again for several months. On the other hand, I was vaguely aware for years after of others basking in the reflected glory of just having known me. Those who were present at the time still claim bonus points.

That episode I probably remember on account of the story having been repeated so many times. In the nature of things the same parents who extol the virtues of their offspring when they are small seem to delight in recalling their misdeeds when they are older and want to forget about them.

But my really big moment happened when I was about five or six years old. I went to the front door along with my mother in order to greet the milkman. For some reason, which no doubt seemed sound enough at the time, I was carrying a large brick at shoulder height.

I well remember the milkman, who I didn't much like anyway, leaning over and patting me on the head in his usual patronising manner.

"What a nice little boy," he said. "Fancy being able to carry a great big brick like that. What *are* you going to do with it?"

The cry of pain as it landed fairly and squarely on his foot was most satisfactory.

He never spoke to me again, although he had a lot to say at the time, and shortly afterwards we started to use another dairy. Either that or he gave up coming to us.

54

Christian Bonington, C.B.E.
Mountaineer, writer and photographer.

During the war I was sent to boarding school in Westmorland near Kirkby Lonsdale. I was quite happy at the school but perhaps showed some indications of an adventurous spirit in being the leader of a mass escape plan. We had not really any clear idea of where we were going to escape to but half a dozen of us decided to run away. We made our plans carefully, hoarding bacon rind from our breakfasts and stealing from the headmistress's pantry a fruit cake and currant loaf which I believe had been specially made for afternoon tea to treat a prospective parent. We made off early one morning before morning school, avoiding the roads and crossing woodland and farmland until eventually we reached a small coppice at the side of a track. I can remember that there was a wonderful big old tree with great gnarled branches and we spent the rest of the day playing in this and also crawling through a culvert underneath the road. By the end of the day, we had eaten our rations and as dark began to fall the realities of escape closed in upon us. We were all convinced that there were wild and savage animals around and therefore decided that we would have to sleep in the tree. Sleeping on a branch is not easy or comfortable. By the time it was twilight the thrill and adventure of escape began to fade. I don't think there was any discussion but somehow we found ourselves trailing back along the road, not at all sure where we were, how far we were from the school or where we were going. It was an immense relief when the headmistress's old car came chugging down the road and we were apprehended. I think I must have been around seven at the time.

Lord Borwick.
Soldier, farmer, yachtsman.

We had been married quite a short time, when I had to fulfil an annual engagement at a Territorial Army Camp, which was held that year at Shorncliffe in Kent. During that fortnight, my wife went over to France with her mother, returning on the cross Channel ferry through Dover.

As it was a weekend, we arranged to stay together on the Sunday night at The White Cliffs Hotel in Dover. It was before the easy days of cash credit cards and my wife was short of ready money, so I agreed to give her £5 to tide her over. I had to be back in Shorncliffe by 7.30 a.m. on the Monday morning, so bidding my wife 'goodbye' at 7 a.m., I left the hotel bedroom locking it behind me.

A short distance down the corridor, I realised I hadn't honoured my promise, so turning back, I knocked loudly on the door. To the query "Who's there?" I answered "It's me, darling, I am sorry I forgot to give you that £5 I promised you."

The face of the chambermaid taking round the early morning tea had to be seen to be believed.

Rev. Canon Peter Bostock, M.A.
Missionary in Kenya, 1935–58, Archdeacon of Doncaster, 1959–67.

When I was 8 years old, recently arrived at a prep. school, I heard a man speaking about the isolation of the islanders on Tristan-da-Cunha, where, if the one boat a year failed to anchor because of heavy seas, the islanders would even run out of soap. That was a turning point in my life. Was it the bliss of not having to wash?

Peter Bowring.
Chairman, Help the Aged, Chairman Aldeburgh Festival—Snape Maltings Foundation, Former Chairman. C. T. Bowring and Co. Ltd.

I had been chosen to play first trumpet in the school orchestra which, it had been decided, should demonstrate its questionable virtuosity on Speech Day by the provision of a musical interlude, the purpose of which was to relieve the monotony of the brand of oratory customary on such

56

occasions. My own particular slot in the programme, of which I can
remember absolutely nothing else whatever, was a much practised but
still far from perfect rendering of what I understand to be Purcell's
Trumpet Air (or was it Voluntary?) accompanied, of course, by the
orchestra. It so happened that my Father had decided to make one of his
rare visits to the school on this particular Speech Day and took me to
lunch in the town's most celebrated hostelry. When he asked me what I
should like to drink with my lunch I suggested, with some temerity, that
a glass of cider might be permitted. In due course what appears in retrospect to have been a magnum of a particularly potent brew arrived. My
Father having tasted it passed the bottle across the table to me and
ordered himself another pink gin.

Just how I found my way to my place in the orchestra pit will for ever
remain a mystery. The events that followed were of such a calamitous
nature as never to be forgotten. I put the trumpet to my lips at precisely
the same moment as the conductor tapped his music stand and raised his
baton. As the trumpet and I approached each other all about me went
dark. This was not entirely because the effects of the cider had reached
an anaethestic level but quite simply because I had
inadvertently chosen the wrong end of the instrument.
By the time that I had found my way round to the input
end, as it were, the orchestra was already in full cry and
to my utter despair and everlasting shame I found the
second trumpet, who quite obviously had been
practising secretly, up on his feet and well into the early
bars of the Air, or Voluntary, or whatever it is called.
Not even Harry Mortimer nor yet Louis Armstrong
in all their glory ever received such thunderous applause as
that which followed this brilliant, polished and completely
faultless performance, by the end of which I was in
the grip of deep remorse and incipient withdrawal
symptoms. Not one of the happiest stories of my
life but one which, when I told it many years after
to the late Benjamin Britten, was dismissed with
a quiet and wholly sympathetic 'Don't let it worry you,
it's almost certain that Purcell never wrote it anyway'.

Sir Harry Boyne, Kt., C.B.E.
Political correspondent, The Daily Telegraph, 1956–76.
Director of Communications, Conservative Central Office, 1980–82.

I must have been about 12 when, walking up Castle Street, Inverness (my native town) I noticed a cigarette packet on the pavement. To notice was, in those days, to kick – which I did, and immediately sensed that the packet seemed heavier than it should have been.

So I picked it up, rather furtively, and put it in my pocket until I reached Old Edinburgh Road, where there were fewer people about. There I examined the find; it contained 15 Player's Medium Navy Cut, intact apart from two or three slightly squashed ones.

I spread the word, and after tea that evening our little Gang of Four assembled at the end of our road, delighted to regale ourselves upon the manna which My Lady Nicotine had chanced to strew in my path. Player's, too! What an improvement on the customary Saturday Woodbine.

We were puffing away, swopping gossip and yarns (like Stanley Baldwin's, our thoughts seemed to grow in the aroma of that particular tobacco, even though it wasn't Presbyterian Mixture) when someone happened to spy a policeman apparently advancing upon us. Having just turned the corner at the other end of the road, he was still at least 100 yards away, but that was quite near enough to create panic among the illicit smokers. Remember, we had an entirely wholesome fear of the police which would seem as strange to the youth of today as our respect for the law which still purports to ban smoking by persons under 16.

As instigator of the crime, it was my responsibility to get rid of the evidence at once. This I did by chucking the packet and its remaining contents into a nearby shrubbery.

Meanwhile the partly smoked cigarettes were stamped and shredded underfoot and we set off on our usual 'training' run round the block. By the time we got back to our starting point the policeman was receding into the distance, having evidently taken no notice of us at all.

Next morning, which happened to be Sunday, I was first up in our household, getting ready for an early Bible class under Boy's Brigade auspices. I was lighting the fire in the kitchen range when the door-bell rang. Who could it be at that hour on a Sunday morning? I unlocked and opened the front door, to be horror-struck at sight of a large and severe-looking constable. I now realise that he couldn't have been our witness-presumptive of the night before, but my guilty conscience leaped to the conclusion that he was none other.

"Is this Mr Boyne's house?" he asked. I nodded, dumbfounded by fright.

Then: "Is he at home? I'd like a word with him".

So this was it; Dad was to be told. A vision of the Training Ship Mars in the river Tay, to which the bad boys of Scotland in those days were sent, flashed into my mind. At the very least, there would be a thrashing across Dad's knee.

I managed to blurt out "Yes, but he's still in bed".

This didn't seem to surprise the policeman. "You'll be a son of his, I suppose", he said. "Well, I don't think we need to get him up right away.

Just you give him this message from the police and that'll save him coming to the door. Tell him we found the front door of the Courier Office ajar this morning, and we think he'd better get down there as soon as he can and make sure that nothing's been stolen during the night. Will you do that?"

I could only nod assent, suffused by such a wave of relief that I instinctively smiled and giggled.

"It's no laughing matter" the constable sternly observed. "For all you know, your father may have lost some valuable property. Don't forget to tell him, now".

I haven't forgotten in 60 years.

59

Gyles Brandreth.
Writer, after dinner speaker.

On the whole I suspect I was a somewhat nauseating goody-goody as a child. School I liked and I know I always did my very best to curry favour with the teachers. However, I'm relieved to say that I was guilty of *occasional* lapses and for some inexplicable reason these all seemed to have involved elderly gentlemen.

I was born in 1948 (a direct result of the 1947 fuel crisis) and my first school was the Lycée Français de Londres, where I was introduced to President de Gaulle aged eight (that was my age at the time, not his) and distinctly let the side down by completely forgetting the words of the Marseillaise on the second line of the second verse. (Well, do *you* know the *first* line of the second verse of the National Anthem?)

After the Lycée, I went on to a Prep School in Kent where I caused the headmaster a few pangs of distress, aged 80. (That was his age at the time, not mine). It was the year when the unexpurgated edition of *Lady Chatterley's Lover* triumphed in the courts and the moment the jury's verdict was out I was on the phone to Penguin Books ordering myself a copy. I felt it would make ideal reading for an eleven-year-old, but when I was found studying it closely (and some of it very closely) in the school chapel I was hauled before the head. He was a most benevolent octogenarian and an enthusiastic classicist. I have no idea what he thought of D. H. Lawrence because he confiscated the book and didn't refer to it for a moment. He simply took it from me, put it in the drawer of his desk, leant forward wide-eyed and remarked, "Brandreth, I have only one thing to say to you: keep that Latin accurate!".

My next school was Bedales in Hampshire, a co-educational establishment at which it is the parents (running from Oscar Wilde to Princess Margaret) who tend to be distinguished rather than the pupils. The school was founded in the 1890s by a great educational pioneer called John Badley and I played Scrabble against him regularly aged one hundred. (You guessed it – that was his age, not mine). By the time I went to Bedales, Mr. Badley was no longer the headmaster, but he still lived in a cottage in the grounds and on Wednesday afternoons I would go down and play him at Scrabble. We played scores of games during the year or two I knew him and invariably he won. He won, a) because he was the better player; b) because I had to let him use obsolete words since he insisted they'd been current in his youth; and c) because his house-keeper kept the score and I rather think she cooked the books (she also cooked the scones and provided physiotherapy so it didn't do to complain). However, I was determined to beat Mr. Badley at least once in my life. I went into serious training, made a determined effort to increase my vocabulary and, just as the great man was entering his hundred and second year, I managed to beat him by four points. A month later he was dead. I have not dared win a game of Scrabble since.

Vincent Brome.
Author and journalist.

I remember a story which circulated in our school concerning a girl called Erica. She had a weak bladder and when the lavatories were occupied, would sometimes – being very young – spend a penny in the passage. Discovering this one day, the mistress said, "Now we will all shut our eyes and whoever was responsible for this puddle will go outside and mop it up, and we'll forget all about it". Eyes were shut: a patter of feet went to the door: a pause and then the feet pattered back. "Excellent", said the teacher, "now you will continue your spelling exercise while I check that all is well".

She went outside, down the corridor and there, beside the first pool was a second one. Written crudely on the wall were the words "The demon strikes again!"

George Mackay Brown, O.B.E., Hon.LL.D., Dundee.
Poet and author.

We were both very young, maybe 4 or 5. We played together a lot, building noisy ships, houses, and castles out of empty tin boxes the tobacconist next door gave us.

We were quite good citizens most of the time, John and I.

On the steep road leading off the main street, called Church Road because there are 3 churches on it, we paused one day beside a derelict building, at the back of the Commercial Hotel. It was plain that nobody had lived in it for a long time. The sole window was grimed with dirt, and

cobwebby – a blind beggar's eyes.

That little house was a blot on the landscape.

Who threw the first stone at the window I can't now remember. A stone flew like a bird out of one small hand – there was a crash and a tiny music of glass fragments falling.

It was our first experience of the dark joy of destruction.

Another stone, and another, and another. Smashings and splinterings of glass! We did not stop in our berserk joy until the last pane in that small sad house was broken – black stars in the middle of every glooming square.

How we were not stopped before the drunkenness of destruction took full possession of us, I do not know. There were houses and shops quite near at hand. (I think it must have been the dinner hour, when all the sober citizens of Hamnavoe were at their broth and mince-and-tatties. . . .)

My chum and I stood half appalled, before the six or eight dark stars that had once been windows. I think we justified our orgy with some devious argument, like "Nobody lives there anyway". . . . "It's all right, nobody saw us". . . .

We crept home for our separate dinners. I can remember my father coming in, a frown on his face. "Do you know anything about the broken windows in Church Road?"

A swift denial (though mounting guilt and shame must have coloured my face).

"You were seen, you and John. Own up."

Shadows of the prison-house, of long blue policemen with handcuffs, gathered suddenly about me.

"New panes will have to be put in. That house belongs to somebody. A fine lot of money it'll cost!"

I'm sure we weren't smacked. I don't think our half-penny pocket money was stopped. But for days afterwards we went about branded

62

with red guilt: glad all the same that the utmost sanctions of justice – jail and policemen – had not been invoked.

'The elastic powers' are strong in 5-year-olds. After a week, maybe, we had forgotten the destruction and the disgrace. We forgave each other. We were gathered once more into the wholesome fabric of our little town.

Then back it was to making positive construction out of empty tobacco tins on the doorstep: ships, towers, sea-planes, cars, piers – whatever the imaginations of children delight in; all negative passion spent (for the time being, anyway).

John Cairney.
Actor, director, writer and lecturer in theatre history and drama.

In those innocent, sunlit dole queue years, just before the second world war, I was a big-eyed pupil of six or seven at a Catholic infant school in the east end of Glasgow. It was a collection of yellow and brown wooden buildings, set in a square 'U'-shape, against the wall of the local scrap merchant's yard. Yet I loved it. I loved the concrete playground, sticky with tar in the summer time. I loved the lady teachers, big-bosomed, black-haired, and all Irish-Scots, heavy with perfume and Catholic guilt!

My teacher from kindergarten to primary was Miss Callaghan, just twenty or so, but seeming ageless to her motley Glasgow ragamuffins. And it was she who set me on the way to a love of reading and writing, and an eventual career in the theatre.

But, at that time, around 1937, I was seven years old, and getting ready to go up into primary at St Michaels, when I committed my first great sin.

As in all Glasgow schools at that time, classes were mixed, but very separated – girls on one side, boys on the other – and like in the ark, we were arranged two by two in the big, wide desks. My companion and best friend was Pat Breslin, who shared a desk and an inkwell with me, and occasionally the rare (very rare) sweetie, when one of us was lucky.

But one day, Pat brought in two cream buns which he was keeping as a playtime treat, and he didn't offer me one. I was appalled – and hurt. So, when he was sent out to collect the milk (we all had a little half pint bottle each, and it cost a halfpenny if your parents could afford it, and nothing, if they couldn't), I took full advantage of his brief absence, and almost in a gulp, ate one of the cream buns. Of course, there was a small riot when he returned, but I acted out my innocence defiantly, and there was nothing he could do about it. After all, wasn't I his pal? Somehow it was all forgotten by the end of the day but that night I had the most dreadful remorse of conscience, and could hardly sleep. Should I tell my mother? The teacher? The priest in confession? No, I couldn't. My crime was too awful. I tried to make it up by giving him a whole bar of Fry's chocolate (it was a small bar), but he wouldn't take it. So I ate half myself, but I couldn't finish it. And after school, I went into the local church and told God all about my terrible deed, and going down to the altar rail, I put the remainder of the chocolate on the wooden ledge, and said Baby Jesus could have it. I felt better at once, and ran out to join the other boys who were playing football in the nearby street. Jesus must have taken it, because it wasn't there when I went to Mass the next Sunday.

Forty years later, I was playing my 'Robert Burns' show in Toronto, and was at the airport after a very successful week in that Canadian city. Some Scots had gathered to see me off, and I was signing autographs for them, as my flight was called. Suddenly a youngish woman with a couple of young children in tow, asked me to sign. As I did so, I asked her name. "Cathy," she said. So I wrote it in her book. As I did so, she said, "My father said he knows you."

"Oh, yes?" I said absently. "What was his name?"

"Breslin. Pat Breslin", she said.

I looked up at once. "Pat Breslin?"

"Aye," she said, blushing a little.

I laughed. "D'you know," I said, "when I was a wee boy, I stole a cream bun from your daddy's play piece when we were in the infant school."

"I know," she said, "My daddy told us all about it every time you were on the T.V.!"

And I thought he was my best pal too!

64

John Cameron.
Film composer.

Once, at the age of thirteen, and very green around the gills, I was on a
Geographical Holiday with the school at a hostel in Northern Ireland.

Also in the hostel was a party from a Buckinghamshire girls' school,
but segregation in the hostel was most strict. On no account were the
boundaries to the different dormitories to be violated!

However, early in the holiday, I managed to rip my trousers climbing
and one of the girls offered to mend them. Later in the week, having
muddied the rest of my clothes, I thought I had better see if they were
indeed repaired.

On approaching the 'Girls' Sector', I was confronted by a formidable
apparition – a large lady teacher intent on preserving her girls' morals.
"And where do you think you are going?" she boomed. "Oh, it's
alright", I smiled "I've just come to get my trousers back . . ."

Daniel Caplan.
Retired senior Civil Servant.

Indolent and inattentive as I was at school, two subjects had their
fascination for me – Geography and History – and rising through school
I became Secretary of the Geographical and Historical Society. It was a
tough task sometimes to muster a respectable audience and I groaned
when the Head told me that Councillor X wished to be one of our
speakers. The Councillor was well-known as a travel bore.

The Councillor had only one leg and this gave me the bright notion
that we might pull in quite a crowd if I let it be known that he had lost the
leg in a fierce battle with a Crocodile. For good measure, I added that
Councillor X would probably show us the remains of his limb complete
with the Croc's teeth marks.

This ploy succeeded and the Head was delighted with the attendance
and my effort was praised. That is, until the time came for the Vote of
Thanks.

The wretched youth who moved this went on to express the general
regret that we had not been shown the Croc's work and teeth marks. As
Councillor X had lost his leg in a road accident, he was indeed taken

aback – and the Head was *not* amused!

The result of the Head's post-mortem was that I smarted – literally – for my bold venture into aggressive advertising. I kept my job but only because the Head knew how hard it would be to get another volunteer!

Fanny Carby.
Actress, films and T.V.

During the war, my school was evacuated to an enormous Gothic Hall in Staffordshire. It had a huge lake where we skated in the winter and it was surrounded by vast hills we could toboggan down.

The road which led to the Hall was cut through these hills and we children could stand on the high wooded banks, with the road quite a few feet below us.

We devised a terrifying game.

As an open lorry drove past below us, we jumped into it – this needed careful timing!

We would then bang on the little glass window behind the driver's head.

He would be struck with terror as he perceived two or three maniacal schoolgirls shrieking with laughter and jumping up and down.

Why we were never killed was a miracle.

This game was our favourite dare.

Ernestine Carter, O.B.E.
Author, journalist, former Associate Editor, The Sunday Times.

My first day at school I was sent off, starched to the eyes, in the charge of a neighbour's older girl and was guided to the first grade classroom where, at the teacher's desk, sat a young woman of unparalleled, at least to my youthful eyes, beauty. Her hair was a soft gold, her eyes a violet blue. I fell in love with her at once. The next day I rose early for I had a purpose in mind. My aunt's front garden had a semi-circular path which led from the street to her front steps. This path was usually bordered with either pansies or violets. This season the choice had been violets. And as Miss Hammond's eyes were violet, I had determined to pick her a bunch with the dew still on them. I picked and picked until I had collected the largest bunch of violets that I could carry, and set off for school. All this picking had made me rather late, to my escort's dismay, and I was the last to enter the classroom. Seated at the desk was not beautiful Miss Hammond but a rather severe looking woman with what seemed to me to be gimlet eyes.

"You're late", she said.

"I know, I'm sorry. Am I in the right class?" I asked.

"This is the first year" she said.

"Where is Miss Hammond, please?" I asked.

She said, "Miss Hammond is not here".

"Is she ill?" I cried.

"No" said the woman coldly, "*I* was ill, she was only a substitute".

I turned round and left the classroom, left the school and came home to find my aunt ruefully contemplating her much depleted borders.

"Ah" she said, "Why have you brought all the violets back?"

I explained, "Because Miss Hammond wasn't there."

"Oh" she said.

"There was another woman there. She said Miss Hammond was only a substitute. What," I asked pitifully, "is a substitute?" and burst into tears.

This incident of the violets had a curious sequel. Many many years later, long after I had married an Englishman, my husband was attached to the British Embassy in Washington. One day the ambassadress asked me if I would help entertain the wives of congressmen. We had tea on the terrace. The wife of one of the congressmen fixed me with a strangely familiar beady eye.

"Did you" she enquired abruptly, "ever go to school in Turbeyville?"

"Yes" I replied. "Briefly."

"Yes" she said, "I recognised you. I was the teacher you refused to give the violets to."

Fortunately I never saw her again.

Field Marshal Lord Carver, G.C.B., C.B.E., D.S.O., M.C.
Chief of the Defence Staff, 1973–76.

My father worked in Manchester and, when I was a boy, the second of four sons close to each other in age, we lived in a village in Cheshire on the outskirts of the cotton-spinning town of Bollington. The outbuildings of our house bordered on the road along which ran the North British Bus Company's service from Bollington to Macclesfield.

We were much taken to the sport of climbing about the roofs of the house and its outbuildings, a practice which was frowned on by our parents and which I personally did not much enjoy, having a bad head for heights. My elder brother, who later joined the Royal Air Force, was the leader of this activity. One day, in the absence of our parents, I and my younger brother (who later became a pilot in the Royal Navy's Fleet Air Arm) were on the roof of the outbuildings and began to amuse ourselves by playing ducks and drakes with stones and bits of brick and old mortar, by bouncing them off the roofs of passing buses, enjoying the reaction of the passengers who could not think what had caused the noise.

Soon after I had boasted to my brother about how skilful I was at this, my aim failed me and the piece of brick that I had thrown broke a window of the bus, fortunately without harming anyone inside. The bus stopped, and the angry conductor stepped out. We were off that roof in a flash, and ran to the bottom of the kitchen garden, where we hid under some sacking behind the manure heap. From our hiding place we could see the conductor walking round the garden with the gardener, our beloved Mr Bretherton, searching for us in vain. Bretherton was not helping him much.

Having waited until we heard the bus drive away, we emerged to face a wigging from Bretherton. But it was nothing compared to the wrath of my father, when he returned from his office in Manchester. It was all vented on me, on the grounds that I had led my brother astray, although I felt that he had put me up to it. My father beat me with his shoe, docked me of my pocket money until I had paid for the damage to the bus, and, worst punishment of all, stopped me from going to see the film of the book 'Owd Bob', a sentimental story about a sheepdog, to which I had been looking forward avidly. Thus was I saved from the life of a vandal, and never threw a brick at a bus again.

Ronnie Cass.
Composer, film and T.V. writer.

When I went to school there, it was called Llanelly Grammar School. Since then, in an upsurge of Welsh Nationalism, it has been altered to Llanelli Grammar School; so that now not only is it unpronounceable, it is also unspellable.

The time was nineteen thirty four and I had reached the tender age of eleven; a quite remarkable fact when you consider that in this year 1983 I have just reached Jack Benny's thirty nine.

Morning prayers – or as it was called in the school 'assembly' – just finishing. Being Jewish I had remained outside, lest hearing such Christian sentiments as are contained in The Sermon on the Mount might forever corrupt me.

But if being Jewish kept me away from Christian Philosophy, it also enabled me to arrive at school at least fifteen minutes later than the unconvinced Christians who were marched, class after class, into 'assembly'.

More and more seconds of that fifteen minutes were frittered away every day, until it became habitual for me to scoot down the corridor to await, with seconds to spare, the finish of 'assembly', because when prayers were over I came into my own.

"Come up Cass", the duty master would call, and I would mount the stage and make my way to the ugly upright piano and launch myself with great gusto into Schubert's March Militaire. Whereupon, the whole school, doubtless inspired by my performance, would – with brilliant precision – file out of the assembly hall.

That's how I started, but that extra fifteen minutes gained for me by my religion had started to corrupt my character. Sloth and laziness came upon me.

Nowhere was this clearer than in my repertoire. Never one to practise easily, the thought of additional practise to learn new marches was not the most attractive prospect, but a 'star' has got his obligations to his public, and I soon realised that an uninterrupted diet of March Militaire – however highly Schubert's mother thought of it – would tend to become monotonous. Then as now it was true, if you want to stay high on the hit parade, then better get some 'fresh material baby'.

In a blinding flash, the solution came to me; how to vary my repertoire and at the same time avoid the necessity of practise. Write my own marches. There was nothing simpler. After all the rhythm is unvarying; there is a first theme almost always in the major, a trio section usually in the relative minor, then back again to the first theme, a four or eight bar build-up to finish and Franz is your uncle.

No sooner thought than done.

Marches poured out of me faster than plays pour out of Ernie Wise, but if I was facile I was also monotonous. One march not only sounded like another, I sometimes would get mixed up and use the opening section of one march and the trio section of another.

Very soon I expected a deputation of masters and boys to come and see me with the message 'Come back Franz Schubert, all is forgiven'.

My ploy to hold my position as top of the hit parade had misfired with a vengeance. I had been playing the piano since the age of six, and had been winning dizzy amounts of money – sometimes five shillings – at local eisteddfodau. I had come to take the easy popularity my piano playing afforded me rather for granted. Suddenly the call ''Come up Cass'' was almost producing a groan of resignation in assembly.

Drastic measures were called for, and as far as Llanelly Grammar School was concerned something drastic was done.

For years I had been improvising as a jazz pianist, and on this momentous morning fate took a hand. I took my place at the piano and realised I had arrived at school minus the spiderlike manuscript that gave a clue to my latest march.

There was nothing for it. Suddenly the strains of 'Sweet Georgia Brown' issued forth. My left hand – even if it's me who says it – was pretty good. I was fast proving that even if I didn't have 'my gal' I did have 'music' and I did have 'rhythm'.

Never had the 'Saints marched out with a springier step'.

Gratefully I accepted the waves of approval I could feel winging their way to the stage.

From 'Sweet Georgia Brown' it was but a stone's throw to 'I Cover the Waterfront' and 'I'm Coming Virginia'. Feeling elated I looked around to see an empty assembly hall and the glowering face of the duty master. The biology master known to all as 'Fungi'.

''That was jazz boy'', he hissed at me.

I felt like saying ''It sure was baby'' but settled instead for a polite ''Yes sir''.

''You'll be hearing more about this'', he said.

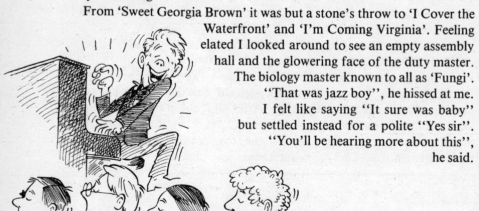

I had no doubt that this boded ill, because I was palpably – in the master's eyes – guilty of some heinous crime, something vastly worse than the mild sounding word 'misdeed'.

Duly the call came to see the headmaster, a very gentle fair and erudite man, Mr. T. V. Shaw, M.A.

"I hear you were playing jazz at assembly this morning, Ronald" he said.

"Yes sir" I replied.

"Well, it is a religious occasion" said Mr. Shaw "and I was wondering if you thought it suitable".

I was rather backed against a wall. I tended to agree with the head-master, but if I was to be barred from playing jazz at the end of assembly it was going to be back to a dreary diet of marches. Suddenly inspiration struck again.

"They do plays and concerts in the assembly hall" I said.

Mr. Shaw agreed but didn't see the relevance. I pressed home my point.

"Well sir" I said. "When assembly is finished the religious part is over, and you can march to jazz as easily as you can to a march."

Not true, of course, but Mr. Shaw's knowledge of jazz was on a par with my knowledge of nuclear physics.

But as I said, he was nothing if not fair.

"Let me think about it Ronald" he said.

All day I waited to hear, and heard nothing.

For the first time in weeks I was early in school. Much to my gratification I was the main topic of conversation in the playground. Requests were flooding in so fast I was beginning to feel like Housewife's Choice. 'Lady Be Good', 'Lover', 'Anything Goes'.

Any second I was waiting to be told "No jazz this morning, Cass" but the message never came.

Eagerly I bounded up to the stage. A bright four bar intro and I was launched into 'South Rampart Street Parade'.

Within a week jazz in assembly was taken for granted, and the 'Great sin of my schooldays' was easily assimilated.

Many years later I returned to the school as an Economics Master and the day came when I took my place on the stage along with the other masters at assembly.

"Come up Jones" called the duty master – Jones, wouldn't you know it – up came a young lad, his face ablaze with acne, who launched himself into Gershwin's 'Somebody Loves Me'.

"It's alright for you mate", I thought to myself "but if it hadn't been for me you'd be playing Schubert's March Militaire".

Rt. Hon. The Earl Cawdor, F.S.A., F.R.I.C.S.

On my fifth birthday, I woke up early, bright and merry. By mid-morning I was in an extremely crotchety mood, exactly why, I forget; it may have been an example of Nanny's tedious dictum,

> Laugh before seven,
> Cry before eleven . . .

Or it may have been caused by some episode in the hellish feud that my older sister and I conducted on and off for upwards of a decade. Perhaps I needed a dose, or maybe the affliction was brought on by eating Edinburgh rock after breakfast, which, except on your birthday, made you Go Blind. No matter, the mood was there.

So, on this glittering September morning, I was loitering by the Summer-house in the garden, with intent as yet undefined, but certainly it was not a good intent.

My cousin, Charlie, of the same age, hove into sight bearing a gift, and most nauseating to behold was his appearance: to my keen and narrowed eye he had clearly been washed and well rinsed in rose-water, his nails cleaned with an orange-stick, his combed hair was held in place to perfection by some adhesive, probably Gripe Water, his clothes were offensively spotless and uncreased, and he affected a special and aggravating walk as befitted the importance of the occasion, unless (Ha!) it was the discomfort of new shining buttoned shoes of patent leather.

With the unconcern of an archangel in a minefield, and the obsequious unction of a Welsh undertaker, he came up the gravel path and presented his offering with a rhythmic, pithy speech: "This is for you . . . Hugh."

It was a tin sword. It was the work of a moment for the connoisseur to see that this was no noble Highland double-handed claymore. One glance revealed that it was a shoddy imitation of a basket-hilted broadsword, of inferior workmanship, probably foreign and worst of all, blunt. A wave at the roses produced a slight rattle from the hilt. The sword was as silvery and as light as a small trout.

I at once decided to cut off my cousin's head. Without warning, I gave a tremendous medieval swipe, striking the donor with admirable aim on the side of his neck. To my horror not only did his head fail to come off and roll away into the lavender beds; he did not even fall over, confirming my opinion of the weapon.

There was not even a drop of blood, and what happened next was this: my cousin's face took on a velvety blush, quite becoming in its own way, like a newly painted putto, and his mouth formed an O shape, like a choirboy's, and from this aperture there now emerged an earsplitting wail pitched at about B sharp in a register unreached in living memory.

There was no time to lose; this fearsome racket was bound to attract the attention of authority, if indeed it did not actually splinter the glass of the Nursery windows above us. I therefore resumed my task with a will, this time using the sword with a vigorous sawing movement and neat wrist-action, upon the stubborn jugular. Suddenly there was an eclipse of the sun which certainly had not been predicted in my copy of Chick's Own. This shadow was caused by a visiting governess who I had immediately recognised as Goliath's mother from her handsome mustache. She seized a handful of my hair and carried me bodily away. Although this did not pain me at all, I thought it ought to, and therefore set up a long-lasting bellow punctuated for good measure by the occasional scream, sobs of self-pity, and groans of thwarted ambition.

Charlie, who remains to this day the greatest of friends in the face of stiff odds, was not so much injured in the neck as hurt in the feelings. There was, to my mortification, much fussing over him; a minute bruise was treated with Pomade Divine, his hair was re-combed, and there was much tutting and tushing; I was in scowling disgrace, surrounded by scolds. The Grown-Ups appeared from time to time to inspect, silently, the martyr and the criminal.

As for the offending sword, it vanished for ever into one of those upper cupboards, Where Things Are Put Away – such a vital feature of the British household – prongless toasting-forks, the arm of a doll, medicine bottles without labels, rolls of corrugated paper, one glove, 49 playing-cards, a broken parasol and the instructions for the use of Friar's Balsam.

Looking at the Visitor's Book for 1937, I see that my cousin Charlie and his family, who had all been staying with us, left on that distant birthday of mine. I wonder if that had been their original plan or did they, like Shakespeare, believe that hospitality at Cawdor was an unknown virtue?

Robert Cecil, C.M.G.
Author, H.M. Diplomatic Service ret'd, Chairman, Institute of Cultural Research.

I was destined early for a diplomatic career. My widowed mother was therefore delighted when she was invited, together with my sister and myself, to spend a week-end with a retired Ambassador and his wife in their country-house near Royston. My mother hoped that, young as I was, I would make a good impression and, perhaps, pick up a few hints about diplomacy. The only warning cloud on the horizon was that my sister and I insisted that we must take our small kitten, Sambo, since none of our neighbours would look after him in our absence. The neighbours' refusal was not entirely unreasonable, as Sambo had already developed some unusual habits. He could climb anything, but had a preference for brocade curtains or rare tapestry; he also loved water and was an accomplished swimmer.

Our reception at the ex-Ambassador's country seat was a little less cordial than my mother had hoped; Sambo was at once consigned to the stables. During the night, however, he made his way onto the roof of an out-house and aroused me by his piteous cries. My sister and I managed, without attracting attention, to haul him up to our window and he spent the rest of the night on my bed, as was his usual practice. Early next morning, inquisitive as ever, he followed me down the passage when I went to the lavatory. The old house had never been modernised, apart from the installation of electric light, and most of the fittings belonged to the mid-nineteenth century. This was certainly true of the lavatory-seat, which consisted of an oval, cut in a solid piece of mahogany. This covered a miniature cistern, which could be emptied by gravity at the appropriate moment by pulling up a brass handle, fitted just below the level of the seat.

I had never encountered such a flushing system and, as I pulled up my pyjama-trousers, I looked around for a few moments until the brass handle caught my eye. My eye also registered the fact that Sambo was nowhere to be seen; a faint mewing from the cistern soon made me aware of what had happened to him. At that moment the door-handle was given a peremptory twist from outside. In my panic I unlocked the door and was confronted by the portly form of His Excellency, clad in a flowered-silk dressing-gown. "Oh, Sir!" I cried, "Sambo has fallen in." The ex-Ambassador, who had seen his country through some awkward situations in his time, was a man of action; he raised the massive lavatory-seat, disclosing Sambo swimming strongly in not very hygenic waters. I snatched up Sambo and we fled, dripping and malodorous, down the passage.

During the remainder of the week-end no word concerning this unsavoury incident – nor indeed concerning any other subject – passed between His Excellency and myself. I noticed, however, that when my mother ventured to raise the question of my having a try at a future date for the Diplomatic Service, our host poured cold water – pure cold water – on the whole idea.

Geoffrey Chater.
Actor of stage and screen.

When I was 5 years old, I used to be taken for a walk with my elder brother in Primrose Hill Park, near the London Zoo.

We would enter by the N.W. entrance and straight away the asphalt path becomes steep for about 40 yards. At this time I was the proud owner of a small tricycle and a very small wheel-barrow. Some days I was allowed to take one or the other to the Park.

One day I noticed that a dog was devouring the thick grass near the entrance. "What's that dog doing?" – I asked my brother. "Oh that grass" – he said, "It's dog's doses". Next day I brought that wheel barrow, filled it with grass and pushed it up and down in front of some people enjoying the sunshine on a park bench, yelling at the top of my voice "Dogs Doses for sale". Eventually, no doubt to bring the performance to an end, a very large lady on the bench offered me tuppence which I gratefully accepted.

On another day, I had the tricycle and decided to have a go at the 40 yard hill (which was strictly forbidden as I hadn't mastered the brake). I was instantly out of control careering down the hill towards the open park gates. I found the hand brake at last, which slowed me down but then I saw the ample form of my benefactor on the path ahead of me. The well up-holstered rear view was a god-send. Pulling hard on the brake I steered towards her and had almost stopped by the time my shoulder and not tricycle brought things to a halt.

"Oh!!" she said – and then, recognising me "I do wish you'd stick to selling grass" – and she walked on.

John Chittock, O.B.E., F.B.K.S., F.R.P.S., F.R.T.S.
Writer, producer, publisher.

My early crimes were mostly harmless events – such as window breaking, stink bombs, even posing as carol singers for the church.

I suppose that my worse misdeeds were all concerned with explosives. I had a perverse desire to blow things up. The problem was that explosives were hard to come by, especially during the war years, and one had to improvise.

My teachers were unco-operative. Innocent attempts to discover the ingredients of explosive mixtures were usually frustrated – or worse, dismissed with such a lack of interest that I became convinced that grown-ups really did lead dull lives.

This problem in accessing information from the traditional founts of learning led me on the path of self-help and self-improvement. If you have the right incentives, learning can suddenly acquire a new dimension and relevance. And so I began to spend much more time at the local reference library. My teachers could not believe this transformation. Chittock was mending his ways.

If my memory serves me correctly, it was through this new dedication to bookishness that I discovered the ingredients of gunpowder: potassium nitrate, sulphur and charcoal. But those early experiments were rather like the proverbial damp squib; it just doesn't work unless you have the sophisticated means of packing the mixture tightly in a metal container.

Screw top bottles with a little carbide and water worked much better, I discovered. The carbide effervesces like something out of Quatermass, and eventually the pressure in the bottle causes it to explode. But even in those days I was a sensible chap and soon came to realise that this was a potentially dangerous route to follow. I needed something safer.

My next innovative attempt worked quite well – magnesium powder and potassium permanganate. The former was often obtained as flash powder from photographic shops and also by filing the outer cases of dud incendiary bombs dropped by the Germans. Did they ever realise, I wonder, how they contributed to my education?

But one day, I at last discovered the perfect explosive. Name – nitrogen iodide. Formula – iodine crystals soaked in ammonia solution. When dry, it is touch-sensitive. Painted on to door knobs, wooden blackboard cleaners, rulers, etc, it could incite agility in the most senile of school-teachers.

Fortunately, my excursions of self-learning (the formal processes in school failed miserably) did get diverted into safer channels before I could actually blow my head off. Mathematics, for example, became a serious business when I discovered the delights of astronomy; that

mysterious science demands a knowledge of mathematics and so at the age of about 14 I surprised all of my teachers by taking a sudden interest in algebra and other branches of numeracy.

Astronomy led to no serious misdeeds as far as I can recall. At least, that's my story and I'm sticking to it. I became the youngest member of the British Astronomical Association, and in attending one of their meetings at Burlington House invoked the curiosity of a passionate BAA member – comedian Will Hay – who in schoolmasterly fashion enquired, disbelievingly, if I really was interested in astronomy.

During that period I discovered a comet, visible to the naked eye. But unfortunately Greenwich Observatory never answered the telephone at nights (due to the war) and I failed to achieve verification, so I cannot go down in history with a comet carrying my name. Eventually Greenwich Observatory acknowledged my letters (when the comet had passed into the galaxy) and clearly regarded me as stupid. "A persistent meteor trail" they said; the words stick in my throat to this day. How could a meteor trail persist over a period of four days?

If anyone recalls any bomb damage to Greenwich Observatory at that time, put it down to the Luftwaffe. By then I was on the straight and narrow.

Tony Christopher.
General Secretary, Inland Revenue Staff Federation, member of T.U.C. General Council, member of Independent Broadcasting Authority.

As my friends know so well, in matters practical, electrical, mechanical or in any way connected with water, I am very little short of a genius. Not so very long ago, for example, having procrastinated for months I was eventually pressed into spending a wet Sunday morning putting up some shelves in a utility cupboard. Carefully I fashioned holes to take my shelves around some pipes, screwed all up tight and looked around for the brush to clear up. No brush; then I spotted it safe and sound. I had carefully cut three shelves around the broom handle.

But that is not really my story. I tell it simply to prove the educationalists' point that some development must come late. I hope.

Around 1940 my mother was in hospital. We were close; her operation was major and, school or not, I visited each afternoon. Cheltenham Hospital in those days had highly polished wood block floors and beds all of three foot high. It was the only way of polishing under them, I supposed – indeed demonstrated. At this point I should explain that another of my attributes is an inability to keep still; walking backwards in shops is something I have always done well, regularly and sometimes disastrously and I tip chairs onto two legs to great effect on occasion.

There I was sitting, comforting my mother (mostly with assurances that I was not starving) and tipping my chair. Then I was gone. Straight under the bed. Bang! Whoosh! The ward was in uproar. One poor woman allegedly burst her stitches. My earliest experience of negotiation was probably the subsequent conversation with the Ward Sister who wasn't all that keen on my evening return visit.

A water story from a year or two earlier comes from Upwey Wishing Well. An elderly lady, who I was certain was a witch, sold glasses of magic water. With kindly care she told the 'little man' to turn around, wish and throw the water over his shoulder. He did – straight into her face. The lesson on that occasion? Witches know bad language as well as spells.

T. E. B. Clarke, O.B.E.
Screen writer (Passport to Pimlico, Lavender Hill Mob, Hue and Cry, etc.).

At Charterhouse I ran a bookmaking business in partnership with a day boy who would pass on risky bets to a town bookie. We were caught and summoned to the headmaster's house on Grand National day, unable to lay off any of our record takings. So ruin faced us on two counts, with the head keeping us sweating for twenty-four hours while he decided whether or not to expel us. As we left his presence an evening paper was thrust through his letter box. The stop press would give the result of the race, which we had not yet heard. Dared we? If he were to

come out of his study our fate would surely be sealed – but the temptation was too great. Two glorious words greeted us: Sergeant Murphy, a rank outsider that nobody had backed. We'd had a skinner! That win went some way towards compensating us for being sentenced to afternoon drill every Saturday of the following summer term.

Trisha Clarke.
Actress, films and T.V.

One of our favourite games at school was 'dare, truth, kiss or promise' – played usually at night after 'lights out'. We would meet with our torches in a large dormitory cupboard, and sit amid suitcases under our hanging clothes dreaming up escapades to get each other to do. One Saturday evening I was dared to put the loaves of bread which were sitting on a shelf in the larder under the shelf – a simple dare! However just as I was finishing the 'dare', I was disturbed and in a panic ran back to the dormitory with an armful of loaves. Nurse was on the prowl, and the loaves got hastily put in the cupboard. Next morning we smelt porridge being cooked for breakfast, and this was a rare event for a Sunday! At breakfast-time after grace, we were informed that as it was the third Sunday in Lent there would only be porridge for breakfast as we would be 'giving up' bread for to-day and so there would be no toast and eggs. As for the bread it didn't even go mouldy; it just took days for the lavatory to swallow it up.

Brian Clemens.
Writer and producer (creator of 'The Avengers', 'The Professionals').

I was, of course, a perfect child – a state that has persisted into my adult life – and so I had no misdeeds, or indeed any blemishes of character (apart from self deception and a tendency to lie a lot). The earliest *misadventure* I can recall was when I was evacuated to Hitchin and a favourite uncle, who was an officer in the RAF, came to call, laden with strange fruits he had brought back from the Middle East. I encountered my first banana (surely one could never eat such a bizarre object?) and oranges, and a lush, ripe pear. I attacked the pear voraciously until I was left with only the stalk – and that little stubby bit that sits in the bottom of a pear. I chewed the stalk to a pulp, then examined that little stubby bit – there were still some pips lurking in there to be eaten. I probed one out, popped it into my mouth and ate it.

Then the other little 'pips' started moving! In my greed I had devoured a large Middle Eastern insect!

Colonel The Lord Clifford of Chudleigh, O.B.E., D.L.
Count of The Holy Roman Empire, farmer and land-owner.

We open our stately house to the public, and get our local friends to keep an eye on the main rooms. In the Morning Room is the medal case which includes the Victoria Cross won by a Clifford in the Crimean War. Latish one afternoon two Dutchmen were looking at the case, so our lady 'guide', trying to be friendly, went up to them and said "You know about the V.C. do you?". A longish pause, and the reply came – "I zink it is just around the corner".

82

Sir John Colville, Kt., C.B., C.V.O.
Private Secretary to three Prime Ministers: Neville Chamberlain 1939–40;
Winston Churchill 1940–41 and Clement Attlee 1945.

When I was fifteen the window of my room at school overlooked the High Street. I had three devilish amusements.

The first was to stick a 1½d. stamp on the pavement. It was surprising how many stopped to pick the stamp up. When they bent down to do so, I poured a jug of water over them. Boys and occasional passers-by were the only safe targets. Masters who tried to recover the stamp had to be spared, discretion being the better part of valour.

The second was to place an old top hat (they were still part of the school dress) on the pavement, topside up and containing two heavy bricks. Passers-by found it irresistible to kick it. The howls of anguish were pure delight.

The third, and the only callous pastime, was to heat pennies in the fire. There is nothing to indicate that copper is searing hot. Retrieved with the tongs and dropped to carol-singers, Halloween performers or penny-for-the-Guy hopefuls, they produced excruciating yells which none but a school-boy would have thought funny.

Had I been caught I should not have thought the retribution funny either.

Patrick Connor.
Actor, National Theatre and T.V.

In 1940 I was evacuated to Uttoxeter. My arrival there does not come into the category of 'misdeeds', though it is indelibly imprinted on my mind. One by one, our 130-strong school party was led away to their billets until I was standing alone, clutching my suitcase. People kept coming up, looking at my identity label which contained my name, school and *religion*, nodding and walking away. Then I heard someone murmur, "He'll do for the Crosses." They, in fact, were a local *Catholic* family who had volunteered to take a *Catholic* evacuee, but only dimly aware that the majority of my school fellows were Protestants, I had this terrible vision of living with the priest and spending my days in North Staffordshire as an acolyte, carrying crosses in church.

No such fate befell me and before long I was one of an irreligious Gang of Four, whose behaviour generally was less than perfect.

Later in 1941, or maybe it was 1942, anyway it was after Hitler had invaded Russia, there was a 'Spitfire Week' in Uttoxeter, during which towns or cities aimed to raise £5000, or more, to buy a Spitfire. (Yes, you could then buy an aircraft for that sum.) The town was bedecked with bunting and in tribute to our Russian allies, the Hammer and Sickle was raised alongside the Union Jack on the Town Hall. We four blood brothers decided something must be done to remove this insult to all true-born Britons – including the half-Irish like me – who were fighting for freedom and democracy. (I may say we were just as xenophobic when our American allies flooded into the area.)

In best military fashion we planned our raid on the Town Hall. We had a 'recce' before deciding to camp out for the duration of our campaign (it must have been during the holidays or over a long weekend). With the owner's permission, we set up our tent in a field outside the compact market town and we had a conference. Everybody was allotted his task, we synchronised our watches, and it was agreed that action would commence at nine pip emma, or whatever time it was, but it was definitely 'pip emma', not p.m. or 'in the evening'. We then walked the mile and a half back into Uttoxeter. Forty years on, I cannot remember who did what, but I know I personally did *not* climb on to the Town Hall roof, but merely kept guard below. I remember feeling drunk with a mixture of excitement and apprehension, frothed up by the patriotism of our mission.

The Hammer and Sickle was removed from its flagpole, and absolutely intoxicated with excitement we tramped back to the field where we tossed the offending alien flag into the air and mock-fought over it, until our hysterical high spirits subsided. Then we went inside the tent where I think we had a drink, probably cocoa, and sat gazing at the Red Flag, wondering what to do with it. Finally, we became solemn. The flag

84

should be cut into four pieces, each of use would take a section away and when the war was over we should meet in Uttoxeter to place the four pieces back into the whole, as the symbol of our undying friendship and patriotism.

That night we didn't actually perform the cutting operation and even before the local newspaper wrote of the *theft* of the flag and the *insult* to our heroic allies fighting for their lives, we had begun to get cold feet. A few days later, sheepishly, we posted the Hammer and Sickle back to the Town Hall intact.

Rearden Conner (Patrick Reardon Connor, M.B.E.)
Novelist and short story writer.

When I was young, in our village in the west, not far from the Atlantic that used to boom against our rocky shores I dreamed of being, not another Columbus, but no less than a poacher. I envied old Joe Lannigan who was said to make a good thing out of his poaching, and whose skill and daring in outwitting the forces of the law made him famous from end to end of the county.

We had a good trout river near my home, and for a long stretch of it the fishing rights were owned by the man who had inherited 'the big house' many years before I was born. He was an irate individual who was seldom seen anywhere without a shotgun over his arm. He had a passionate hatred, it was said, for poachers and individuals of that sort, and a burning desire to blow holes in them and let the fresh air into them.

Nevertheless, I was determined on one thing . . . to catch the old trout that lived at the top end of the river. It was a long and fat trout and not too active. Yet it was cunning, so cunning that even Joe Lannigan had failed to catch it, and all his efforts had disturbed it no more than the patter of raindrops.

The river was narrow at the spot where the trout lived, and not too deep. It was spanned by a one-arched stone bridge which humped its course over the water like the back of a huge, grey cat. I leant over the low wall of the bridge for hours, flicking the line of my fishing rod along the water. I had tried book flies and stone flies, live and dead bait, since early morning . . . but the trout had not budged. There it lay, alone, moving its tail slightly as if to taunt me. Sometimes I could see the gentle

motion of its gills as it brooded in the shadow of the bridge.

When the sun began to shine strongly I climbed down to the river bank and hid behind a bush, casting my line artfully towards the trout. The coloured fly on the hook seemed really to dip down and skim the water so practised had I become at making a cast. But the old trout was not to be deceived. It did not even attempt to rise towards the bait. Only when one of the countless water flies dipped down above its nose did it rise, slowly and heavily, to engulf it.

By around mid-day I had grown to hate it. I shouted abuse at it in an effort to arouse it from its coma. Once I thrashed the water with my rod, and it glided away into the shadow of the bridge. I broke a branch off a bush and followed it into the cool water beneath the arch. I beat at the water with the widespread branch, churning it into a white, foam-like surf. But the trout did not seem terrified. It glided away under the long drifts of water-weed, leaving me to spend my rage on startled minnows.

In the afternoon when I returned to the bridge the trout was there once more, brooding serenely, as though it had never been disturbed in its rest. The sight of it made me tremble. I wanted to catch it in my hands and crush it for daring to defy me. I picked up a handful of stones and began to pelt it. It dodged the first and the second with incomparable ease. At the third it turned and slid under the bridge, languidly, as though in patient boredom.

I was furious now. The old trout had become an obsession. I decided to dam the river at this point. I was so intent on victory over the trout

that I had forgotten any danger from the anger of the owner of the big house and his inevitable shotgun.

I rushed home and searched for old potato sacks. These I fastened end to mouth with long, pointed sticks. When I returned to the river the trout was still there. The sun was shining strongly on the water, making it look like a polished shield. But my face felt brighter even than the surface of the water with eagerness. Now I knew that I was going to best the trout. In a little while it would be entrapped, at my mercy.

I worked quickly, driving rough stakes broken from a nearby ash into the river bed at the top of each bank. I stretched the sacks between them and weighed the sacks with stones so that they could not lift with the flow of the water. As I worked my face felt drawn and tense from excitement and sweat stood out on my forehead.

I finished the first dam and found it a success. The water flowed through the canvas of the sacks, bellying them out. I looked to see that there was no hole through which the trout could escape. I saw, too, that the trout was still there, brooding under the bridge, completely unaware of its approaching fate. "Ah, my fine boyo," I said aloud, "you'll soon be in the frying pan!"

I went back to the bridge and climbed down to the bank on the other side. Here I began my second dam. Then I took my cap and waded into the cool, deep water under the arch. I told myself that I could use the cap to scoop up the trout. But when I reached the spot where the trout lived I saw that the clear space of water was vacant. I waded around, poked under weeds, examined my first dam, returned to my second, but the oblong of water seemed uninhabited except for a score of minnows and one young eel.

The trout must have turned lazily and swum up river under the long grasses on the river bank while I had been fixing the first stake of my second dam. I did not realise that it had been able to match its cunning against my artfulness. I was convinced that it could not have got away unobserved.

It was then that I began to grow afraid of it. There were still men in our district who told tales of fairy fish which vanished if not kept constantly under observation, but which, if caught, were found to hold pearls or rare jewels in their bellies.

I began to think that the old trout was such a fairy fish. It was strange, I reflected, how it lived all by itself near the bridge, not under the bridge and yet not in the open river, as though it wished to keep an eye on all who peered over the low stone wall above it.

I removed the two dams and went home heavy-hearted. I had been defeated, just as the renowned Joe Lannigan himself had been defeated by that very rascal of a trout. The trout had made a laughing-stock of me. True, there had been no observer of my effort, but there was always my secret opinion of my own prowess, and that had been shaken badly.

I lay awake that night thinking of the trout that had now become my enemy, planning how I might outwit it and destroy it once and for all. Finally, I had an inspiration. I had read somewhere that the natives of the South Sea islands caught fish by means of a bow and arrow. I would make a bow and arrow! The night seemed endless after that thought had gripped me. I tossed and turned in my narrow bed as though the thought were one of great magnitude beating down upon my mind like a wave upon a small craft.

At dawn I was up and had cut myself a thin, tough sapling. It was easy work fashioning arrows. I smoothed them and pointed them well, working feathers into the ends so that they would fly true to aim. Then I practised for an hour, aiming at a dock leaf, blunting the points against buried stones and resharpening them.

I was on my way to the river before the men had begun their labours in the fields. The old trout was there, brooding near the arch. It was a dull morning. The sun did not shine on the water to dazzle me. I could have sung a song of joy as I saw my victim, now unsuspecting, moving its tail gently down below. My heart beat wildly with excitement. I took careful aim, conscious all the time of the beating of my heart. I felt my eyeballs pressing against their sockets as though they, too, wished to leap down with the arrow and put an end to this fish that had so tantalised them. Then I released the string and saw the arrow flash down, white and straight. It hit the water with a plunging, hollow sound and transfixed the fish well below the gills.

The old trout leaped as if it were awakening from a queer dream. It thrashed the water with its tail, whitening it as I had whitened it with the whipping branch. Then it fell down and lay still, suddenly as inanimate as a fish on a slab, held to its favourite spot by the thin arrow now embedded in the river bed.

Half an hour later I made a good meal off the old trout. It was not as appetising as I had hoped, not by a long way, but to my everlasting regret as I grew older, I found satisfaction that morning in devouring my enemy.

A day later neighbours were saying that I was lucky not to have been taken in my youth, and I would have been too only for old Doctor Roche. "Such pain he suffered," they said, "and he screaming like a poisoned pup for hours on end!" They went on to say, or so I was told long afterwards, "For what did the young blackguard do but eat the old trout from the bridge that had been there for years and years and that some said was a witch, a trout that was so rotten with disease that it was unable to swim more than a dozen yards at a time, and must have been near the point of death before ever he caught it!"

Jilly Cooper.
Author and Mail on Sunday columnist.

There was an incident when we had a chair at home which you could remove the seat from and my mother was having some very grand people to a bridge party and a lot of fuss and preparation went into it. She probably didn't have enough time that morning to talk to me because she was making cakes and sandwiches and tidying up the drawing room. So I got sulky and removed the seat of this particular arm chair where my mother often sat and placed a blue and purple silk cushion over it. The time duly arrived and all these smart ladies turned up and were all talking in their ringing voices in the drawing room and Mummy swept them in

and brought in the tea things and she was just about to pick up the silver tea pot when she stepped back and sat down on the chair, and of course because there was only just a cushion she went straight through, so her legs were sticking up in the air and her knees were against her face. All

the women looked at her with great surprise and amazement before they pulled her out. I remember I was spanked by my father for this and I felt very guilty and ashamed of myself and I don't think I've ever really mobbed anyone up in public since. But my mother, to give her credit always tells this story with screams of laughter today so there were no hard feelings really.

The Right Rev. Roderic Coote.
Bishop of Colchester, Irish champion hurdler, pianist and broadcaster.

The school at which I did my secondary studies was in the middle of a sizeable town which was quite proud of its school and followed its football and cricket matches and other activities with eager interest. One of those other activities was the annual school play performed to packed audiences on the Wednesday, Friday and Saturday nights of one week in the Spring.

For umpteen years one member or other of the Coote family acted in the school play. My great year was when I was cast as the son of Mary Rose (in J. M. Barrie's play of that name), the tough young Australian soldier who returned to the old home and encountered the ghost of his mother Mary Rose. During the play I had to balance on my knee a very bony fellow student, who was very un-ghostlike.

I experienced a mixture of excitement and apprehension when the English master who produced the play told me that I would have to smoke a pipe during the performance. I had to cut some plug tobacco with a clasp knife that played an important role in the plot. I didn't smoke the plug tobacco. I had a packet of very mild stuff to smoke. I put my hand into my pocket with which I had rolled the plug tobacco, and deftly took out the mild substitute which I put into the pipe and smoked. Even so, I only just got off the stage in time on each of the three nights, for I had never smoked anything in my life except the odd cigarette behind the hedge.

It was the very first scene, and I was understandably a bit nervous. I cut my plug tobacco, rolled it in my hand, substituted it for the mild stuff, packed my pipe, lit a match, lit the pipe, shook the match and threw it into the stage fire of red tissue paper with an electric bulb in the middle. It didn't go out! Mercifully the fire had a wooden base raised about half an inch from the stage, and the match went underneath. Even so, I spent the entire first scene on my hands and knees frantically trying to pat it out. The drama critic of the local press seemed to think that it was not the best scene in the play!

Paul Copley.
Actor of stage and screen, teacher and writer.

At the age of 7, I seemed to have everything included in my surroundings that anyone could possibly wish for.

I had two sisters, so our family of five lived claustrophobically in a two-up/two-down terraced cottage, on a budget which would have taxed the ingenuity of a fasting penitent! However, the terrace was in the rich dairy farming belt of the West Riding of Yorkshire, and our tiny oblong garden (which had a 4' × 4' square of grass – 'the lawn' and a muddy bit!) was augmented by the 75 acre dairy farm, whose buildings adjoined our terrace. We kids had the run of the farm; its barns with clamberable machinery and dusty cornbins, its sheds with rough-tongued calves and steaming, smelly bull; and its seemingly endless fields and woods, stone walls and hedges, ankle-turning ploughed fields and hide-and-seeking cornfields. The only limitation on our freedom was that we must not cross the road alone, and we must not venture into the grounds of the big house across the road, built long ago by the owner of the local woollen mill. The house was a mansion, the grounds dark and brooding with laurel and rhododendrons.

One of my favourite haunts at this time was a one-acre wood, a triangle of trees on sloping ground, where free-range hens scratched during the day and huddled in the hen-houses at night.

Alongside the wood a stream gurgled in what seemed like a ravine to me. The stream bounced out of a large hole in a banking and this hole, my 'cave', intrigued me more and more; but its darkness and dankness put me off more than the most cursory investigation. Until, one Sunday, I was given a huge, battered torch with a searchlight of a beam, by my Uncle Jack. The power of this torch gave me the courage to satisfy my curiosity to know where the stream came from.

On the Monday morning, it being school holidays, I left our backyard, dodging our flapping, wet sheets hung out to dry, carrying my torch. I also had five 'Marie' biscuits wrapped in greaseproof paper in an old gas mask bag.

I entered the cave, astride the stream. Water dripped, mud sucked at my feet, slimy hand-holds slipped away. But my trusty torch showed me the way forward. I sloshed ahead, crouching as the roof of the tunnel got lower. I shivered at the sight of a frog, and looked back to the entrance for reassurance. I'd obviously rounded a bend with no entrance in sight. Slight panic – go on or turn back? Deep breath – plunge on. My shoes were full of water as I was now obliged to walk in the stream. The roof got lower still, one knee dipped in the water.

By the time I saw light again I was on all-fours, wet through, covered in mud, 'Marie' biscuits lost along with gas mask bag. The light at the end of the tunnel had me whimpering with relief. When I reached it, bars of iron blocked my escape! The idea of going back was unthinkable!

I pushed at the bars in desperation, they gave way. The tunnel spat me out on top of them; bedraggled, muddy, and lost.

I was in a dark green jungle; a gloomy alien land! I crawled along under the bushes not daring to think of what I may meet.

Suddenly, through the branches and leaves I saw – wet, white sheets flapping in the breeze. I scrambled out of the bushes, there was mother, hanging out more clothes. I shouted across the road to her in glee.

The telling-off, the smacks, the rough stand-up bath I was given, were all accepted with relief and joy.

Now the farm buildings are town houses, the mansion is an office

92

building, the free-range hens scratch no more; but the tunnel from the big-house grounds, housing the stream that runs down past one acre wood, the land drain, remains.

Lt. Gen. Sir John Cowley, G.C., K.B.E., C.B.
Controller of Munitions, Ministry of Supply 1957–1960.
Master-General of the Ordnance, War Office 1960–1962.

Between the age of 8 and 13 years, I was educated at a splendid preparatory school, from which most of the boys went to Osborne, Dartmouth and the Royal Navy. My years there corresponded almost exactly with the years of the Great War of 1914–1918.

The success of this school was due to the character of the Headmaster, who was a fiery-tempered Welshman. He was a powerful man who had won two Blues at Oxford for football and putting the weight. He was also a formidable thrasher of any small boy who had incurred his wrath – and to him the mortal sin was 'idleness', a complaint I have suffered from all my life.

Fortunately, I escaped with only six thrashings – well below the average – and even these were modified by the loving care of my mother, who sewed cotton wool pads inside the seats of all my trousers.

My last thrashing was unusual, even for him. He entered the school hall with his cane, stood up in front of the seventy boys, and said:

"Tonight I will thrash somebody. If any of you are willing to step forward and be thrashed in front of the school, I will give that boy sixpence."

I volunteered, as sixpence in 1918 was a considerable sum of money. After five strokes, I had had enough and got up. He said "Stay down, boy, you have one stroke more to go". When he had finished, he handed me 6 pence and said "I hope in your future life you will earn money as honourably as you have earned this".

The strange part of this story is that the great majority of the boys admired him. He made us work and play games as well as we could – and most of the boys left the school knowing that they had been taught to do their best, or suffer the consequences. (Modern psychologists, please note!)

Pauline Crabbe, O.B.E., J.P.
Vice Chairman, Brook Advisory Centres, writer, broadcaster, member of Advisory Council on Race Relations.

I always say – although I am not sure it is true – that my family were the first Jamaican immigrants to settle in this country. We came here in 1919: a large extended family consisting of my mother and father, six children, a grandfather on one side, grandmother on the other, an aunt, a cousin and a couple of elderly women who claimed to be related to my mother but whose exact degree of kinship was never discovered. We were the only black family in the neighbourhood; we were the only black children in our schools and as we grew up in the white world of London in the twenties we somehow never thought of ourselves as strange or different. At least I didn't – until one winter morning which remains fixed in my mind to this day.

I can't remember how old I was but I had already been at school for some years. I loved everything about school but especially the opportunities it offered me for acting both on and off the stage. I had always been one of those ghastly children prepared to recite to visitors when called upon to do so and always ready not just with my party piece but with an encore or two as I felt certain I should be well applauded. And so I took for granted the admiration I received for my dramatic renderings. My vanity allowed me to consider myself a remarkable actress and both teachers and class mates pandered to me by a tacit agreement that I should always have the lead in the annual school play. Being chosen in this way seemed to emphasise the fact that I was of course acknowledged as the best actress the school had.

Quite suddenly one year another girl was chosen to play the most important part in the school play. I remember vividly when this was announced my sense of shock, of outrage and the frightening flash of fear in my mind that perhaps people thought I was no longer a talented actress.

In the middle of morning lessons I rushed out of school without stopping to seek permission. I cried bitterly all the way home and arrived at our house to hurl myself into my mother's arms as she opened the door. I poured out my pain and disappointment about not getting the best part in the play – about my fear that without knowing how I had perhaps lost my cherished acting ability. I remember the warmth of my mother's embrace as she slowly and carefully helped me to understand that perhaps there was another reason why I had not been chosen to play the lead in the school play that year as it happened to be a production of Snow White and the Seven Dwarfs.

Gemma Craven.
Actress and musical star.

One of my early misdeeds embarrassed my mother more than it did me. When I was about five she had a friend to tea who presented me with an absolutely outsize bag of sweets. I staggered out into the street and rounded up all my playmates, letting each of them touch and admire the bag but not to eat any of the sweets. Then I went back into the house and returned the bag to my mother's friend, saying: "Thank you. You can have it back now. I've shown it to all my friends but they're the kind of sweets I really hate"!

Anna Cropper.
Actress.

I was brought up in the Rossendale Valley, a small industrial valley north of Manchester. The War had ended, but we were still on rations. My best friend Anne Disley's father, Fred, owned a soft drinks and pickling factory at Water Barn Mill, and one Sunday he said that he would take Anne and me to catch tiddlers at Mill Lodge, so after lunch at Anne's, armed with scoop nets and jam jars, we set off. Fred said he'd go for a walk after we'd settled ourselves on the bank. Within half-an-hour, having caught hundreds of tiddlers, we began to get bored, and Fred not having come back, we wandered off to find better sport. We hadn't to look far, for we found the Mill door was open and Fred not being there, we began to explore. Soon, we were gazing at hundreds of bottles of lemonade, cream soda, Tizer, dandelion and burdock, sarsaparilla – all in crates, and *all* unlabelled. I can't remember *who* thought of it, but we decided to do what hadn't been done before work stopped the previous Friday. We would label them, but with a difference. Difference, being the operative word, we found the boxes of labels and set to, giggling at the confusion that would be caused in Rossendale when people bought lemonade and found it was cream soda; dandelion and burdock, sarsaparilla etc. "Just think of it," said Anne: "I tell you it's *Tizer,* Mrs. Ramsbottom. It says so on the *label!*" "I tell *you,* Mr. Eckersley, Tizer's orange *not* red, and doesn't taste of raspberries!" "Now look here, it could be *pee* for all I know, but if it says Tizer on the *label,* then it's *Tizer!*" "And talking of *pee* Mr. Eckersley, sarsaparilla's my mother's favourite tonic, but what was in that *other* bottle made her wet the bed, but not before blowing her stomach up!" "Just *think!*" said Anne, and we did, our imaginations running riot. The only thing we *didn't* think about was the consequence that poor Fred would have to bear. There'd be trouble 't Mill all right! Such was our excitement that when the labels ran out, we had to find something to create more chaos with. We soon found it: crates of *empty* bottles – but what could we fill them with? "I know," said Anne, "Vinegar!" "Where?" said I. "There!" She pointed to two huge vats. Soon, we had turned on the taps and were filling the empty bottles, little knowing, caught up as we were in our escapade, what Fate had in pickle for us. . . . The last bottles filled, we soon found out. "I can't turn off the tap!" yelled Anne. A terrible pause. "Nor can I, mine!" yelled I. To our horror, both had stuck. Not even our combined strength could budge them. There we stood, two frightened little eight-year-olds, transfixed by an uncontrollable rush of vinegar, splashing round our ankles and on to the floor. It seemed we stood there for ages before our screams brought Fred on to the scene. "What the bloody hell!" he shouted. "You young buggers! Just wait till I lay me hands on you!" Whereupon, having turned off the taps, he proceeded to chase us all over the Mill. When he finally caught us, he gave us a good hiding. "Just look at it!" he said, the brown, acrid sea swashing round and over his best Sunday boots and into the turn-ups of his trousers. "Just look at it! And look at *you!*" he said as we stood there shivering, sodden with vinegar. "You'll *die,* that's all I can say! Just like them did in Revelations in that sea of wormwood! It'll dry up your skin and then your blood it will!" We were already whimpering, now we were howling. He frowned fiercely for a moment, relishing our terror then, suddenly, burst out laughing before taking us home. "Here's two pickled gherkins for you, mother!" he said to his wife when we arrived. Mrs. Disley proceeded to bath us and wash out our clothes. Mine having been dried by the fire, I was taken home smelling as sweet, if not looking as innocent, as when I left. The following Tuesday, we took delivery of four bottles of dandelion and burdock. They were accompanied by a note from Fred: "Sweets to the sweet . . ." When I opened the first bottle and tried it though, it was far from sweet, despite the label! It was malt vinegar. Ugh! I'd got my come-uppance! It's now 1983, and four weeks ago I was filming in Manchester so I went to visit my best friend Anne, for we never lost touch and the friendship founded on our first day at school is still as solid as a rock. I knocked on the door. Who should open it but old Fred! "Eee – our Anna! Come in! Hey, do you remember that day when you and our Anne emptied vinegar vats all over Water Barn floor?!"

Leslie Crowther.
Actor, comedian.

Like most little boys, I developed the usual healthy interest in the opposite sex. I spent hours wondering what they looked like without their clothes on. The fact that one could see little girls wandering about in local paddling pools, or by the seaside, stark naked, was unimpressive. They were only toddlers, so they didn't count! It was one's contemporaries at school that one mentally stripped in the playground. I had my first break at the age of eight, when a nubile lady of the same age – or maybe she was a year or two older – virtually picked me up in the school holidays, and invited herself round for tea. My mother suggested that we should go upstairs and play in my bedroom after tea; a suggestion which Deirdre Bosworth seized upon eagerly. You see, I even remember her name! Once upstairs, she offered me a tour of inspection. Breathlessly I accepted her offer, and she divested herself of her blouse and vest. "Those are called breasts," she declared. I was not impressed. I'd seen fat boys in the showers who were bigger than she was! This is probably why, when I was twelve and at a co-educational school in Twickenham, I evolved *my plan*. Not only were the girls of my age infinitely shapelier by then, but we all used to go to the same public swimming baths for swimming lessons. Our changing rooms were divided by a wooden screen which started at the ceiling but didn't quite reach the ground. There was the kind of gap that exists under the doors of the WCs in public loos. The kind of gap that enterprising West Indians are said to Limbo underneath and so get in free! I bought a pocket mirror and instructed my mates to do the same. At the next opportunity, we placed our mirrors in a row on the floor under the screen which divided us from the girls, and by skilfully tilting them we saw the lot! The following week we were surprised to hear sounds of uncontrolled mirth coming from the other side of the screen. Staring aghast at the floor, we saw a row of mirrors tilted towards us. It wasn't their retaliation that rankled – it was their laughter! Mind you, it was a very cold day!

Constance Cummings.
Actress.

In my early days in the theatre, one of my first engagements was in the Touring Company of "Old Kay".

I was one of a group of fourteen girls who did four speciality dances. A friend of mine in the line-up and I conceived an idea that we thought would be a hilarious joke for the last night.

There was a scene where Kay, the leading lady, pretended to be a maid serving lunch, and she went round the table with a large bowl of lettuce dishing out lettuce leaves in a slap-dash manner to the guests in turn.

My friend and I thought what fun it would be to hide a toy mouse in the salad bowl – what a lark – wouldn't the leading lady laugh when she saw it. Talk about *my* salad days – as I write this, I can hardly believe that I was ever so green in judgment and so awful as to have done such a thing.

But I did!

When the leading lady, who was circling the table, dealing out lettuce leaves and delighting the audience with her comedy, lifted the fourth leaf, she saw the mouse, gave a shriek, dropped the bowl and fled from the stage. 'Consternation' does not describe what took place. The actors managed to ad-lib. The leading man, who was the leading lady's husband, was beside himself as he

dared not leave the stage and was frantic to know what had happened to his wife.

My friend and I stood in the wings, horrified at the extent to which our little joke had misfired. We confessed, of course, and when the show was over we went to apologise. The leading lady was a lady indeed; she did not scold us at all. She just said perhaps *she* had been a bit silly, but we would be wise not to do anything like that again as it might go wrong a second time. We didn't need telling that!

The next morning, Sunday, we managed to find a flower shop open and we spent most of our last week's salary on a great bunch of roses which we took to her hotel before she left town.

Sir Charles Davis, C.B.
Counsel to the Speaker (European legislation etc.), formerly Legal Adviser, Ministry of Agriculture, Fisheries and Food.

There was a very pretty girl who worked in a camera shop in Cambridge, and during my last weeks as an undergraduate I decided to 'chat her up' and ask her to partner me at the May Ball. In those days, I was very shy where pretty girls were concerned (in my old age I am less shy) and it took me several days to summon up the necessary courage. During that time I confided my intention to an Australian friend called John, who gave me much encouragement. When I finally managed to stammer out my invitation, she replied "I am so sorry, but yesterday I agreed to go with John to the Ball''. A few weeks later, I went down from Cambridge for good, and I have never seen or heard from John (or the girl) since then . . . over fifty years ago. An early lesson, perhaps, in the importance of security – careless talk costs dates ?

The Ven. Peter S. Dawes.
Archdeacon of West Ham.

Since it was wartime, we all had to be members of the Cadet Corps. Once a term there was a Field Day and this one was special in that we had all been transported to some rather more distant place, instead of the area surrounding the school. I, as Lance Corporal, was leading a small Section reconnoitring the enemy positions. I was armed with a 'thunder-flash' which was like a very large firework banger. The exercise had not gone on long when to my delight I found myself overlooking the enemy Headquarters in a group of bushes. It was the matter of a moment to light the thunderflash and drop it among them, but then it set fire to the neighbouring bushes. Instantly there was a shout of "Fire" and although it was very minor and soon got under control, the whole Field Day was ruined, since everyone had come out of their positions. With the senior Officers (Masters) I was distinctly unpopular, though in the end it was conceded that no-one had ever known a thunderflash to set fire to things before, and so everyone's wrath gradually cooled down.

Curiously, one thing was not noticed then, or indeed subsequently, and I thought it wiser not to draw attention to it myself. Only as the thunderflash left my hand did I realise that in fact it was the Headquarters of my own side and not the enemy's.

Perhaps it was just as well the war ended two months before I joined up!

The Lord De Freyne.

I succeeded to my father as the seventh Baron when I was only eight years of age, in 1935. He died on Christmas Eve, which was a particularly sad time. Also he died in London.

I think one of the things that stand out in my memory on my return to my home, French Park, in the remote West of Ireland some months later, was being called 'His Lordship' or 'Your little Lordship' which was the local custom of house servants and outdoor staff of that time. Looking back, I suspect there was some sympathy for a little boy ruled, as some may say, by a 'Petticoat' regime, being the youngest with four sisters, in a household under the sway of my mother. The school-room came under Miss Lilly, my youngest sister Faith's governess and mine, and finally Nanny Steel, though in theory retired, but still active in nursery matters.

It comes therefore as no surprise that Faith and myself were usually up to no good (she being next to me in age). The following summer, I remember Faith and I had been joined in the school-room by a girl friend of hers to share lessons. Long summer evenings added possibilities for trouble-making, so when the first ever cinema came to the village once a week, this was it.

As I remember, a film with George Raft in the leading role was to be shown at the village hall. This was an opportunity not to be missed, and certainly permission to view this delight would have been met with a firm refusal. Not daunted and greatly daring, our ringleader laid plans. Bikes were hidden in the partly-unused kitchen basement, ready for the 'off'.

School-room supper eaten in a hurry, which pleased Miss Lilly – keen to play Bezique with our mother before their dinner – a fond good-night to Nanny, splashing sounds of water, teeth cleaned and then to bed, but not finally! Dummy beds made up with pillows – and we were off.

The village was downhill and the three keen culprits soon presented themselves at the box office – "Good evening to your Lordship and Miss Faith". Seats for three to include Faith's friend, and we were ushered free to raised benches which were the Grand Circle. The film started and we were in the seventh heaven.

Alas, back at home nanny was checking on her chicks. All were not present and correct. Miss Lilly was alerted, who clearly had her own shrewd suspicions. She climbed on her trusty steed and biked in pursuit.

When she arrived at the door of the village hall, all was in confusion. "Delay the woman" was the general cry. "Get his Lordship and Miss Faith out". Through the back door and on to our bikes, off we fled, but we were seen pedalling like mad up the hill and around the corner of the demesne wall. Faith yelled "Come on, we can make it".

We didn't, and the next morning found three children on the carpet. (Oh, why was nanny not asleep.) Our mother did take us to the cinema in later years, but she did have to pay to get us in.

Lord Deramore.
Architect, navigator RAFVR, 1940–45.

Sir Jamsetjee Jejeebhoy, the 6th. Baronet of that name, was at a 'crammers' in Suffolk and up at Cambridge with me. He was the head of the Parsee community in Bombay and of the Zoroastrian faith. He was a delightful person and possessed of a great sense of humour. In his room at Caius he had a large photograph of the Taj Mahal above the fireplace. One undergraduate, seeing this picture for the first time, gazed at it in awe and asked, "Is that where you live in India, Jejee?" Deadpan came the answer, "Yes, old boy, my father had the swimming pool in the foreground built about five years ago."

On an earlier occasion, while driving back to the 'crammers' from Cambridge with one of the tutors, he was faced with an imminent head-on collision while his Hyper-sports Lea-Francis was travelling at more than a mile a minute. With lightning reactions he swerved left off the road on to Newmarket Heath, coming to rest several hundred yards later. Without a word he switched off the ignition, extracted a gold cigarette box from an inner pocket, opened it and offered his shaken passenger a cigarette, saying, "Icy calm, old boy, icy calm."

Alan Devereux, C.B.E.
Chairman, Scottish Tourist Board.

Growing up in wartime had its anxious moments for my parents too, but my attempted electrocution of Auntie in the loo, our gang's secret store of Howitzer shells and even our spirited efforts to blow a sea mine were more childish games compared with the goldfish incident.

It seemed such a bargain at the time. Our fishpond down to a few scruffy carp and this chap offering any quantity of prize goldfish at sixpence a dozen – all, he assured me, honestly caught in a "river stiff with 'em". It was perhaps an unfortunate coincidence that the very celebrated owner of a prized collection of goldfish should find his stock depleting at the same time that my parents were experiencing such plenty. It was even more unfortunate that this celebrated person should be so well connected with the police and at the very time the CID were following the fishy trail, the ten-year-old middleman spoiled it all by vanishing. A police party, horrified parents and my quaking self stared into the pond. A hush fell. The sergeant took off his helmet – I thought he was going to dip it in and catch fish. "Well Sir," he said pointing down to the hundreds of happy swimming goldfish, "I just don't rightly know which would be yours and even if I did know – I don't rightly know how to get hold of them." Nor did the celebrated owner. But my parents knew how to get hold of me. Yes, growing up in wartime had its hard moments for me.

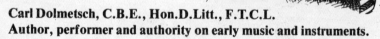

Carl Dolmetsch, C.B.E., Hon.D.Litt., F.T.C.L.
Author, performer and authority on early music and instruments.

I was seven years old. After a concert in London, my father gave me his bag to hold while we awaited our homeward train at Waterloo

Station. En route, he checked our baggage and instruments and alas, one was missing. The sleepy seven-year-old had left the bag on the platform. It contained my father's 18th century Bressan recorder, which he had used in his concerts since 1905.

After fruitless advertising for its recovery, he decided there was nothing for it but to make a new one. Thus was born, on platform 7, the whole of the modern recorder movement which has since encircled the globe.

The Bressan? It was returned to my father by a friend a couple of years later; he had bought it in a bric-à-brac shop near Waterloo for five shillings (25p). Its present-day value is nearer £8000!

Maestro Antal Dorati.
Conductor and Composer.

I was about ten or twelve years old when it happened. Our school, a large red-brick building on a broad, chestnut-tree-lined street in Budapest – my native city – happened to be in the vicinity of a big market place, often the scene of large, colourful fairs. It was easy to run to the fair-grounds during the ten-minute intervals between lessons, amuse oneself for five minutes, and be back in the classroom in time for the next lesson.

During one of these quick excursions, I could not resist to buy, with savings from my small monthly allowance, an especially alluring 'souvenir'. It was a rather large balloon, in the shape of a pig when the balloon was blown up. When the air was let out of it, it escaped through a whistle which gave a long, tearful squeal, very similar to the squealing of young pigs in agony. It was a terrible, terrible noise.

Very proud of my acquisition, I inflated it in the classroom to the great acclaim of my fifty-three classmates. The pig was, just once more, blown into its full, imposing shape when suddenly our teacher appeared. We all fled to our benches – I, with the fingers of my left hand holding tight on to the pig-balloon, safely hidden under the bench. So far so good – I only had to hold it tight for fifty minutes and everything would be alright.

But destiny intervened. I was called up to report on our homework. I stood up, rather frightened, always holding on to the pig under the bench. But things did not go too well. I was, understandably, rather flustered and in my embarrassment, I messed up my report – it was a lesson in arithmetic, by the way. The teacher, full of goodwill, invited me to come out to the blackboard, which loomed forebodingly at the other end of the room, behind the cathedra, to write out the problem and its solution in chalk.

"Oh no, thank you", I said. "I can do it from here", and I got more and more mixed up.

Finally, the teacher's patience was wearing thin. "Stop that nonsensical stuttering. Come out and write it up on the board right away".

This was a command. I had to obey it. I did. But was I to go with or without the pig? I decided that the shame would be smaller if I marched alone. I let the pig go and advanced – with the accompaniment of that horrible squeal – joined a second later by the guffaw of the class.

Luckily, the teacher laughed too! Bless his soul.

Robert Dougall.
Former senior newsreader, BBC Television, and President, Royal Society for the Protection of Birds.
Now, author and freelance broadcaster.

I went to my first school in 1917 at the age of four. My parents were then living in South Croydon. It was called St John's School and was run by three generations of Polleys. Grandpa Polley was 99 and so his running days were really over. He was an engaging old boy with a white beard and a passion for bonfires. In fact, he liked them so much that in summer and autumn, when meal times came round, nothing would induce him to leave his favourite site at the bottom of the garden. There he sat on his straight-backed chair, wreathed in smoke, happily munching his sandwiches.

Next in seniority came Mr and Mrs Polley, who were in their seventies, and whom we regarded with awe. Their daughter, Miss Ethel Polley, aged about 30, was the Headmistress. She wore ankle-length skirts, nipped in at the waist; her straight hair was parted in the middle with Pre-Raphaelite loops on either side. Her billowing skirts impeded her not at all as she rushed nimbly about an adjoining field teaching us, among other things, the rudiments of hockey.

The school had only been in existence for two years when I joined it as their sixth pupil, so we got plenty of individual attention. Of all the authoritarian figures, the one of whom we lived in most dread was undoubtedly Mrs Polley. She was a distinctly formidable old lady with steely-grey hair and a stoop. Our classroom was situated on the first floor of the house, overlooking the garden at the back. Artwork was one of the subjects taught and at the end of one of our sessions, when clearing up, it seemed to me a perfectly reasonable idea to empty my pot of paint water out of the open window. As luck would have it, the formidable Mrs Polley was passing by immediately below at the precise moment when the contents of my pot were on the way down. In fact, she received them smack on her steely-grey cranium.

Unfortunately, no one would believe that I hadn't perpetrated the deed with fell intent. Retribution was swift. For some time after that 'sitting comfortably' was quite a problem for me!

Brian Doyle.
Author of 'The Who's Who of Children's Literature', writer, broadcaster and film publicist.

I grew up on English public school stories and, between the ages of about 9 to 15, regularly devoured at least three such novels a week, mostly borrowed from the Junior Department of Plumstead Public Library, in South London, but some presented to me on birthdays and at Christmas by a fond Mother who knew and appreciated my tastes.

Far and away my favourite reading in my chosen literary genre was 'The Magnet', that marvellous weekly boys' paper written by 'Frank Richards' (real name Charles Hamilton) and chronicling the colourful happenings at Greyfriars School in Kent. It ran from 1908 until 1940, when the wartime paper shortage closed it down. It was nearing its demise when I discovered it, but I later managed to buy (or 'swap') stacks of old 'Magnets' from friends and secondhand book-dealers (it was easy then, but they're collectors' items today).

What magical names I recall from those halcyon days when I was a blissful but passive honorary pupil at Greyfriars. . . .

Billy Bunter (the Fat Owl of the Remove Form and possessor of the tightest pair of trousers at Greyfriars), Harry Wharton and Co. (otherwise known as the Famous Five and comprising Wharton, Bob

Cherry, Frank Nugent, Johnny Bull and Hurree Jamset Ram Singh), Herbert Vernon-Smith (the Bounder of the Remove), the indolent but nice Lord Mauleverer, Horace Coker (the brawny Duffer of the Fifth), Gerald Loder (the Cad of the Sixth), George Wingate (the Captain of the School), that odious trio Skinner, Snoop and Stott, and such masters as Dr Locke (the Head), Henry Samuel Quelch ('a beast – but a just beast'), Prout and Hacker. And not forgetting Gosling, the school porter ("Wot I sez is this 'ere. . . .").

Life at my Grammar School in South-East London, though pleasant, wasn't much like that at Greyfriars, or Greyminster, though. I was pleased that the masters wore gowns and that the Head wore a mortarboard on occasion. We even had a fat boy who was actually nicknamed Bunter. But at 4 p.m. we all went home (if we weren't delayed by detention) and there wasn't much social life, as there was at Greyfriars and all the other fictional schools I adored. And there certainly weren't any 'Midnight feasts in the Dorm,' for the simple reason that we were all day-boys and there weren't any Dorms.

The single most dramatic moment I recall at my school was when a studious, bespectacled boy named Castleton, who was something of a chemistry wizard and forever pottering about in the labs, took a pocketful of homemade fireworks into Morning Assembly and, by some mischance, set them off accidentally midway through the Lord's Prayer. He suddenly jumped up like a Jack-in-the-Box surrounded by bangs, fizzes, showers of Golden Rain, and flames, accompanied by the pungent smell of burning school blazer (aptly-named on this occasion) and literally erupted in the centre of the packed school hall.

Neighbouring boys leapt away from him, no doubt thinking that here was a convincing and practical demonstration of spontaneous combustion in their midst, until he was left alone, frantically tearing his

blazer off and then stamping on it. There he stood, thoughtfully gazing down and surrounded by smoke, for all the world like a pantomime Demon King who hasn't disappeared on cue and wondering what his next move should be, before the audience started jeering and throwing pennies on to the stage. Far from being upset, Castleton grinned and waved as he was led away by two grim-faced masters. "They worked all right, didn't they?" he was heard to hiss to a friend as he disappeared up the centre aisle, still smoking slightly and carrying his smouldering blazer gingerly but proudly as though he had just won a prized and coveted trophy.

Rumours were rife throughout the school that morning. "Castleton's been expelled, have you heard?", "Castleton's dead, they say," went the whispers. But all Castleton got was a severe talking-to by the Head, 'Six-of-the-Best' from the Head's most pliable cane, and a dispensation to wear a somewhat loud checked sports-jacket at school for the next few days until his Mother could buy him a new (non-blazing) blazer. ("The new one's going to be made of asbestos" went the rumour.)

If it had happened at Greyfriars, Castleton would have been doused by the school hose-pipe and then have fled from the school and the consequences. The next couple of issues of the 'Magnet' would have been devoted to his mysterious disappearance and his eventual discovery (via a secret passage) in an old dungeon beneath the cloisters, busy manufacturing bigger and better fireworks.

Bunter, of course, would have stolen his tuck.

Charles Dyer.
Writer, dramatist.

After Mr Guthridge died, I decided to raise him from the dead whilst Chuffy Gosport and Milky Moe kept cavey.

Mr Guthridge taught Arithmetic at Highlands School for Boys and Girls. Asphalt playground. Iron railings. His sister took Bible Class (we were up to Lazarus); and the lonely Guthridges shared a victorian house in Lennox Road, a stone's throw from Grundy's corner store. Chuffy and I occasionally lunched there, supplementing our mothers' jam sandwiches with a halfpenny bag of broken biscuits. On lucky days, for pudding, Mr Grundy would slice us a penny ice-lolly into two. Marvellous.

Because of his sudden death, the funeral and such, Mr Guthridge's class was granted an extended lunch-hour. Wonderful. And a bee-buzzing summer's day, too. I hated school; dreaded it; useless at school. Once, the Headmaster upset my mother by deriding my mediocrity: "An incredibly uninspired child, Mrs Dyer". True. True, it had to be said. Chuffy Gosport could at least spit further than any kid in the district; but I excelled at nothing. I could not even fail stylishly: couldn't even make bottom in class. Forty-eighth out of forty-nine. Milky Moe was bottom, but one of her eyes moved independently *and* she could hypnotise frogs. Milky Moe was ten years old, I think, and us others were nine-and-three-quarters.

In company with Milky Moe and, to be fair, Scrubber Parkyns – who was quite bright but somehow always smelled of damp rot, neither Chuffy nor I had ever enjoyed Mr Guthridge's blessings: not the palest "well-done!" nor thinnest of smirks in those thousand years of his tutorship. He despised us, and nourished a venomous contempt for me in particular.

Chuffy Gosport couldn't understand why I wanted him back.

For the glory; just to have done something right; anything. Well, Milky Moe made a sexy remark about my chances; and Chuffy, panting, coerced me into a wager: my dancing frog against Milky Moe letting us all see her titties. By heck, she was a sizzler. But I loved my frog; didn't want it hypnotised. Still, it was a 'God's Honour' bet, and barely had I spat over my wrist before I was being shuffled ahead of a sudden multitude towards Lennox Road. Pimples Winthram had appeared, Stuffy Hesba and her brother Syd, Virgin Connie and Ginger Grappeley and, oh dozens, the bulk of whom bivouacked at Grundy's Stores, leaving Chuffy'n me'n Milky Moe to slink like cartoon cats, dodging gate to gate along the walls until we reached that fateful house. . . . And there it was! No garden: just a small paved area for the parking of the late Mr Guthridge's BSA-with-sidecar.

The Guthridge's parlour curtains had been part-drawn, but the sash windows were open; so was their front door. Everything seemed quiet. I prayed the funeral was over, perhaps, and our teacher safely under the sod. But Chuffy smelled death, he claimed, and was feeling sick. Anyway, the three of us clambered on to the motor bike and peeped into that parlour.

Oh heck, he was still at home.

Mr Guthridge was entrestled in a mound of wreaths. His coffin was mahogany. Lid-less. Through divided doors beyond, we saw a hundred plates of boiled ham'n piccalilli in rows on the dining room table. Lettuce and beetroot. Somewhere a bluebottle was buzzing.

It was either him or my frog, so I tumbled frightened into the room, and crept towards his remains. I must have been quite small. My chin was but inches above the coffin's edge; my eyeline was the blue-black steel jungle up Mr Guthridge's nose. Hairs which had quivered through yesterday's rages. . . . "Hundred lines, Dyer! Fifty more for arguing! Stand up! Wake up! Shut up! Is dyer-ere? ha-ha-ha-ha-ha! . . ." Now he was framed in dead-white satin. Pin-stripe suit. Crossed hairy hands. Sunday shoes (my dad could've used them on his Territory); fancy burying 'em dust to dust! Mr Guthridge's neck of plucked chicken, scruffed'n wrinkled, jutted like a tortoise's from his overtight collar; and his clamped face was pale leather, shiny-white-ish; purple in places. And he was still Never Wrong! Still annoyed. Pursed mouth, with his teeth looking funny. Then the bluebottle landed to rub its feet on Mr Guthridge's forehead. I blew it off, puffing it into a hysteria of zizzing among the flowers, from whence it zoomed up and away towards the Funeral Ham. Quiet again. Weird. Yet strangely, a peacefulness came over me.

"Hey, things aren't too rough. Come'n look at his funny teeth!"

Chuffy moaned in green. And Milky Moe said "Holy Mother o' God". Milky's mum was a Catholic and a very pious woman.

So! Gripping the coffin's edge, and squeezing my eyes to fierce and holy slits, tightening my lips until they smarted, forcing vibrations into the muscles of my arms'n legs and shoulders'n chest, and drawing close to Mr Guthridge's ear, I hissed:

"Pick up thy bed'n walk. Pick up thy bed, sir, please, sir, and walk, sir. Pick up thy bed, sir. Pick up thy — "

But there came a shriek, a screaming yowl of horrors. It shredded my moment. Tubes of prickly ice spiralled from my stomach to shatter around my heart. Chuffy Gosport and Milky Moe fled, yelping. And I, quaking, thudding, fell backwards into the flowers. There, from between the trestle legs, I peered upwards at Mr Guthridge's Sister. She was aghast in the dining room, open-mouthed after her scream. In each hand was another plate of boiled ham'n piccalilli. Eight feet tall, she seemed, all shocked bones and old lace, eyebrows banished under the brim of her mourning hat. Sepulchral and black, she was; but starkest black was her dreadful stare. I struggled out of the mangled ruins of a wreath from 'The Headmaster and Staff'. Oh heck!

So many years ago; and Time has frilled my memories. Yet I swear her lips had frothed. She was shivering. Paper thin lids circled her bulging eyes; the white parts were dirty brown and pink-shot. She howled at me: "Wasn't killing him enough for you, Dyer?" She called me a vile brat, a monster, a necrophiliac (as I gathered in later years). And I started to whimper, to squeak:

"I just wanted to c-call him back, Miss. F-from the dead, please, Miss. Like L-Lazarus".

Her brows fell to a crunched vee, screwing her eyes into fearsome holes of crow-footed hatred. "He's embalmed," she snarled. "*Embalmed.*" The word puckered her lips to a wet red square. Now, still clutching her plates of boiled ham'n piccalilli, she began clapping her elbows into her ribs, and stamping her feet. *Embalmed.* I burst into tears; I rushed past her, dodging her kicks. Out! Through the hall, and out. Out, racing the wind to around Grundy's corner. Behind me, Miss Guthridge was at her window, ham and all, still shrieking "Embalmed!" Over and again and again. "Embalmed . . . embalmed . . . embalmed."

Mad. They were all mad.

Milky Moe had squatted on the pavement outside Mr Grundy's; an ashen Chuffy Gosport was cradled to her breast. He had been sick into his school hat. We had to rinse it in the playground drinking fountain; then scrub his jacket, his splashed boots. Nothing more was ever said by anyone; so that was lucky-that . . . save for having to give Milky Moe my dancing frog.

Nice Miss Briault took us for Arithmetic that afternoon. Such a pretty frock she wore! Even so, I couldn't concentrate for wondering if Lazarus had been embalmed . . . and if being necro-what's'it was worse than being ordinary?

Commander Sir John Eardley-Wilmot, M.V.O., D.S.C.

My father was a very good Contract Bridge player at the end of the 1920s; he had four children at that time and he taught them all to play. Their ages ranged from four to eleven and on rainy days, three little old men and an old lady aged seven would huddle round the table and explore the 'losing count system' and Mr Culbertson's 4 and 5 No Trumps.

On his fifth birthday, the youngest boy, after impoverishing his father by consuming many cream cakes at either Gunters or Buzzards, or perhaps Rumplemayers, was allowed to sit by the side of a very famous player at Crockfords and watch him bid and call a small slam in no trumps against my father and his partner. "What do you think about that?" said the maestro. "You could have got seven", said the five-year-old. "How come?" "By playing low in dummy to the first lead and trapping Daddy".

"He'll remember that in future", said my father, somewhat sourly.

The Revd Nick Earle, M.A.
Headmaster, Bromsgrove School.

One of my predecessors prided himself on having a good memory for faces but he was not always successful in connecting the face or even the name with the exploit. He met someone at a reunion whose face he knew very well but he could remember nothing about him except that he had a twin brother and that he (the headmaster) always used to confuse the two.

As he was wondering what to say it did occur to him that someone had told him something about the two brothers – or at least about one of them. Imagine his horror when he found himself addressing a comparative stranger by his name and adding the words – "Just remind me – was it you or your brother who was killed in the War?"

Sir George Edwards, O.M., C.B.E., F.R.S., D.L.
Chairman, British Aircraft Corporation, 1963–75.

One of my earliest recollections, though not a very humorous one (I was probably about 6 years of age at the time) was when I was walking home from school round the lake in Hyams Park, where I lived, which was in the process of being drained. Wishing to take a short cut I walked on what looked like dry ground covered with leaves only to find I was fast sinking in mud; it progressively reached up to my neck, and I was still sinking, when, fortunately, a man with a dog came along. He threw the dog's lead to me which, one arm having struggled free, reached my outstretched hand; I was pulled to safety, smelling like a pole-cat, and sent off home.

I arrived on the doorstep, dripping mud and leaves and was promptly hosed down before being allowed inside the house.

During my later years as an aircraft designer, and when dealing with Governments, before walking across any political ground at the invitation of an Official or a Minister, I would always 'turn the leaves over' to see what sort of morass unsuspectedly lay beneath.

Robert Edwards, M.P., (Wolverhampton S.E.).
Member of European Parliament, 1977–79.

This city of Liverpool was a marvellous place to be born. I should imagine there is something in the chemistry of the air of this cosmopolitan town that creates people of strong character and independence. I suppose it is a mixture of Irish, Welsh and of most countries of the world that has created an atmosphere of new thinking, opposition to establishment and revolt.

Thinking back, there were periods of unhappiness for me and periods of great joy and interest. I was born on the Mersey Dock Estate, right on the banks of the Mersey, in an old manor that was owned by the Mersey Dock and Harbour Board, and I learned to swim like a fish at the age of about four. Water and rivers and oceans had no fear for me at all.

Two incidents are still clear in my mind. The first occurred when I was about six or seven when swimming in the upper reaches of the Mersey at Cast Ironshore. One of my friends got caught in a whirlpool and was drowned. There were all kinds of warning notices about the dangers of the river, and even a police patrol, but we always ignored them and I remember well explaining time and time again to the police just how one of my friends had disappeared. Despite this incident and all warnings, we continued to swim in these dangerous waters.

Another incident clear in my mind was taking a small boat out with a friend into the Mersey and being swept out into the Irish Sea among the ocean-going liners. There was an awful panic, but finally police boats surrounded us and we were brought back to Liverpool. Everybody thought we had been drowned and I got a terrific spanking, which I resented very much because I was blamed for this incident although my companion was three years older than me and he got off scot free. I never believed there was any danger until years afterwards.

For adventurous youngsters Liverpool abounded in places of interest. There was Eastern Woods on the other side of the Mersey, Morcombe, and the Wirral where a rich aunt had a wooden weekend holiday lodge which we used frequently, and which I am afraid I rather carelessly burned to the ground. When it was not in use, we used to sneak across and steal potatoes from a farmer's field and cook them over a primus stove. On the occasion I have in mind, we lost control of the primus stove, flames reached the ceiling, set the hut on fire and burned it to the ground. In our panic we got back to Liverpool as quickly as possible and I sneaked off to bed, but not to sleep. It was not many hours before my aunt came to the house because my cousin, who had little affection for

me, swore I was responsible. The police had informed my aunt of what had happened to her holiday hut, which was completely uninsured. My mother insisted that I had not left the district and that I was asleep in bed so it could not have been me. They came upstairs and found me apparently fast asleep and my aunt was reassured, but not my cousin, with whom I was always in conflict. She always tried to boss the place as she was six years older than me.

There was a famous old-fashioned music hall theatre in the town and it was the custom of my parents to go there every Saturday evening. They went to spend this particular night at the music hall and left my cousin in charge of the house. To my annoyance, she found me wide awake, put on the lights and spotted that my hair and eyebrows were singed! This was her great opportunity. She seized me fiercely and gave me a terrific tanning until I was ready to admit that I was responsible for burning the hut. In great triumph she recounted to my parents and aunt when they returned that she had beaten the truth out of me.

As far as I remember this was the most miserable period of my youth. A family conference was called and I was deprived of my pocket money for a month; all comics and the little books I enjoyed reading so much were cancelled and I had to be in bed by 8 p.m. every night. It had one value to me as I was forced to learn to tell the time which hitherto had been of no importance to me.

Outside Liverpool was a country district called Mossley Hill where we used to spend camping weekends and I am afraid we usually lived off the land. We had a wooden cart which we packed with a tent and cooking utensils, and the nearby farms invariably provided our food. One shocking incident ended these happy excursions. A nearby church was raided during a weekend when we were not camping, indeed, I was on holiday in the Isle of Man, and the collecting box had been stolen. We were accused of this theft and the police came to the school to interview the five boys who used to camp in the Mossley Hill area. I managed to convince them that it could not possibly have been us as I was away on holiday, but unfortunately one of our group, feeling lonely, did go to Mossley Hill on the Sunday and had been caught by a farmer stealing apples, and he was accused of the crime. It was a surprise to us to learn that he had actually been in the area and all of us had to go to the Juvenile Court, which involved staying the night before the hearing in a remand home in Dale Street. I remember well what an undignified experience it was, particularly as we were completely innocent, and this was known, apart from the one boy who had made the Sunday visit. We had to take off all our clothes, which were fumigated quite unnecessarily, and were literally scrubbed in a huge wooden bath all in the same water.

Our friend was found guilty and received six strokes of the birch. He was a happy, gentle boy until this happened. It made a big impression on me. In later years, as a member of the Juvenile Employment Committee I campaigned for the abolition of the birch and I think Liverpool was the first city in the country to abolish it. The tragedy was that about a month later, the real culprits were discovered – a local gang of hooligans – but no redress was possible for the boy who had been the victim of this miscarriage of justice. I lost touch with him completely, but I know he was involved in quite a lot of incidents with the police which I attribute to the effect of this unjust and callous punishment. In later years I heard he went to prison in America.

Denholm Elliott.
Actor of stage and screen.

When I was about six years old I lived with my father and mother and my elder brother in a flat in West Ealing. My father, who was an intelligent, sensitive man, was a Barrister. It was not a profession he particularly enjoyed or excelled at. My grandfather had been an eminent King's Counsel with many famous cases to his credit. My father as his eldest son had been expected to follow in his footsteps or, should I say, in his shadow. And this, indeed, he did. However there was one thing that my father excelled in . . . he was a superb gardener. His flower beds were like billiard tables with sloping sides and filled with flowers and vegetables of all descriptions. He had been given an allotment in a field behind our flat, and he had turned this into a veritable cornucopia of produce. It

116

was his passion.

My family which had, at one time, been extremely wealthy, had fallen into hard times. By this, I mean, we only ate pheasant on Tuesdays and Thursdays. Overhearing my parents discussing our financial situation suggested to any young mind that we were about to enter a world of Dickensian poverty and horror. I determined to do my bit to save the family from ruin, waited until my father had gone to work and then, entering his garden proceeded to cut every one of his flowers. I tied them into small bunches with cotton and made off to Ealing Broadway where, half an hour later, my piping treble voice could be heard shouting "lovely flowers, halfpenny a bunch"! I sold the lot in minutes, and started off home with the money. On entering the flat, I found my family, ashen faced, having discovered what I had done, and predicting some terrible vengeance my father would inevitably exact in retribution. I waited alone in my room for his return. Finally the door opened and he came in and stood in front of me looking at me. And then slowly a gentle smile spread from his eyes to his face, and I felt he was looking at me for the first time.

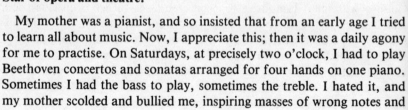

Mary Ellis.
Star of opera and theatre.

My mother was a pianist, and so insisted that from an early age I tried to learn all about music. Now, I appreciate this; then it was a daily agony for me to practise. On Saturdays, at precisely two o'clock, I had to play Beethoven concertos and sonatas arranged for four hands on one piano. Sometimes I had the bass to play, sometimes the treble. I hated it, and my mother scolded and bullied me, inspiring masses of wrong notes and juvenile rebellion. I was seven years old and planned revenge. So one Saturday, when she was out shopping in the morning, I stuffed hard bundles of tissue paper between all the strings of that poor piano, and sat down later with her, all innocence to play the duets. The sound as you can imagine, was a ping and twang; great glee for me, and weeping fury from my mother, who threatened: "Wait till your father comes home." Which I did in fear and trembling. My relief when he laughed heartily, and helped her to remove all the tissue paper, made me adore him more than ever, especially as he winked at me over my mother's furiously rigid shoulder. Of course I said I was sorry. My punishment was never to be allowed to play duets again. How wonderful that was!

Robin Ellis.
Actor.

One afternoon in November when I was 4, my mother had told me she was expecting Auntie Rita to call round for tea. It was a Monday and she had spent the morning doing the washing in the scullery on a corrugated surface by the sink – no washing machines in those days. We had had our lunch and I was playing in the hall with my Dinky army trucks, while she was hanging up the clothes on the pulley-operated system over the stove. Dad's shirts, vests and pants, her 'smalls' and blouses and the fiddly little clothes that belonged to me. These last ones were giving her some trouble – they kept falling off. Exasperated she said, "Oh heavens – I wish Rita wasn't coming this afternoon – I've got nothing in – I'll never be ready." Dinky-playing big ears was listening to this and at 4 o'clock when the front door bell rang – being quite tall for my age – I went off to do my party piece of the moment – opening the front door.

"Hello Auntie Rita – mummy doesn't want you to come to tea this afternoon".

Years later my mother told me that poor Auntie Rita was not amused.

I thought – wouldn't it be fun to be 4 again.

Professor H. J. Eysenck.
**Professor of Psychology, University of London; Psychologist, Maudsley
and Bethlem Royal Hospital; Director of the Psychological Laboratories,
Institute of Psychiatry.**

The fairies who stood around at my birth presented me with many
gifts, but they left out one which to me would have been very important,
namely musical ability. I never managed to learn an instrument, I never
learnt to sing in tune, or even whistle; all that comes out when I try to
carry a melody is a croaking sound which leaves other people guessing
vainly what the tune might be that I am trying to carry.

I was quite conscious of this defect when I was 8 years old, and when
Herr Meier, the new music teacher in our class, asked me to sing a tune, a
feat successfully performed by everyone else in the class, I declined
gracefully, pointing out my disability. He was a fat, pompous little man,
short-tempered and irascible; he simply told me to get on with it and
obediently I started to croak my way through 'Oh Tannenbaum, Oh
Tannenbaum . . .' a German Christmas Carol better known in England
as the rather blood-thirsty 'Red Flag' sung at the end of Labour Party
Meetings.

Herr Meier couldn't believe his ears. He stopped me and told me in no
uncertain terms to stop clowning and get down to business. I told him
this was the best I could do, and getting red in the face he asked me to step
up to his desk and hold out my hand. He then got hold of a heavy ruler
and tried to hit my hand. Feeling that this was rather unjust I quickly
withdrew it, and he managed to hit his own hand instead. This infuriated
him so much that he grabbed my hand again, lifted the ruler and
threatened to really hurt me. My reaction was quite instinctive; I put
down my head and bit the fleshy part of his hand just below the thumb. I

was a big, strong lad even then, and although only 8 years old my jaw muscles were well developed. Herr Meier paled visibly, dropped the ruler, and let out an agonised shriek. When this did not produce any effect, he started shaking his hand frantically, with me hanging on like a terrier.

By this time the class was in an uproar of course, shouting and shrieking hysterically, jumping up and down on their seats, and generally misbehaving. I had no thought in mind other than to hang on like grim death, and this I succeeded in doing.

At this precise moment the Headmaster was passing the classroom, his head full of those august thoughts which characterise headmasters in general. He heard the uproar, opened the door to the classroom, and was greeted by a sight which in 40 years as a schoolmaster had never met his eyes before. Having satisfied himself that he was not hallucinating, he came in and tried to separate the vicious young thug from the visibly tiring Herr Meier, but without much success. He called for help, and finally a whole group of teachers, caretakers, and other employees managed to pull me off, not without doing considerable damage to Herr Meier's hand. By this time he was not far from fainting, and sat down on the floor with his head between his knees. I was standing by the desk, none the worse for wear, and when the Headmaster asked me what happened I told him the story, adding that I was not going to be unjustly punished, and that in any case the law did not allow teachers to hit pupils. (This did not much inhibit Prussian teachers at that time from doing precisely that, but nevertheless if a pupil was intent on being awkward this might produce difficulties for the teacher).

The Headmaster, who was no fool, realised that I was not likely to knuckle under, and would create endless difficulties for him, for the school, and the unfortunate Herr Meier if he didn't use some tact. Herr Meier was sent home, in the care of a nurse, to stay away from school for several weeks, suffering from attacks of nerves. The Headmaster himself took over the class, I went back to my seat, quite happy with the outcome of the event and quite calm in the certainty that I was in the right. What I had not anticipated was that the story would spread through the whole school, and other schools as well, and I became known, rather as in the caption of a Bateman cartoon, as 'The Boy Who Bit His Teacher'.

Nothing of a disciplinary nature followed; the Headmaster knew full well that Herr Meier had been in the wrong, and that any attempt to punish me might prove very counterproductive. Psychologists often wonder about the degree to which a person's behaviour shows consistency over the years. In my own case the whole affair was perhaps rather prophetic; when I felt that I was in the right I have always stood up to the establishment, or the powers that be; Herr Meier was only the unfortunate forerunner of more important and more highly placed figures!

Lynn Farleigh.
Actress.

Sitting at Vidal Sassoon's having a 1920s hair trim for the rôle I'm currently playing, I remembered a blush-making incident.

I had, and have, very fine, very straight, very greasy, very boring hair. Aged five, I hated it. I also hated parties, as I loathed the food, my dresses and my hair.

One Saturday afternoon, about an hour before one of those late-forties icecream-cake girls' parties, Jane, a school friend, came to our house so that we could go partying together. Jane had on a red dress – my favourite colour, but a colour I never wore. Jane also had fair, curly hair – the hair of my dreams. I took Jane to my mother's bedroom and there, with nail scissors I 'improved' her hairstyle. I have no idea why she allowed me to do it; I don't think I would have used force! But she certainly looked different afterwards. I also changed my own appearance to that of a Joan of Arc chewed by the dog. I did not go to the party – Jane did, tear-stained. I had to apologise to Jane's mother and explain all at school, and of course live with my own haircut.

Hair salons are to this day places of agony for me but perhaps writing this down will relieve the torture and even, who knows, make my hair curl.

Terence Feely.
Playwright, novelist and television writer.

When I was at school we had a Latin teacher who was a master of the Times crossword. Every day he would sweep in, give us some fiendish piece to construe to keep us quiet while he addressed himself to the cross-word, which he prided himself on polishing off in 15 minutes.

One morning we intercepted his Times before he got it. We were already armed with an unblemished copy of the Times of the day before, from which we carefully cut that part of the crossword which one fills in. Then, with the aid of a delicate adhesive, we very skilfully so arranged things that, when he got down to it, he found himself struggling with a combination of today's clues and yesterday's spaces.

Oh, the grunts and groans, the sighs, hair-twisting and muted curses that came from his desk as he wrestled with his impossible task while the rest of us sat in a state of imminent explosion as we ached with stifled laughter!

He finally screwed up the paper, flung it into a corner and strode from the room. At which point he earned our undying admiration: we found he had managed to complete half of it – and in a way that actually made sense.

Dame Honor Fell, D.B.E., F.R.S.
Director, Strangeways Research Laboratory, Cambridge, 1929–70;
Fellow, Girton College, Cambs.

When I got into trouble with my elders it was usually because of some unfortunate mishap rather than an intentional misdeed. The misadventure of the eels was a case in point. I had parked them temporarily in a hand washbasin while I cleaned out my aquarium, but unfortunately I had overlooked the fact that the basin was equipped with an overflow. Eels being what they are, mine soon discovered this escape-route and vanished forever into the drains. When I told my mother of my loss, she was extremely annoyed. One of her chief interests was domestic architecture, from the technological rather than the aesthetic standpoint, and in particular all her long life she was fascinated by drains (in my mind I can see her now as a very old lady, an imposing figure poised precariously on a slippery mound of wet clay watching the construction of a new sewer).

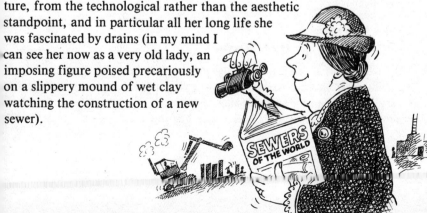

122

Where the eels were concerned, she considered that, thanks to my carelessness, our drains were now seriously at risk. The eels, she said, would probably breed down there and eventually block the whole system. In my defence I pointed out that such a disaster was unlikely because eels did not breed in fresh water but migrated far into the ocean for this purpose. Having pondered this for a moment, she said firmly "I don't believe it"; to this there was no valid reply.

I recall only one instance when I deliberately defied authority – not my mother's, that would have been unthinkable. First I must introduce my ferret Janie, who was my partner in wrongdoing on this occasion. She had been given to me by my father to enable me to keep down the rats on the place. Janie was a charming animal and became so gentle and friendly that I used to carry her about on my shoulder. She must have been unique among ferrets in her unnatural liking for jam puffs which we would share bite for bite when I happened to have one for elevenses. Where rats were concerned, however, she remained the ruthless professional. One afternoon I had taken her and one of the dogs to a haystack at the bottom of our land, which often harboured rats. I put the ferret on top of the stack and almost immediately a rat shot out of the thatch, ran a short distance then plunged back into the hay with Janie in hot pursuit. The chase was prolonged and I realised with dismay that it was time to return home for a lesson; failure to appear would mean a serious row and punishment. But how could I leave the drama on the stack at this critical stage? Having carefully weighed the pros and cons of the situation, I decided to stay where I was and take the consequences, disagreeable though I knew they would be. Eventually the end came; the rat was despatched, I retrieved Janie and went home to my unpleasant welcome, wondering rather dismally whether after all I had made the wise decision.

Hilda Fenemore.
Comic actress of stage and screen.

I was about seven years old and in love with being a 'famous' actress, as that is what my beloved mother wanted me to be. She was Irish/Swedish, very excitable and longed for the stage herself. We were doing the school pantomime, 'Cinderella', and I was busting to get a part in it – when finally it came!

I rushed home to my mother. "I've got a part in Cinderella". My mother was very happy until I told her, "It's the Page; I have one line". My mother, crestfallen, said this was not good enough for me – "Go back to the teacher and tell her you should have the leading part".

I was a terribly shy and nervous little girl, but I adored my mother. So I girded up my loins, went to the teacher and asked for the leading part. I said the Page was "too small". I remember the teacher's face – she could see how earnest and sincere I was. I *really* thought I should have the lead because my mother had told me so!

The teacher very quietly explained to me that the part of the Page was *very* important – if I had not found Cinderella's shoe, there would not have been a happy ending. It was a good part and very crucial to the play.

I was seven years old and was well satisfied with this explanation – and I went on to give it all I'd got.

As a matter of fact, I am now a grandmother, still in the business after thirty-two years, still loving it, and still being told how important my small character parts are!

I remember the line to this day –

"I have found this shoe upon the stair,
Someone must have dropped it there".

See what I mean.

David Filkin.
Editor: 'Tomorrow's World', British Broadcasting Corporation.

George Washington's moment of truth came when he chopped down a tree. Mine was when I first tried shaving. I am sure, for both of us, the momentous factor was simply that we did not lie. The event itself pales into insignificance next to that unforgettable ethical decision. I had scrambled over the yawning gaps of a sixty-foot-high fire escape at the age of two, and pushed a girl down steps at three – but they meant nothing. I was ten before I was really wicked.

I do not know about George Washington: but in my case it was all my father's fault. He would stand there every morning, methodically smothering his face in foam and then meticulously scraping it all off again. He never shut the bathroom door; and I was completely mesmerised. I too had to try it. The trouble was I could not find the shaving soap.

The clean, conscientious Fifties produced a spate of solid antiseptic materials for leaving everything pristine and sparkling. Every decent household had a collection of cleaners. And our bathroom sported a bright pink, abrasive gritty cream guaranteed to leave bath, wash basin and lavatory bowl mirror-bright and spotless. What is more it was accessible – unlike the shaving cream.

I still do not quite know what possessed an intelligent ten-year-old to smear his bristleless, marble smooth jaw and cheeks with the destructive dehydrating devastation of a lavatory cleaner – but I did. It started to set like clay on my face before I had even explored the technological complexities of the safety razor. As my skin seemed to be sucked away from my face, in a panic I grabbed the razor and furiously strove to scrape off what felt increasingly like powdering pink sandpaper. Almost inevitably the pink became stained with thin lines of red as the blood found its way from the slender cuts which my haste had inflicted all over my face. In a flash of amazing inspiration it occurred to me that I could wash off everything – cleaner, blood and all – with cold water. But the scars remained.

Worse still, the razor was still clogged with impacted cleaner. No amount of rinsing under the tap could remove it. What appeared to vanish comfortably from the side of baths, leaving them clean and desirable, seemed to have the opposite qualities on a razor blade. Time rushed by. The school bus was imminent. There was no elegant way out. I put the razor back in its place, made one last desperate cold water attack on my face – and somewhat hesitatingly made my way to breakfast.

The few seconds before anyone commented felt like hours. When it came, the first remark was devastatingly uninspired. "David, what have you done to your face." The response was devastatingly absurd. "Nothing – why?" With more restraint and puzzlement than I can still comprehend, my mother went on to point out that school boys do not normally start the day with a face like a seat belt advertisement and that it was not unreasonable for her to want an explanation. But I stuck to my guns and gave none.

I had a giddy brief moment of triumph as I sat on the school bus, somehow foolishly convincing myself that I had got away with it. But then reason began to dawn. The clogged up razor would soon be discovered. The cuts would not miraculously disappear. Even a doting parent had to come to the inevitable conclusion. There was no alternative. When I got home that evening, I had to own up.

Not surprisingly, it was only with incoherent embarrassment that the whole story was blurted out. Surprisingly, it did not produce the expected deprecating disapproval. Telling the truth had its compensations.

I like to believe that George Washington found a more laudable motive for his honesty than simply a realistic appraisal of the situation. It would be sad if the ethics of the free world were based on mere pragmatism.

Penelope Fitzgerald.
Biographer and novelist.

When I went, at the age of seven, to my first boarding-school, there were – indeed there were at that time in all English boarding-schools – a number of 'Indian children.' This meant that their fathers were in the Indian Army or the Indian Civil Service and that they had been deposited, like packages, until it was convenient to call for them. When they were tiny they had lived in India, looked after by indulgent servants, and had been ecstatically happy. But time was their enemy and now they had been sent Home because they must have a healthier climate and a proper education.

They were very pale children, not so much fair or blonde as pallid, as though they had been reared in a conservatory. Their manner struck the rest of us as strange. They expected to have everything done for them, often didn't know the most elementary things, such as how to buy a halfpenny worth of sweets, and yet they could not be laughed at, having a certain air of dignity. They were miserable beyond words, and indeed could scarcely be expected to have words for what they felt.

Lois, however, told me that her parents didn't expect to come home on leave from India for the next two years, a span of time so long that we couldn't envisage it. She would be nine then and so would I. We couldn't imagine being nine. Lois got up in the middle of every night, and, rather than waste time crying, climbed onto the wooden rail at the foot of her bed and sat there rocking to and fro in her Liberty sleeping-suit. She was riding her pony in the chilly English moonlight and darkness. After a bit I used to implore her to put her pony away and get into bed, or they might come round the dormitory and catch her.

"The *sais* will put him away," said Lois. She gave a few words of command in Hindi.

"I shan't stay here," she told me one day in break. We were in a secret place, the evergreen bushes, with their distinctive smell of dust and gin, which bounded the school garden.

"How can you stop staying here?" I asked her. We should all of us have liked to know this. At that precise moment, for example, we were all aware that there were sixty-nine days, seven hours and three and a half minutes until the beginning of the holidays.

Lois told me that she had some money and intended to run away. "I shall go to the station and get a ticket to Victoria." So much she had learned, even in a short time. "Then I'll go to the docks and take the P&O to Bombay. The inside cabins are much cheaper, you know. We had an outside cabin coming over here, but I don't mind hardship."

I was afraid for Lois and offered to accompany her at least as far as London, where my own parents lived. It was quite true that she had some money – not pocket-money, that was taken away and looked after for us by the headmistress – no, she had acquired it by helping herself from the velvet bag which was handed round in church while she was putting in her own collection. She knew what our half-price tickets would come to, and she also – this was the weakest part of the scheme – thought that we ought to pretend to be boys. The first Shakespeare that was ever read to us had been *Twelfth Night,* and the teacher had explained that "of course, no-one has any idea that Viola is really a girl in disguise." To effect this, we simply put on the pea-green linen shorts which were our uniform for rounders and sports days. Both of us had short hair, shingled (whose wasn't?) to a feathery point on the nape of the neck. (I can still remember the scrape of the hairdresser's clippers.)

We set out after lunch. It was the rest period, during which we were supposed to be lying down on rugs on the wooden floor of the gym. It strikes me now that it was really a rest period for the staff.

"Are you two little girls travelling by yourselves?" the booking-clerk asked us.

"We are little boys," said Lois.

"You don't look much like my little boy," he said.

"You have no right to stop us getting on the train. We have given you our money."

"I'm going to give it back, young lady."

Lois fixed him with a memsahib's glance and spoke with dignity and precision, though with an intonation that was not quite English.

"I am being parted from those I care for most, now I am returning to them. If you try to give back the money, I shall spit upon it. You are only a second-grade railway clerk, you will be dismissed."

It is a fact that the man did not argue any further with Lois. The train was nearly empty, we had a carriage to ourselves all the way to London, and sat there looking at the skimming fields and houses, and counting the telegraph poles – wasn't it sixty-six to the mile?

I was a little worried – though Lois was not – by the question of the P&O – I knew that it cost quite a lot to travel by sea, having been taken the year before to the Isle of Wight. However, the headmistress met us at Victoria. The stationmaster had informed on us – he knew the uniforms of all Eastbourne's myriad prep-schools, and he knew the green shorts. The headmistress had acted promptly, hiring a car. She wore a coat-and-skirt of unyielding material which neither of us had ever seen before, and a hat pierced by some tortoiseshell ornament. The hat seemed to unnerve Lois for a moment, and she cried out that it was my fault and that I had suggested the whole thing. I don't remember resenting this, for I loved her.

"That's an extremely foolish thing to say. You don't do something wrong, indeed wicked, just because someone else tells you to." The headmistress gave a slight, gracious laugh to bring us both to our senses – "Supposing Penny took it into her head to tell you to jump under that train."

The heavy coaches had just begun to move. "Well?" said Lois.

The headmistress did not meet her blue despairing gaze, but led the way to the hired car.

Lois was 'taken away' at the end of term. Her scheme had succeeded, after all. I missed you, Lois. I know that this is a story of your misdeed, not mine. But you were the first person to show me that if one cares enough one can challenge any authority on this earth. I hope that at this moment, wherever you are, you are surrounded by those you care for most and that nothing will separate you from them.

Cyril Fletcher.
Broadcaster, entertainer, author.
(Excerpt from his autobiography, *Nice One Cyril*, published by Corgi.)

I am now a small boy of six and a half and I am in a great rage. I am beside myself with fury and frustration. I am crying and shouting and swearing and throwing myself about and wishing my parents were dead. Perhaps it would be better if I were dead, then they will be sorry. How can I kill myself before this indignity that they are about to thrust upon me? I am to be page at a wedding, my aunt's wedding, and I am to wear a pale-beige tussore suit I have not worn for at least two years. I have been told to get into it and be quiet and get on with it or they will all be late. (A small child has great dignity which one should always respect. I have remembered this hurt vividly for over fifty years.)

I have now got into my tussore suit and my hair is neatly brushed and I have strict instructions to keep clean and look as if I am enjoying myself. The whole grown-up charade seems absurd to me. Why all this fuss about getting married? Why do they all have to dress up? Why do I have to dress up? I am then given my instructions. I am to be the only attendant and as there are no bridesmaids I have to carry my aunt's gloves, prayer book and bouquet. I already look cissy enough in my tussore suit, but now I have to hold a bunch of flowers. In front of everyone, too.

I remember arriving at the parish church. We assembled. We walked slowly up the aisle, I was given the gloves; hurriedly taken off and with the fingers inside-out, the white prayer book and the flowers. The service, with full musical honours, was quite a long one. There seemed to be a lot of kneeling. I knelt with my arms full. My arms got very tired indeed. I can feel the dull ache of them now. I decided after some cowardly looks all round that the best thing for me to do was to put the flowers carefully on the floor and still hold the gloves and prayer book. It was the flowers that were so heavy. So I gently put them on the paving stones of the aisle in front of me.

I was quite tiny kneeling there in my tussore suit, and the grown-ups on either side seemed to tower over me. On my left-hand side, that is to say the bride's side of the aisle, and looking even larger than usual, was the largest of my aunts. She was married to my mother's brother and was also my godmother. She was not 'of the family' as she had merely married into it and was, consequently, although I had known her all my life, 'a stranger'. Her face always had a certain hauteur and she whispered from within the pendulous folds of it to my uncle: "Cyril has thrown the flowers down." It was the word 'thrown' which angered me. Because the flowers were making my arms ache I had quite reasonably, and gently, put them on the cold pavement in front of me. My large aunt moved her enormous form a little towards me. There was the edge of the pew, the heating grating and half the aisle between us. "Pick those flowers up," she hissed. I pretended not to hear. (Thrown indeed!) She tried again. I still pretended not to hear. She tried to draw my attention by striking out at me with her long glove. I took no notice. She must by then have demanded at least six times that I should pick up the flowers. I have very large brown eyes, they were even larger when I was a child as my face was smaller. I turned them on my aunt with a blank stare. She glared back in fury. I then turned my face to the front and began to break off the heads of the flowers from the bouquet and one by one stuff them down the grating. I followed my bridal aunt out of the church holding her gloves, her prayer book and a bunch of stalks.

Sir Denis Follows, C.B.E.
Chairman, The British Olympic Association.

I recall an incident when I was a schoolmaster and was Captain of The Old Boys Cricket Club. At that time, we had a Dalmation bitch whose kennel name was Barouche Dorothy Perkins. We called her 'Rosie'.

It was my practice on a Friday night to clean the cricket pads for use the following day. They were cleaned with blanco and water, and after a fair application of blanco, I must confess that the pads had a rather unpleasant smell.

I had quite a wag as a member of the team. His name was Geoffrey Hall. He took a pair of pads out of the bag to put on, to open the innings. As he took them out, he exclaimed: "Gosh! These pads do stink! What did you clean them with?" I replied, "The same as usual, blanco and water". His retort, as quick as a flash, was: "Rosewater, I presume". (. . . Rosie, you will recall, was the name of the bitch!)

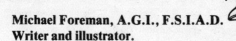

Michael Foreman, A.G.I., F.S.I.A.D.
Writer and illustrator.

First day at Sunday school, six years old. Eight-year-old John Moore arrives red with excitement.

"You should see the apples" he whispered. "Millions of them. Easy. Just down the lane from here. Get over the fence easy."

Tom and Billy Botwright, eyes shining, nod.

"Yeh, on our way home."

The hot sunny afternoon, the droning vicar, the little pictures we were given to look at, and the Lord's Prayer full of words I didn't know the meaning of, and all the time my head full of apples and fences and fear.

Billy Botwright was my classmate and tough and I valued his friendship. I would do anything not to appear chicken in his eyes. Anything he would do, I would do.

The fence was bigger than I expected and I couldn't see any apples at first. John Moore pointed out a few shrivelled little green ones at the tops of high branches. (My mother was the village greengrocer with crates of apples. Why was I trying to scrump these?) Around the trees was a quagmire liberally covered with chicken droppings. The chickens were as ominous as vultures.

Billy Botwright was first over the gate. We followed in a heap. By the time we reached the trees our boots were covered in so much slippery goo, climbing the trees was impossible.

Suddenly, the sunny Sunday afternoon was blotted out by a shape all black and dracula. The Vengeance of the Lord – the Vicar defending his shrivelled cookers – had me by the throat.

The Botwrights had disappeared. John Moore was dropping to freedom from the top of the fence.

"Come back" yelled the vicar, Strather Hunt, "I know who you are."

"No fear!"

The vicar pointed to a notice –Trespassers will be Prosecuted.

I was marched into the ghostly porch of the vicarage – not inside because of the state of my boots.

"What's your name?" he asked through his fangs. I hoped there was a strong chain attached to his dog collar.

He knew who I was so I told him.

"And who were the others?" Ah my chance to be brave. Actually, I was too scared of Billy Botwright to ever split on him.

The next day the village policeman, P.C. 'Pal' Whiteman arrived at our door. I hid under the front room table and my mother said I was out. I heard P.C. Pal laugh and say something about "as we forgive them who trespass against us."

I should have paid more attention to the Lord's Prayer.

So should the Vicar.

Christina Foyle.
M.D. of Foyle's bookshop and daughter of founder; originator, aged 19 and hostess for 50 years of Foyle's Literary Luncheons whose guests have included Bernard Shaw, H. G. Wells and General de Gaulle.

My parents, anxious really to be rid of us, decided that languages would be useful for our future life in the Book Trade and we were sent abroad to school – my brother to Dresden, and my sister and me to Switzerland.

Our school was owned by two elderly French ladies – the mesdames Boutibonne, daughters of the court painter to Franz Joseph. They were always talking about their nephew Robert, who lived in Paris – how completely perfect he was – his brilliance, his looks, his goodness, indeed a real saint.

One day there was great excitement. Robert was coming to stay. Everything was polished, delicious provisions were ordered. The great day came. Robert arrived. He was indeed extraordinarily good looking, about twenty-five, tall, blond, debonair. He lived up to all we had heard about him.

I was a pretty little girl of fifteen, and Robert was especially kind to me. We often met in the garden and he would congratulate me on my good command of French.

Every day we schoolgirls were escorted by a German Fräulein for an afternoon's walk. Robert surprised me by asking if I could give the party the slip and meet him at a café in Interlaken for tea.

It was not difficult. Fräulein Olga led the crocodile and was very trusting. It was quite easy for me to loiter behind and disappear down a side turning, and make my way to Interlaken where I met Robert at the

Café Schatz. After tea we went to see a film 'Ergieb dich mir' – Let me possess you – full of fiery passion, and all through the film we held hands.

Afterwards he took me to supper at the Kursaal. I had my first glass of champagne. When we arrived back, very late, at the school, we tried to slip in through the kitchen unobserved, but Sophie, the Cook, was still up and she told the mesdames Boutibonne that we were home.

Robert was packed off to Paris the next day and I was in disgrace for weeks.

I wonder if Robert Widmir, who would be about eighty if he is alive, remembers the schoolgirl at the Villa Unspunnen in Wilderswil all those years ago.

Professor Sir Charles Frank, O.B.E., F.R.S.
Emeritus Professor of Physics, formerly Director of H. H. Wills
Physics Laboratory, University of Bristol.

I was about nine, I think, when two younger brothers and I found access, behind a chimney-stack in the attic, into a previously unexplored roof-space. There was very little light in there and presently I missed my footing, putting a foot through the ceiling below me, and so depositing a mass of broken plaster on the spare-room bed, newly made up for father's uncle Garney, who was coming down from London to stay a week with us on the farm.

Father had already left to meet him at the station. Mother had barely half an hour, I think, to clear up the mess, boil up flour-paste, and paste a large square of white paper over the hole in the ceiling.

Most of sixty years later, driving through Suffolk, I deviated from my route to look at the old farmhouse. It was unoccupied, but presently the owner of the farm appeared, the son of the man who took over from my father.

His mother had lived on in the house as a widow till two or three months before and now it was being substantially refurbished for him to move into.

He showed us round. Refurbishment work had not reached the spare bedroom yet, and mother's paper patch on the ceiling was still in place.

Helen Fraser.
Film actress.

The most valuable possession to a small girl at boarding school, apart from her teddy bear of course, was her tuck. This precious ambrosia was closely guarded, occasionally swapped, but rarely shared. There were two courses of action: to gobble it down immediately or to eke it out bit by bit as a little treat each day. In either event it helped to stem the continuous waves of homesickness.

I took the thrifty course, rationing my intake of treasured sweets to one or two a day. Having received a tin of assorted caramels for a birthday present I counted out the contents and with joy, found I had at least three weeks of comfort. The tin took pride of place on my dormitory locker and the highlight of each day was to decide which flavoured caramel would lessen my misery.

Late one afternoon, after my dreaded solitary piano practice, I returned to the dormitory where the other girls were already changing for supper. When I came in they all seemed to be sniggering and in my wild imagination, chewing with teeth clenched as if interwoven with sticky strands of caramels.

I took one look in my tin of treasures and rushed, with wild accusations, to our matron in the laundry room. She listened sternly to my story of theft, led me firmly by the hand back to the dormitory to face the guilty band of robbers and after a long and loud lecture on the penalties of stealing, she asked me for some proof. I picked up my tin, opened the lid and wailed "when I left the dormitory the tin was half full and now it's half empty."

The sniggering grew into raucous, wide-mouthed laughter and the open mouths showed no trace of caramels; the chewing had been a teasing pretence.

Matron's face grew sterner and as a punishment for my false accusations the tin of caramels had to be shared out equally among my room mates.

That night, as I soaked my pillow with tears of homesickness, I realised with despair that I had no more sweet comforts to help me until the next tuck parcel arrived at mid-term. Thank goodness for teddy bears.

Christopher Fry.
Playwright.

I can only suppose that my father's death when I was three-and-a-half years old took some of the high spirits out of me, and that may be why my mother's stories of my misdeeds all belong to the six months or so before he died: such as getting hold of a pair of scissors and cutting off the hair of a little girl of my own age when we were playing in the conservatory – and the two stories about my brother's tin soldiers. He was five years older than I was, and very proud of his collection of infantry, cavalry, bandsmen, stretcher-bearers, kilted warriors running with fixed bayonets, Zulus with spears, even Russians in green uniforms, representatives of the Russo-Japanese war. They fascinated me too, but not to display them in ordered ranks as on a parade ground. My mother had prepared a tea-table for visitors, and came into the room to find that I had stuck soldiers into the butter, into the bread, into the cakes, and was jumping up and down, clapping my hands and calling "Look what me done!"

But this anti-war demonstration, or at any rate lack of proper respect for military dignity, was taken even further. My mother had been making jam. A large saucepan of the stuff was simmering on the stove. She left it unguarded for a few minutes and came back to find that I had thrown a mixed regiment of soldiers into the bubbling cauldron where the glory of their uniforms was lost for ever.

136

Peter Fry, M.P.
Member of Parliament for Wellingborough.

My school like many others, while escaping any direct damage, none-the-less had an extremely difficult war period. Standards had actually been improved despite the fact that the great majority of the masters had been taken away for war service. The result was that the Headmaster had to recruit a large number of ladies, which when they first arrived were considered a very great novelty in an all-boys school.

At the first Speech Day at the end of the war the Headmaster felt that he should pay tribute to all the help that he had received to get him through those very difficult years and in his opening remarks, before the assembled Governors, Parents and school, he declared "I don't know how I would have got through the war if it had not been for all my mistresses!"

Sir Vivian Fuchs, F.R.S.
Leader of the Commonwealth Trans-Antarctic Expedition, 1955–58 and lately Director of the British Antarctic Survey.

In the early 1920s all the Houses at Brighton College except ours had changed from gas to electric lighting. Whenever the electric supply failed, as frequently happened, our somewhat old fashioned House-master would gleefully point out that his retention of gas lighting assured that we were the only ones who could present ourselves in class next day with 'prep' completed. To us this seemed very unfair – after some thought we devised our revenge.

In my study a capped gas pipe protruded from the wall. Without much difficulty I removed the cap, and four of us took turns to blow into the pipe with all our might. First our light, then all lights in the passages went out. Our efforts were crowned with success when the large multiple-mantle lights in the prep-room flickered and died. The House was in total darkness, and next day *we* were the only ones excused prep.

With hindsight I realise that it had all been a very dangerous exercise but luck had remained with us. We were never found out, and the next year electricity was installed – as a result of which our fortunes then coincided with the rest of the school.

Major-General Edward Fursdon, C.B., M.B.E., D.Litt.
Defence Correspondent on the Daily Telegraph, London.

I was on a family beach picnic at Croyde Bay, North Devon, in August 1927. It was a bright, sunny, seaside day and even at the age of two-and-a-half, I was car mad.

With the older children, I had tried to help make the circle of full-size chairs in sand which were my father's annual speciality and on which we were to picnic. I remember we had also constructed the traditional series of successively draining pools which refilled at each exploratory but inexorable surging in of the tidal wavelets.

Soon overwhelmed, we retired for the rest of the day to the sand dunes where, more happily, I could exercise my formidable collection of toy cars up and down convenient sandy hill climbs and runs and rest them in parks sited between the tufts of sea-grass.

Surprisingly – with a notion simply years ahead of the times! – I suddenly buried all my cars into a deep sand underground car park. Just

as the task was completed, I was called in to the spread rugs to eat our jammy tea – one in which many marauding hungry wasps shared. Soon it was time to pack up and carry all the assorted beach and picnic paraphernalia back to the car and return to our lodgings with the local postman at nearby Georgeham.

"My cars!" I remember crying out despairingly to an initially rather unsympathetic family, when I realised I could not remember where, before tea, I had buried my collection. At that tender age, the more I looked the more the sand dunes all looked alike and, after all, I was the one who was supposed to know where I'd been.

But, when the utter depth of my misery became loudly apparent and overtook all else, five pairs of eyes joined in – but their combined efforts were to no avail. The burial job had been too well done and its concealment was perfect. Eventually, the family discipline of return and routine had to over-ride a reluctant and red-eyed unremembering 2½-year-old – who miserably rode home.

So, amateur adventurers, if any of you live near Croyde Bay and have an electronic metal detector, there is a hidden collection of valuable cars awaiting you out there, which by now will have acquired the vintage flavour of real treasure. It's over to you – they are yours for the finding! But if you do discover them, then please let me have back just one – for old time's sake – and I'll not be fussy about the make of the one you give me; they'll all be antiques by now.

L. Marsland Gander.
War Correspondent for the Daily Telegraph, 1941–45; first newspaper Television Correspondent, 1935.

It was 1918, the last year of world war one. By some chance I had reached the top form at the City of London College. Discipline was slack to put it mildly. We didn't know it would be the last year of the war; life was cheap and we were all expecting to be called up shortly. Cannon fodder in the classroom.

Thus it was extremely difficult if not impossible to take exams seriously. I was confronted with a mathematical question about some ridiculous hypothetical problem. X little 2; y little 2. What the hell did it mean? There was a swarthy lad sitting next to me whose name ended in 'ski.' He was bound to know. So I brazenly consulted him and we agreed on the answer. The only snag was that it was completely wrong. Thus we scored a pair – a couple of ducks. But curiously there were no punishments at the time.

When a learner reporter on the Stratford Express my chief vice was motor-cycling. Girls on the pillion decorously sat side saddle but this tended to make the machine unstable and spills were numerous. I counted my wounds like a Red Indian notching his scalps. But one day the charmer on the back shot across a wet road in one direction and I went the other way. She scraped her behind rather badly whereas I was virtually unscathed. She was a good sport and made little fuss as she limped round the local library where she worked. But, O dear, her father was not amused.

My motor cycling continued in Bombay when I was Chief Reporter of the Times of India. I had also taken up the less dangerous hobby of amateur theatricals and was in the chorus of 'The Gondoliers.' One day I was passing close to a car parked by the kerb when the door was suddenly flung open and I crashed into it. "You bloody fool" I yelled. The driver was my girl partner in The Gondoliers. When next I clutched her round the waist and chanted "Here we are at risk of our lives" she was distinctly frigid.

My worst folly was to come. In Bombay I shared what we called a chummery over the Times of India office, a neglected barn of a place with a minimum of furniture and a maximum of servants. Eric Linklater dour, quiet, reserved, introspective was one companion there, another was an alcoholic Scottish sub editor. A third was a fellow Cockney who had come to India to sell printing machinery. Before leaving England he had become engaged to be married. I had been friendly with a pretty brunette who had seen me off at Tilbury and somehow the two girls got together. "Wouldn't it be nice if you also got engaged," remarked Bill, my Cockney friend. What a good idea, I thought and promptly wrote off asking my brunette to marry me. She agreed and I bought the ring.

Immediately things began to go wrong. I sent her an alabaster model of the Taj Mahal and it arrived in a thousand pieces. Then I reported a story of murder and attempted abduction and scored a triumph by getting a picture of the woman in the case Mumtaz Begum, mistress of the Maharajah of Indore. I also got into a front page display of the Illustrated Weekly looking lovingly at the girl who, of course, I had never seen before in my life. My fiancée, who did not understand the demands of publicity in the field of journalism, was livid.

When after a severe operation I returned to England I quickly realised it had all been a ghastly mistake. We agreed to call it off. Inviting this contribution the compiler talked of events which "seemed dreadful at the time but will make you chuckle today." Well I don't chuckle over these reminiscences. I think I was just a silly young fool.

140

Andrew Gardner.
Journalist, newscaster and television interviewer.

I hate fireworks. If I had my way they'd all be banned. But as a child I adored them. The day war broke out, as dear old Rob Wilton used to say, I was seven. And during the war years there were no fireworks – other than those provided by a combination of the Luftwaffe, the RAF and the Ack Ack batteries near my home! Oh, and the Home Guard too, they let off the occasional banger.

I was a keen student of chemistry and by the time I was 11 years old I was determined to have some fireworks on Guy Fawkes night. They couldn't be outside ones because of the blackout regulations, so I worked secretly in the garden shed producing an elaborate box of indoor fireworks. It was to be a surprise for my unsuspecting family.

I had a spot of luck because a school friend had given me a supply of cordite he'd prised out of an unexploded shell. I added this precious ingredient to black powder, sulphur, saltpetre, iron fillings and anything else I could lay my hands on from my impressive chemistry set. With the help of fuses, paper, cardboard, glue and my paint box I soon had a box full of very exciting looking cones, tubes and oblongs. The big night arrived and the family assembled round the hearth for 'Andy's surprise'. I think most of them had forgotten it was 5th November, although they soon remembered.

I started off with 'Golden rain' which was a bit of a disappointment. It burnt with a fierce roar and produced a lot of smoke. My Father opened the French windows. The next one was called 'Eastern Magic' and should have been a snake that grew from a cone of fire. Unfortunately the 'snake' emerged rather faster than I had expected and raced across the living room carpet in a gooey fire ball. My Father stamped on it and my Mother said "Are you sure these are quite safe dear?" The next three or four did more or less what I intended. But my undoing came when I lit the fuse of my 'Volcano surprise'. The Volcano was bad enough . . . the surprise was devastating! It set light to the curtains, the hearth rug, the cat and my Father's favourite armchair. Aunt Molly said it was much worse than being in an air raid, I was sent to bed, and we didn't see Tiddles for three days! At least it was a night to remember!

Donald Gee.
Actor.

King George the Sixth had just died, and Scouts and Cubs throughout the land were asked to distribute a special brochure to raise money for a charity – King George The Sixth Foundation. Johnny Littlefair and I were Cubs waiting, wanting to be Scouts. The Cub or Scout had to knock on the householders' door, explain the reason for disturbing them – "It is a very important project and young people in the Scout Movement will benefit. Please sign here and commit yourself." And so after work and longing to get back to their teas and Dick Barton, with no money to hand over, they signed.

What attracted Johnny and myself about the prospect was the medal. Each Scout or Cub got a medal for every fifty signatures we were to take back to the Church Hall, Aspinall, Gorton Second Scouts – six hundred such commitments. We had succumbed to the gong at an early age, and like the man who started each Rank film, put everything into it.

We were due six medals each. Mr Dobbs, the Scoutmaster, glowed at our achievement. "Lads, you've done the best for miles around. I want you to come into the Scout Room – I'm going to cover you both with glory."

We weren't used to such words, but we went to the Scout Room. Gathered in a circle: fifteen Scouts, two Cubs. It was like a Junior League Football result. But we were the Lions, the winners, the best. Mr Dobbs' long khaki shorts covered his knees. "Lads" he began in praise.

"We have here two Cubs who I'm proud to say will very shortly be Scouts. They have set an example to you all. The industry and ingenuity which they have achieved is staggering."

He went on in this fashion, and suddenly Johnny and I found the whole thing absurdly funny. I don't know why. Inexplicable. His shorts, his Mounties' hat, which was too big. We looked at each other and smiled. And a laugh which exploded in the nasal passage. And then the laugh direct.

Mr Dobbs heeled round, looked at us in disbelief. "I think" he measured, "we will draw your praise to a close. This is disgraceful behaviour. Stand outside while we carry on proper Scout business."

We were banished, never again to enter that inner Sanctum. Johnny and I decided that while Mr Dobbs was in charge of overall Scouting policy for the 2nd Gortons, we'd give the khaki hats a miss. But not the medals.

We knew where he lived. He'd got eight of us round to move a mangle and a wardrobe. After the dust had settled we were to knock on his door. "Mr Dobbs, can you tell us, please, when do we get our medals?" "They haven't been cast yet and I doubt whether any will be coming your way."

"Why, Mr Dobbs?" The concern and politeness were to alter. We'd wait for him to get off the tram and shout "Hey, Dobbsies, where's our medals?" and pedal off.

We never did get our true recognition. Mr Dobbs' trousers grew shinier and shinier. We grew up and discovered the Speedway.

Sir John Gielgud.
Actor.

I vividly remember, while I was at a preparatory school near Godalming, I was isolated for some epidemic or other – measles or scarlet fever – and was allowed to sit out on the terrace which led from the Headmaster's drawing room.

I used to drape the rug on which I was sitting round my shoulders and over one arm, and march royally up and down the shallow steps that led into the garden.

In those far-off days I think I had no idea of wanting to become an actor and I was terrified that someone might catch me posing in this way, but the urge was not to be denied. I suppose it was an unmistakable sign of things to come.

Sir John Gilmour, Bt., D.S.O.
M.P. for East Fife, 1961–79, Lord Lieutenant of Fife since 1980.

When at Eton 1925–1931 there was a very nice Master who had a bit of a squint. One day, rounding a corner, a small boy ran into him full tilt. "Heavens, please boy" said the Beak "look where you are going". To this the small boy replied; "Heavens, please Sir, go where you are looking!"

Sir Leslie Glass, K.C.M.G.
British Ambassador to Romania, 1965–1967.
High Commissioner in Nigeria, 1969–1971.

When I was a small prep. school boy I was staying one Christmas with the family of a Rector in Wales. Wishing to pay his two sons out for some trick they had played on me, I set out in the dark corridors of the rectory at midnight on Christmas Eve to hang a stocking at the end of one of their

beds. It contained a package of turkey gizzards. Unfortunately, in the dark I mistook the room, and hung the stocking at the end of the bed of a visiting Bishop. The good Rector was very cross with me.

The Rt. Hon. Lord Glendevon, P.C.
As Lord John Hope, M.P., 1945–64.
Minister in Governments of Churchill, Eden, Macmillan at Foreign Office,
Commonwealth Office, Scottish Office and finally as Minister of Works.

I was born and brought up at Hopetoun House, on the Firth of Forth, a beautiful Adam house (some of it earlier) where my family have lived for over two hundred and fifty years.

To Hopetoun there came, one day in 1919, the Emir Feisal, who was over here in connection with peace terms after the First World War. He was staying on board the Flagship of that part of the Fleet which was stationed in the Firth, and he was brought ashore by the Navy in a barge which landed him just below the house, which was apparently to be the first European house he had ever seen.

My twin brother Charlie and I were just seven and we were playing on the lawn near the wood, from which the party would emerge as they walked up from the shore. We knew nothing of the visit, so were totally unnerved by the appearance of the Arab leader in his robes, accompanied by the famous T. E. Lawrence (Lawrence of Arabia) and others, as they burst through the bushes.

My father being away on military service, my mother was supposed to meet the visitors. She had, however, forgotten that they were coming and was playing squash rackets in a pair of my father's pyjamas when they were first sighted. She rushed back to the house and changed in time.

Feisal was taken through the house. It was full of lovely things, but what really interested him was a stuffed seal's head (long since destroyed, I am happy to say) over a door in the hall. I remember him pointing up at the head and talking animatedly to Lawrence.

The next thing I remember was that we all went out again on to the lawn. Feisal then said something in Arabic to us boys. Lawrence said, "He asks if you will go back to Arabia with him". At that disastrous moment, Feisal seized each of us by the hand and started running across the lawn away from the house. We were terrified and yelled blue murder as we tried unavailingly to free ourselves, and I can smell now the spicy aroma of his robes as they enveloped me. Mercifully, he soon turned back and we were safe.

Lawrence was laughing as he scratched his nose. We felt rather ashamed of ourselves, I think, but it had been quite an ordeal.

John Glenister.
Film and T.V. director.

I must have been something less than ten years old when I was evacuated away from the early days of the war in London to Wellingborough in Northamptonshire, the home of both my parents' families. I stayed with an uncle and aunt who kept a grocers shop in the Northampton Road.

The shelves of Newman's Stores were stocked with most of the necessary items for the neighbouring houses, but my particular favourite was the ice-cream, packed into two deep, metal tubs in a refrigerated chest and topped by heavy, circular lids.

It happened one family Sunday. Lunch was finished and tea was far away. Uncles and aunts sat talking with my grandparents. I felt left out and bored. My thoughts turned towards the ice-cream, unattended in the closed shop.

I made some excuse and was soon passing through the door that led from the house to the shop, darkened by drawn blinds. The cold chest was only two steps away and then all that stood between me and unlimited ice-cream was the heavy lid of the container. It was quite difficult to lift it clear and rest it on the far edge.

The ice-cream must have been in great demand the day before: the level was so low that I had to hitch myself up in order to reach into the tub. The scoop had not even touched bottom when my arm caught the lid and knocked it over the back and on to the floor.

At least, that is where it should have fallen but I knew by the sound that things had gone wrong. The sound was softer, cracklier, squashier than I expected.

I went round to look and discovered that I had just heard the unusual noise made when a heavy, metal object falls on what, to my young and guilty eyes, looked like at least five thousand eggs. They were newly laid, freshly delivered and, until quite recently, neatly arranged in large, square pallets the other side of the ice-cream chest.

I only hesitated a moment before deciding to leave everything as it was, in the thin hope that the shop cat might take the rap. I fled upstairs and hid under a bed. For nearly two hours I lay there, trembling with fear and listening in vain for the sound of voices raised in anger against the cat.

At last I was found – but my time under the bed must have served as sufficient penance because I had become a missing person, presumed dead, and the consequent relief by-passed any intended punishment.

I still like ice-cream. And I'm very partial to scrambled eggs.

Air Marshal Sir Victor Goddard, K.C.B., C.B.E., M.A.
Chief of the Air Staff, New Zealand. Member, Air Council. Author.

I was about four. My brother, nearly two years older than me, used to give me the round end of the bath. Nanny was in attendance. My brother got into the bath first. So he was already sitting at the tap end when I, absent-mindedly, and not wishing any harm, turned on the hot tap, scalding my brother all down the backbone.

He leapt out of the bath, screaming, went down the back stairs, ran along the passage to the hall and out to the drive and the Harrow road. He ran towards the village, still screaming and starko. But suddenly, realising where he was, he stopped screaming, turned round, and ran back to the house, and into the bath again; that being the warmest place.

I had already been sent to bed. That was a non-bath night so far as I was concerned.

Johnny Goodman.
T.V. and film producer.

Fourteen years old and only just out of school, I enrolled as an A.R.P. messenger during those dark, yet strangely exciting days of the London

Blitz. This activity involved one or two nights a week sleeping in the underground headquarters in Shepherds Bush. On this particular occasion it wasn't one of Hitler's bombs that roused me from my slumber on the floor but contact from a warm female hand that had gently taken mine and proceeded to tenderly squeeze and caress it for some fifteen minutes or so. The perpetrator of this outrage was a rather attractive lady warden lying next to her husband on a slightly raised section close by. As we were all fully clothed apart from our steel helmets it was probably not the most erotic setting for such a seduction.

I recall those heady moments today with amusement and, perhaps, just a shade of chauvinistic pride, but at the time my feelings were a lethal combination of sexual excitement and stark fear at the mortal sin I was involved in. The following morning I awoke convinced I would be confronted by an outraged husband and probably horse-whipped. Happily, he seemed to have slept like a log, oblivious of the explosions outside and his wife's outrageous but (sadly) singular lapse within. My, how times have changed!

The Very Rev. Thomas Goss.
Dean of Jersey since 1971. Chaplain RAFVR, 1941–7.

The piano was always a feature in our family. We all had a go on it from time to time, and on Sunday evenings my father would sit down and play hymns while we three children, my two sisters and I, sang lustily, each of us choosing in turn a favourite hymn. When I was about 8 years old I was given my first pen-knife, of which I was tremendously proud, and of course I wanted to put it to use as soon as possible. Alone in the drawing room and toying with my knife, I looked round for a suitable piece of wood to experiment on, and the only piece of wood that seemed readily available was the piano. So with scarcely a thought I carefully scratched on the inside of the open lid my initial, 'T'. As soon as I had done it I realised I had made a mistake and tried to expunge it with my probably rather dirty finger, to no avail. Had I been older and wiser I might have written the initial of one of my sisters, or perhaps even chosen some other article to adorn. But the 'T' was there, very plainly, for all to see.

And of course all did see it. My father held an identity parade and asked each one of us if we were responsible, and I am sorry to confess that none of us owned up. Not that it mattered. It was all too obvious who the culprit was, and he was duly punished, and there the 'T' remained, a permanent witness to my folly and my falsehood.

When my father died at the age of 89 the piano was still there with the 'T' a little mellowed but still very visible. But now it had taken on a new character and become a source of family amusement and a slice of family history. The guilt, somehow, is no longer there.

If I may improve the shining hour, is not this the way things happen. The disastrous earthquakes of millions of years ago which must have struck terror into the hearts of whatever beasts were there, have become the beauty-spots of the world, Himalayas, Alps, the Lake District and so forth. Historical disasters have become woven into the fabric of the world and even a source of pride. Just like the 'T' on the piano.

The Lord Granville of Eye.
M.P., Eye Div. of Suffolk, 1929–51.

I was acting as a stand-in P.P.S to Ramsay MacDonald when he was Prime Minister in the 1931 Coalition.

He had an important speech to make in the House of Commons. In each of his two waistcoat pockets he carried a pill – one a *stimulant*, the other something of a *sleeping* pill.

I was in the Prime Minister's private room behind the Speaker's chair, when he suddenly exclaimed "I've taken the wrong pill!"

We walked into the Chamber and took our seats.

I decided to go out and telephone his personal doctor, whose address I got from Rosie Rosenberg, his Private Secretary at Number 10.

The doctor assured me that taking the wrong pill *did not matter* – they were for the same purpose, which information I transmitted quickly to the P.M. by a hurried whisper from the second bench.

He made a really good speech, winding up for the Government.

On returning to his private room, his doctor was there. I told him that I had conveyed his assurance to the P.M. that it did not matter which pill he took.

He smiled and replied: "Oh yes it did – but just as well he didn't know!"

Sylvia Gray, C.B.E.
Creator of Bay Tree Hotel, Burford. Chairman, National Federation of Women's Institutes, 1969–74.

When I was a small girl, I was told at lunchtime one day to clear my plate by eating some fat which I did not fancy – "No, I won't" I said – "I don't like it". "Do as you are told", said my father, "or go straight up to your room". "No I won't", I replied again. "I'll go into the garden and eat worms!"

It is a remark that has lasted in the family until this day when faced with doing something we don't fancy!

Sir Hugh Greene, K.C.M.G., O.B.E.
Author, journalist, broadcaster and publisher, Dir. Gen. BBC, 1960–69.

I am afraid that I was a disgustingly good and rather timid little boy. Some of my enemies would say, perhaps rightly, that I have spent the rest of my life making up for it.

So my misdeeds as a child were few. I do, however, remember an occasion when with my cousin Barbara, who was a couple of years older than me, I was caught by my nurse in the kitchen garden at the School House, Berkhamsted, eating large quantities of green gooseberries. (I belong to that unhappy class and generation which spent years in the grip of often horrid nurses and nursemaids.)

As a good little boy should, I knew my Bible well. I said to my nurse "The woman tempted me."

Lord Grey of Naunton, G.C.M.G., G.C.V.O., O.B.E.
Chancellor, New University of Ulster, Governor of Northern Ireland, 1968–73.

Tauromachy has its eminent supporters – in literature as well as in practice – and it has also, of course, its vehement critics. But in the New Zealand of my youth the bull was a useful, valuable asset, not to be trifled with. My only essay at bull-fighting thus owed nothing to custom, fashion, intellect or valour: its only cause was original sin.

Aged seven, I went with my mother from the small country town in which we lived to the farm of friends. Our conveyance was horse-and-gig. When the grown-ups settled to their own affairs and there was no one of my age to occupy me, my wish for action was unhappily aggravated by the sight of a bull in a paddock near the house. The bull wore, as was the local winter custom, a canvas cover. Satan suggested that if I crept through the wire fence and stealthily approached the bull from behind I might flick it with the gig-whip just where his cover ended and some excitement would follow. It did. No doubt the bull was even-tempered enough but the application of the whip did not please him. He made it clear that flight would be in my best interests.
Hampered by the whip, which was taller than I was but which I dared not leave behind, I made good time towards the fence. But the bull was gaining on me ominously. An undignified scramble through the wires was achieved just in time, with the bull roaring his displeasure.

To have been caught by the bull would have had consequences unknown but doubtless disagreeable. The consequences of parental disapproval, both of the folly of my act and of the damage to our good standing with our hosts, were all too well known and likewise disagreeable.

I have not engaged in tauromachy since then; nor do I have pleasure in reading of it in the works of Hemingway or other *aficionados*. Little and early has proved more than sufficient.

General Sir John Hackett.
Commander-in-Chief, British Army of the Rhine, 1966–68.
Principal, King's College, London, 1968–75.
President, UK Classical Association, 1971 and English Assn, 1973–74.

As a young Oxford undergraduate at the very beginning of the thirties, still as I might think today a child, I was fascinated by the large amber globes then recently erected in busy streets at pedestrian crossings. 'Belisha Beacons' they were called and I wanted one. I soon had it too, and with half-a-dozen little goldfish and a packet of ants' eggs set up a small aquarium in 13 King Edward St which gave much innocent pleasure to us all.

One day the Proctor's bulldogs called. Had I been betrayed? It was the work of only a few moments to run upstairs and tip my little friends into a wash basin (a *real* wash basin in those days, mind you: none of your plug- and-running-water things) and tie a table lamp flex around the flanged rim of the amber globe. I then gently hung it out of the window and closed the sash, just like the man with the forbidden whisky bottle in 'Lost Weekend'. The bulldogs had called about something else. They left and we could all come together again.

But the end of term was close. I could hardly ask my landlady . . . What I wanted was a light and cheerful glass vessel furnished with a frequent change of water. Where could I possibly find such a thing? Behind the market, in Market St, there was (and is) a public convenience, the male section presided over in those days by a one-eyed elderly man in a yachting cap. We knew him as the Rear Admiral. Upon the wall above the customer's heads was fixed a generously proportioned glass cistern, regularly emptied and filled. The very thing!

I brought my little friends round in a jam jar with two accomplices. One attracted the Rear Admiral's interest, the other gave me a leg-up. It was done! After more than 50 years my memory may be at fault in this but I rather think that one little fish went out on the tide the first time it ebbed. The rest soon got the hang of it . . . We left.

Next day I called. There they were, in full view, happy as could be.

"Hullo," I said to the Rear Admiral. "Goldfish, eh? Now that *does* brighten the place up!"

"Yes," he replied with an enigmatic look. "Can't be much grub in there. What do they eat?"

"Well, these look the same as mine. They eat ants' eggs. As it happens I'm taking some home. Want a few? Here, have these."

Again the enigmatic look.

I went down from Oxford for the Vac.

The first day of the next term I called round. There they were, loving it.

"Yes," the Rear Admiral was saying to a visitor, rather proudly I thought. "Brightens the place up, don't it?"

The week after that they were gone. "What happened?" I asked.

"The inspector," he said. "Didn't care for it."

We looked at one another. In the Rear Admiral's one good eye was the merest hint of a shared sorrow.

"Inspector said he didn't *want* the place brightened up. Could easily draw crowds."

"Pity," I said, and meant it.

I never saw the Rear Admiral again.

Willis Hall,
Writer for theatre and screen; author of children's books.

They were the early days of the war and, like every other eleven-year-

old at that time, I was a zealous little patriot.
 I collected waste-paper.
 I hunted out scrap metal to make Spitfires.
 I studied first-aid with a local group.
 I even pored over purloined Home
Guard manuals which explained how to
decapitate German motor-cyclists with cheese-wire.
 I was a loyal Boy Scout.
 In short, I did everything within my power to aid the war-effort –
except for one thing.
 I didn't eat liver.
 Wednesday was liver-day in the school-dinner cycle. I hated liver.
Under the eagle-eye of the maths-master who supervised my particular
table, a thick rubbery wodge of liver was placed in front of me every
week. To return a plate down the table with the food uneaten was a
cardinal sin.
 We were exhorted both on the wireless and in the newspapers *not* to
waste food. Huge billboard posters glowered down at me on my way to
school, pointing out that wasting food was tantamount to helping Hitler
win the war.
 The actual act of liver-evading was quite simple but at the time it
caused me many sleepless conscience-stricken nights.
 I smuggled the liver, gravy and all, into my blazer-pocket when
attentions were directed towards the arrival of the steamed-pudding.
After school, on my way home, I made a detour through the local park
where I unloaded the foul offal, surreptitiously, into a waste-paper
basket.
 Over the years, I have managed to conquer my hatred for liver. But I

shall never forget the curious smell of stale liver-gravy in a blazer-pocket. Nor shall I ever forget the torments I suffered whenever I considered how I, personally, was prolonging World War 2.

Leslie Halliwell.
Author, T.V. film buyer.

I remember an embarrassing occasion when I incurred my headmaster's displeasure. Being a film buff then as well as now, I was running a school film society at the age of thirteen, and the indulgent master in charge went along blithely with my choice of programmes. Thus it was that one Monday after school we trundled a 16mm projector into the library and ran an Aldwych farce called A CUCKOO IN THE NEST, which I remembered as an infant thinking positively hilarious; it had practically sent my mother into hysterics.

I hadn't seen the movie for eight years, and as it unspooled I realized that my childish innocence on the previous occasion had failed to detect a rather large dose of sexual innuendo which adolescent society members were clearly enjoying. Doubling as projector operator, I was standing at the back, near the double doors, and it was unfortunate that just as a gale of laughter greeted the pyjama-clad antics of Ralph Lynn, trapped in a double bed with a lady not his wife, I felt a warm breeze on the back of my neck. I turned, to find our magnificently leonine headmaster breathing extremely heavily in my direction. I think he was too astonished to speak there and then; at any rate, he turned abruptly on his heel and departed. I was too apprehensive to join in the remaining laughter, and of course there was an inquest next day during which the future policy of the Film Society was brought rather strictly under review. I believe the attractions for the following term were in fact KING OF KINGS, REMBRANDT, a Russian silent documentary called TURKSIB and D. W. Griffith's THE BIRTH OF A NATION. None were quite so much fun as A CUCKOO IN THE NEST, but the last of them at any rate brought us a record attendance which included the headmaster, who was extremely puzzled to find that the Ku Klux Klan were depicted by Griffith as heroes. He gave us a corrective lecture on the subject on the following Friday, but I think after that he abandoned the world of the cinema as rather too puzzling.

Admiral Sir John Hamilton, G.B.E., C.B.
C. in C. Mediterranean, 1964–67.

During the First World War my mother lived for a while in rooms in Southsea when my father, a regular soldier, was away at the front. I was seven at the time. One wild and stormy winter's afternoon I was playing alone on Southsea common, which was virtually deserted. What fascinated me was throwing the metal top of a tin into the wind and seeing it soaring up and back over my head. I was experimenting to try and determine which angle of throw achieved the longest wind-borne flight. Without realising it, each throw and subsequent recovery inevitably brought me further and further down wind away from the seaward edge of the common and closer to the road which bordered its inland edge. Great was my delight when, after my most successful throw, I found, near where my tin top landed, a larger tin top (which I now presume to have been the top of a small oil drum). I launched this forth into the wind with all my might. Caught by the wind, it soared beautifully, high over my head, and then to my horror went straight for a tall street lamp at the side of the road. It cut the glass clean as a whistle and the whole heavy globe fell to the ground with a resounding crash.

I took to my heels and ran flat-out off the common, past the Queen's Hotel and down one or two streets, heading for home. I rounded the last corner into our own street head down and going like a bat from hell – straight, head first, into the midriff of a large policeman, pacing his beat with measured tread. Convinced that he had been put there for the specific purpose of arresting me and sending me to prison, I rushed on past him shouting, "I didn't mean to do it! I didn't mean to do it!" until I reached the sanctuary of our lodgings and slammed the front door, terrified that the Law would follow.

Nothing more happened.

I have often wondered what that bobby, unsuspectingly walking his beat, thought of that small and frightened tornado of a boy who disturbed the even tenor of his peaceful afternoon's round.

Sir Richard Hamilton, Bt., M.A.
Landowner, playwright.

I remember three severe shocks in my early school days.

When the two minutes' silence was observed at my prep. School, it was the custom for the pupils to turn their backs on the staff assembled on the dais and to face the wall at the end of the room.

On one occasion, when the eleven o'clock siren sounded, I duly about-turned, prepared to stand in silence during the two minutes which seemed to most of us an age. It so happened that I was one of the boys immediately nearest the wall. My prayers for the fallen – if any – were suddenly broken off by the sight of a curious round wooden object attached to the wall. What was it? Why did it contain two inviting little holes? Eager to probe the mystery, I inserted two inquisitive young fingers. The stabbing, seering pain that shot up through my fingers to my arm and shoulder gave me literally the shock of a lifetime. Mercifully no anguished scream escaped my lips to jarr upon the hallowed silence. Had it done so, in the best traditions of that spartan academy, further pain would inevitably have come my way.

But at that tender age one seldom learns. Shortly afterwards I was recovering from 'flu in a small dormitory with two or three other sufferers. One evening, when about to clean my teeth, I noticed that one of the electric lights had no bulb, so what more natural than to set it swinging? When I thought I might as well stop it, I thrust my tooth paste tube up the empty socket, metal top and all. There followed an unearthly

flash – this time the shock was mercifully only mental – and total darkness descended upon the face of the land. (I learnt afterwards that the whole of the Prep-room had been plunged into Stygian gloom.) I groped my way back to my bed and feigned sleep. Enter shortly an agitated Matron with lighted candle. "Did any of you boys know anything about this?" "No, Matron," we all assured her. I supposed that electricity would take days and days to restore, but the worthy boot-cleaner, Mr Pople, soon had the situation in hand; the fuse was replaced, light returned and this little liar got away with it.

But nemesis followed. Next day cups of hot milk were brought to the invalids. I disliked hot milk and threw my ration smartly out of the window. Alas, it bespattered the laurel leaves outside the boot-hole where Mr Pople was busily at work. This time the culprit was all too easily traced and interrogated, and a lie could no longer avail. The ex-invalid returned to normal life next day and his programme included a short visit to the Head-magisterial study. Shock number three.

Richard Hamilton.
Recorder of the Crown Court, Chancellor of Liverpool Diocese, author and film critic.

It was all Shorthouse's fault; things usually were. He was a rat-faced youth of a devious nature. – In an earlier age he would have sold to French aristocrats return tickets to the Guillotine, but at the age of 9 he was as corrupt as I was naive and innocent.

By then I had read few if any of the novels of Dostoievsky, and the satires of Saltykov-Schedrin were a closed book to me. I certainly never assumed that our School Matron was well versed in Russian Literature. To me as a small schoolboy she seemed an ancient crone – she must have been twenty-five if she was a day. She used to preside sternly during the mid-morning break over the cold milk, to make sure that we drank it and liked it.

Anyway, at Shorthouse's suggestion, I approached her with a question. "Please, Sister," I enquired timidly, though after careful coaching by Shorthouse, "have you read *Baby's Revenge,* by Nora Titsoff?"

"What did you say?" she said, her cheeks flaming scarlet. I repeated the question. I should have guessed that any question framed by Shorthouse was tainted, but the double meaning never occurred to me. There was a

158

pause, followed by a stinging slap on the ear, and the words "You little monkey!"

She seized me by the hair and dragged me all the way to the headmaster's study. Time has mercifully erased the memory of what happened next.

I am willing to lay good money that Shorthouse went unpunished. I have lost touch with him over the years; if he has lived up to his early promise, he must soon become a Cabinet Minister.

Nor since that day have I ever come across the works of Comrade N. Titsoff. Perhaps she fell foul of the Russian authorities just before the Twentieth Party Congress of 1956, and had her Party Card withdrawn for writing work of a bourgeois and revisionist tendency.

There's no justice.

Peter Hawkins.
Actor, creator of 1000 'voices' on television incl. the Daleks and Capt. Pugwash.

The year I took my School Certificate, at the age of about 15, I was in 5b; a form for the neither brilliant nor hopeless, that had a somewhat rowdy element of which I was no small part.

It all started during Oral French (how naughty that sounds today!), when we sat along the benches in the Chemistry Lab. waiting to suffer the torture singly in the Balance Room. At the back of the class, far from 'Doggy' Druce's eagle eye, we waited . . . bored. To while away the time, we extracted a lump of pure sodium from its bottle of protective oil (one of its properties is that water ignites it), and proceeded to cut off tiny particles, on which we dropped small amounts of water. The ensuing 'fire-work display' was not noticed by 'Doggy' deep in his book; the accompanying smoke was and we were brought nearer to the front of the class and warned that anyone caught smoking would be taken to the headmaster.

There had been no time to return the remaining lump to its bottle and it had been hastily shoved into a pocket wrapped in a handkerchief. When eventually we were released, we decided to have some fun with it down in the 'bog'. We again cut off a tiny piece but this time it barely fizzled – one nameless idiot put his foot on it. The unexpected explosion which immediately took place slightly damaged his shoe. Two of us decided we had to get rid of it quickly and safely, not to mention anonymously. We hurried to the local Common.

On the small, peaceful lake around the central island floated the paddle boats; each propelled by its tiny occupant. By this time we had transfered the still large, lethal lump to an old paper sweet-bag that we'd picked up. Then, after weighing the 'pros and cons', we hurled it, far from any craft, into the centre of the lake. Relieved, and, after a few seconds, slightly disappointed by the faint trace of tell-tale bubbles, we turned to go.

We were amazed; first by the great plume of water that rose as if from a depth-charge and then by the almighty roar which followed it. There was a silence . . . and then the air was shrill with screaming from the terrified children, while parents flew about in panic. Keeping calm, we walked for several yards . . . then ran . . . then sprinted for all we were worth – remembering to keep a tight hold on the school-caps in our pockets.

Nigel Hawthorne.
Actor.

I was lucky enough to have been brought up by the sea. When my younger brother and I were kids, we used to steal sheets of corrugated iron from building sites, bend them in two, block up the ends with pieces of wood made water-proof with tar scraped off the road on a hot day, and, in these home-made boats, we'd put out to sea. This meant paddling across the bay. We had a bright idea one day. We fashioned a shark's fin out of a piece of wood which we painted grey. We then attached it to the rear of one of the canoes with a piece of string. Then I paddled like fury while both my brother and I screamed out . . . "Help! Help! Shark!"

People who lived in the vicinity, and passers-by, looked down on the drama with patience tinged with pity. "Just those Hawthornes up to mischief again. And the one paddling, the older of the two . . . really ought to go on the stage. . . ."

160

The Venerable W. S. Hayman, M.A.
Canon Emeritus of Southwark, formerly Rector of Cheam,
Archdeacon of Lewisham, Chaplain to H.M. The Queen.

As a chorister of Salisbury Cathedral from 1911–1917, I had little time for mischief. We were kept too much at it, with singing, lessons and compulsory games. One incident, however, comes to my mind.

Our organist, C. F. South, died during my time in the choir. He was a kind and gentle soul and we boys would have done anything for him. We would not have misbehaved, either in Cathedral or at practice. It was just not done.

After his death there was a fairly long interregnum before his successor, Dr (later Sir Walter) Alcock arrived, and the services and choir practices were conducted by various organists from the city of Salisbury. We regarded ourselves as professional singers and had a high sense of our own prestige. One temporary organist, the possessor of over-long red hair and a sweeping moustache, to our great indignation set us some lines for making a mistake at practice. This unusual procedure was greatly resented by us and we consulted with one of the masters at the Choristers' School as to the best course to pursue in the circumstances. He thought for a time, and then came up with the view that the lines must be written, but that they could consist of the following extract from 'Measure for Measure':

"But man, proud man!
drest in a little brief authority,
most ignorant of what he's most assured,
his glassy essence – like an angry ape,
plays such fantastic tricks before high heaven,
as make the angels weep."

We took this brilliant advice and the temporary organist had the wisdom to accept the lines without comment.

M. R. Haynes-Dixon (Rumer Godden).
Novelist and poet (story from 'Two Under the Indian Sun, Macmillan).

"Why didn't you use your sense?" said Aunt Mary as Rumer sobbed, "How was I to know?"

We, four sisters, had been given four rabbits, white ones with pink eyes. They hopped about and lived in a long run with four hutches and grew tame, especially one called Betty who belonged to Nancy, and Connie who was Rumer's. One day Betty in her separate hutch produced four young – something none of the others had done. "Why Nancy's rabbit?" we older ones asked at once. At first the babies were squirming and pink, not much more interesting than worms, but in a trice it seemed, they were delicious little hopping balls of whiteness with swansdown tails and ears lined with shell pink. "Mine!" said Nancy in a glow of pride. Now she had five rabbits of her own, four of them these entrancing young ones. It was not fair, and, one early morning, Rumer went into the run and caught Connie by her ears, shut her in the hutch next to Betty's and then removed two of the fluffy young and gave them to Connie. Triumphantly Rumer shut the hutch doors – and was rooted to the spot.

Connie sniffed at the babies with her twitching nose; they squeaked and suddenly, before Rumer's horror-struck eyes, Connie changed from a soft furred nibbling cuddlesome rabbit into a fiend, a white sinewy arch of fury with blazing red eyes and, set close together, two of the longest sharpest teeth Rumer had ever seen which tore and mangled the babies to bloody pulp. Bits of fluff and flesh were tossed to the hutch roof and stuck on to the netting; blood and tiny entrails were stamped into the straw, blood spattered the hutch walls. Once only Connie lifted her head and glared, a baby's ear and half its cheek dangling from her jaws, her whiskers red. Rumer gave a terrified cry and fled.

"She was a buck, stupid, a he-rabbit. Didn't you know that?"

"Then why was she called Connie?" sobbed Rumer.

"You called her that." said Aunt Mary.

"Why didn't somebody tell me? They might have told me . . . someone might have told me!"

162

Barry Henderson.
Member of Parliament, East Fife.

My housemaster, Alasdair Macdonald, wondered what my parents would feel about his news that: "Barry has distinguished himself in his first week by becoming bottom of the school", and was relieved when my father replied philosophically: "At least he has everything in front of him".

Rachael Heyhoe Flint.
Captain, England Women's Cricket Team, 1966–77, England hockey player. Public speaker, journalist and broadcaster.

My whole childhood seemed to be a series of naughty happenings, mainly because I was a terrible tom-boy and I always used to play with my brother and his friends rather than play 'dollies' with any girls in our neighbourhood.

We used to have milk delivered to our home by a horse and cart; one particular horse went absolutely wild if she heard a whistle, so my brother and I would hide behind the hedge in our front garden and when the 'milk' horse drew alongside and

stopped to make a delivery, we would issue piercing whistles; this resulted in the horse bolting up the road with the poor farmer sprinting along behind trying to catch up!

We played a lot of football and cricket in the road; one household objected to us having 'Cup Finals and Test Matches' outside their house. They complained to the police and we registered our objections by pushing frog-spawn through their letter box; so that they would get a slimy surprise when they put their hands inside the box to collect the mail!

Another group of residents in our road who annoyed our 'gang' were treated to the 'cotton on the door knocker joke'. We would attach cotton (or rather black thread because it was stronger) to the door knocker then would run the reel of cotton down their drive and round the corner of their fence. We would then pull the cotton to rattle the knocker – and rush off in fits of giggles when the occupiers opened their door to find that there was no-one there.

When our games of cricket or football in the road became 'raided' by the police we would all rush to hide behind hedges and garden fences. On one such occasion the police car stopped, the officers got out of the car and dragged all the Wynn Road Gang out of their hiding places and proceeded to book them for playing games in the road. They didn't ask me for my name, so I went up to the one policeman and asked him if he would like my name because I was playing cricket; he replied rather sneeringly that girls didn't play cricket – so from then on, I was determined to make my name as a cricketer to prove the policeman wrong!

Bernard Hepton.
Actor.

The first time I set foot on a stage was at a very tender age; about five or six. I was to be a blackbird, but whether it was the blackbird which pecked off the maid's nose, or one of the twenty four baked in a pie I can't quite remember. I think it must have been one of the twenty four: the singularity of the blackbird which 'pecked off her nose' amounted to star status. I certainly didn't have that.

The one thing I can remember is that I cried. I actually walked on to the stage in the ancient St Cuthbert's Rooms and cried. The indignity of standing there in front of the whole world – the world at that age is mercifully small – in an ill-fitting piece of black material which seemed to be hopelessly inadequate to go even halfway to impersonating a blackbird, the whole creation topped off with an enormous yellow cardboard beak! I thought I looked a fool. But as far as I can remember I was the only one, and after I was pulled off and abandoned in a corner the concert went on to its triumphant conclusion.

Or perhaps I ruined it. I can't remember. It is probably just as well that my memory is and always has been a most deficient mechanism in times of crisis.

Perhaps the people in charge of such things learned their lesson, because I didn't appear on a stage again until I had passed from the tender care of Saint Cuthbert's and progressed to Saint Bede's where the only time I was allowed on a stage was to play Schubert in a playlet about the great composer for St Cecilia's Day. I sang a song called 'Peace'. I was a treble. By the end of the song I was a baritone. The humiliation! I had warned Mr Boylan but . . .

But before the great events at St Bede's, I played cigarette cards in the yard at St Cuthbert's with all the other slackers, was thwacked by Miss Kempley, deservedly, and I remember to this day the noise her cane made as it came down on her tight, ankle-length skirt. I was very good at cigarette cards and finished up with every collection then available. If only I had them now: they'd be worth a fortune! I was always caught out with a devilish torture called 'mental arithmetic' and was inevitably among the last two or three to sit down having solved the problem. The dreaded corner, where you stood with your back to the class as a sign of imbecility and shame, loomed and added a panicky incentive to get the answer. I am ashamed to admit it but I think I spent some time in that corner for biting someone. I'm afraid I can't remember who it was or why. I only hope that my atonement in that wretched corner was sufficient to forgive such an anti-social crime.

I remember the sounds of those iron stairs, and the sickness when I ran into one of the sloping girders and split open my forehead just at the hairline. The scar has always been a marker for how much hair I was losing over the years. Now it stands out white and alone while its companionable hair has vanished. Under those stairs, – on the boy's side of course – Lord, amuse yourself on the girls' side? Impossible! – the cigarette cards fluttered and thumped as fortunes were won and lost, and the marbles and glass allies skinnered in the gutters in the yard.

The Yard. Come to think of it, it was rather like a prison yard where we were let out to exercise. But that is unfair. This school, somehow slotted between crowded dwellings in what would now be looked upon as a deprived area at 'back o't'mill', on two levels with a playground, a shed and reasonable sanitation, was pretty good for 1898. How were they to know that we would have to suffer two World Wars, severe depressions and the vagaries of Town Planning experts when the school was

---

built? It served the community efficiently, seeing many thousands of children leave to take their places in an increasingly troubled world, most of them hoarding memories of that tiny overcrowded place, some happy, some sad, some humiliating.

Like the awesome happiness of being taken from school to a performance of 'Toad of Toad Hall', presented by some intrepid thespians, long forgotten, the magic of which so impressed itself on my mind that, months later, whilst under anaesthetic having my tonsils removed, I was frying sausages over an open fire with Toad, his canary and his caravan on the Open Road. What a disappointment to wake up bloody and sore to be fed ice-cream and syrup of figs!

But in my case the memories are mainly humiliating. I must have been a terrible little boy, shy and retiring on the outside, with little to say for himself, but inside, burning with a consuming awareness of himself, a self, woefully deficient in the things considered to be of value, and given little opportunity of finding other means of expression, and perhaps not being able to recognise them when they came. Like that damned blackbird. How was I to know that standing up dressed as a blackbird in front of the whole world was to be my life?

Christopher Hibbert.
Author.

The worst of many grave misdemeanours of my childhood, which I now recall with shame, was when I and my brother put our baby sister in the dustbin in the hope, fortunately vain, that this tiresome arrival in our family, the apple of our parents' eyes, would be removed.

James Hill.
Oscar-winning producer & director, films and T.V.

I was about 14 or 15 years old at the Bradford Belle Vue Secondary School, when the idea occurred to me and a bunch of my cronies.

About a mile away from our School was the more prestigious Grammar School – the 'posh' school as it was known.

I reckoned that it was possible, with a little inside help, just to walk into the school and spend an entire day there, going through all the classes as a new boy, and be undetected.

There was a lot of discussion about it, and there was a bet of a shilling (a large amount in those days) that the ruse was not possible.

I was to attend the Grammar School, hair parted in the middle, and wearing glasses. One of the Grammar School's regular pupils, a youth called Donnington (I think his name was) would go with me through the various classes – seven during the course of the day. If undetected, I would collect my reward.

On the agreed day, I think it was a Monday, I walked through the gates of the Grammar School with Donnington. Meanwhile at my own Bradford Secondary School, one of my close friends covered up my absence.

When I walked into the first class-room at the unfamiliar Grammar School with Donnington, I was acutely nervous. I was ignored for a time by the Master, until he suddenly noticed me.

"And who are you?" he said staring at me with curiosity.

"New boy, sir."

"Nobody told me about you."

"Sorry, sir – not my fault. Just moved into the district."

"Oh, well, I wish someone had mentioned it. Have you any books?"

"No, sir"

"Come over here and I'll give you some."

It was as easy as that. The Master gave me a piercing look, then brought me some note-books and text-books, and the lesson continued normally.

And so I went through the day. No problems. Seven classes in all, and a pile of books at the end of it.

Later that evening, I collected my shilling wager from my cronies at my Secondary School, modestly acknowledged many grins and congratulations, and thought that was that!

But not quite!

A few days later, I was quietly sitting in a mathematics-class at my own Secondary School, when there was a message that the Headmaster, Dr Fisher, wished to see me in his study immediately.

It appeared one of the Yorkshire newspapers had somehow got hold of the story and printed it in its columns.

Doctor Fisher was not amused. He told me in no uncertain terms that he thought it the most appalling behaviour he'd ever heard of in his entire scholastic career, and would give me two choices only.

"I can either expel you on the spot – or you will go immediately to the Grammar School and apologise to each and every one of the masters concerned!"

"I'm on my way, sir" I replied, grabbing my cap.

But as I hurried out of the Headmaster's Study, I fancied there was a smile on Dr Fisher's lips.

Susan Hill.
Author, playwright for T.V. and radio.

I was about 2½ at the time, and still in my big, coach pram, if we went any distance; we didn't have a car and there were no buggies, then. That would put it in the last year of the war, when bread, like everything else, was still strictly rationed.

When my mother went shopping, she put all her purchases in the pram, at my feet, under the rug (no shopping-trays). I can still remember the bumpy feel of tins, the crackle of brown paper bags, as I pushed against them with my toes. Best of all was the bread though; a large, white loaf, wrapped in tissue, still warm from the baker's oven and smelling quite wonderful. Smelling marvellous. Smelling mouth-wateringly delicious.

While my mother was in another shop, I felt down with my little feet, and pulled that loaf just a bit nearer to me, so that I could enjoy its warmth, like a hot water bottle on the cold winter day. And its smell curled up into my nostrils tantalisingly. I was very hungry. *Very* hungry.

I pulled it just a little nearer, within reach of my fingers, and broke off a tiny, crumbly bit of crust. And ate it. – Ah!

But it was not actually the crust I like best, it was the warm, soft doughy inside of the loaf. So I made a hole; a very *small* hole, and pulled out a few strands of the interior of that loaf. And then a few more. Every time my mother reappeared, I stopped doing it, and every time she went into another shop, leaving me parked outside, I started doing it again. The hole grew just a bit bigger each time.

You can probably guess the rest. We got home. My mother took out her shopping. The loaf felt strangely light. She examined it. A perfectly hollowed-out crust, without any inside. Our only bread for the rest of that week. Ah, that bread. Never has bread tasted like it. My tummy was quite full.

Then she took me out of the pram. And then, as my daughter Jessica would say, "let's not talk about the rest."

Admiral of the Fleet The Lord Hill-Norton, G.C.B.
Chairman, Military Committee of N.A.T.O., 1974–77.

In my days boys joined the Royal Naval College, Dartmouth at the tender (if that is the right word) age of 13. Apropos of which, someone once had the temerity to say to Lord Mountbatten "of course when you went to Dartmouth you were too young to know any better", to which the great man replied "And I've been doing it for fifty years and still can't think of anything better"; my sentiments precisely.

Cadets joined the College, lived and worked and played as 'a term', and there were 56 of us in mine. Each term had as its recreation space, for writing letters and other off-duty pastimes, a large room called the Gunroom, so called because in the days of the wooden walls the cadets and midshipmen at sea berthed (in great discomfort) behind the great broadside guns.

In my fourth term, by which time I was fourteen and a half, a number of us were in our Gunroom one evening doing nothing much when another boy pointed out a shiny screw, just under the main light switch. Several of us peered rather doubtfully at this, which had not been noticed before, and it was suggested that it might be live. I hit on the brilliant idea of demonstrating that it would be quite safe to touch it, so long as one was insulated, which my mates took leave to doubt.

Trapped, by myself, I had to test the notion. We wore uniform of course and part of it was a white rope lanyard at the end of which might be kept keys, or a whistle. I accordingly applied my key ring to the shiny screw, holding on to my lanyard. There was instantly an enormous blue flash, a loud bang and some smoke, though neither I nor the small knot of interested spectators were damaged. Good news, one might suppose, for me.

Not at all. Every light in the College went out, just as the Wardroom officers were having their pre-dinner drinks, to say nothing of the Captain whose large house was plunged into darkness too. There was nothing to do but own up, but it was made difficult by the total darkness to find anyone to whom I could confess. By the time I had done so, some twenty minutes later, the whole affair – certainly to me – seemed nothing like so amusing as it had at the time.

I was at once, or rather as soon as the lights had been restored, soundly beaten. I have always thought this was a bit hard for a young scientific experimenter whose experiment had, in fact, proved his point.

Simon Hoggart.
Writer, contributor to the Observer and Punch.

I don't think anyone was terribly wicked at my grammar school, though somebody once let off a small bomb in the organ loft. Bad behaviour was, so to speak, in its infancy then, and an offence as minuscule as talking back to a master (they were never called 'teachers' in schools which had pretensions) would send a frisson of delighted horror around the class. The pleasure came, I think, from watching the enactment of an ageless ritual while knowing that you were not fated to play the central role as the sacrifice.

For this reason, the punishments were not so much harsh as formalised. Writing lines was a bore, being detained for half-an-hour (or more likely twenty minutes; it never crossed our minds that the master who was keeping us in might want to get home too) was merely a nuisance. Caning was very rare, and most classes contained no more than two or three people who had ever been caned. Even then there were no signs that it hurt very much. The boys who were caned would come back with awesome tales of the vast range of thrashing devices kept under the headmaster's sofa: the thick one, the bamboo, and the dreaded 'split pea' which delivered a thin, double slice to the buttocks. But in retrospect I don't believe these stories which were, I suspect, designed to heighten the already considerable prestige of the victims.

The Divinity master used a unique form of punishment in which ritual was much the more important part. When someone behaved badly – talking in class, flicking ink pellets at other boys, and other forms of childish misdemeanour which nowadays seem almost Elysian, even pre-lapsarian – he would take a copy of Hymns Ancient & Modern and tuck it into a corner of a threadbare, floppy document case he possessed, made out of one of the earliest kinds of plastic. The thin material, folded over, allowed him to take an appropriate swing, and the hymn book provided the necessary weight for bashing. We called him 'Ichabod' because it meant 'the glory has departed', and he was bald. Ichabod stood majestically with his feet almost a yard apart, as if about to flog a mutineer. His arm, as stiff as a pendulum, swung round, and hymnal met grey worsted with a faint dull thud. It was only the ritual which fascinated, delighted, and I suppose, ultimately managed to control us. For the punishment, unlike five minutes of football in the school yard, did not hurt at all.

The Venerable Gerald Hollis.
Archdeacon of Birmingham.

As a young Naval Officer on the Staff of the RN College, Dartmouth, early in World War 2, I found myself, one Sunday morning before luncheon, entertaining a seemingly elderly civilian visitor by the name of Ruttledge in the Wardroom Mess. "Are you any relation to the chap who climbs a bit?" I asked breezily. "I did have the honour of leading His Majesty's last Expedition up Mount Everest" my guest replied gently. . . .

Antony Hopkins, C.B.E., F.R.C.M., Hon.R.A.M., D.Univ. Stirling.
Fellow of Robinson College, Cambridge, composer and broadcaster.

I suppose I must have been about 5 or 6 on the day of The Great Scream. Owing to my father's early death I had been adopted (temporarily it was assumed at the time) by a kindly school master and his wife, rather older than my natural parents would have been. It was a strange upbringing for there were some 40 adolescent boys boarding in the house. I was so much younger than this somewhat noisy horde that I became a sort of mascot. My adopted father, a serious and almost silent man, reluctant to speak a single word unless it was absolutely necessary, nevertheless set about educating me with such dedication that I was soon precocious beyond my years. By the time I went to my first school, then known as a kindergarten rather than a common primary, I could read fluently and would sustain remarkably 'grown up' conversations with any adults I encountered. It was this feeling that I was intellectually far beyond my actual years that undoubtedly accounted for The Great Scream.

I had suffered some sort of tummy upset, enough at any rate to justify a visit from the school doctor. He requested that I should provide what to this day is euphemistically referred to as a 'specimen'. To my horror I discovered that this entailed sitting on a chamber pot until such time as I delivered the goods. This reversion to babyhood was more than I could stomach; to spend a penny into the offending vessel might have been tolerable, but 'the other' was unthinkable to one of my exceptional

maturity. I refused point-blank. The first request had come from my adopted mother. On meeting with my obdurate refusal she summoned reinforcements. 'Matron' came in a white coat and nun-like headdress. I was more than a match for two women. Next on the scene came my adopted father, shortly followed by the assistant house-master whose curiosity had been roused by the considerable noise that was now emanating from the region of the bathroom. Now, it is one thing for Queens to give birth in the presence of witnesses representing both the Church and Body Politic, but quite another for a small boy to have to sit on a jerry surrounded by a group of increasingly impatient adults. It was at this critical moment in my life that I was impelled to give vent to The Great Scream. Once I had begun I could not stop. With something of the volume of a train-whistle entering the Watford tunnel I continued to emit the most ear-piercing yells, virtually without pause for breath. I was forcibly shaken, but that only increased the volume. My audience soon grew in number as butler, cook and housemaids joined the fascinated throng. The ultimate achievement was still to come however, for someone, glancing out of the window, saw the local vicar cassocked in black running down the lane from the vicarage. Since it was situated at least 200 yards away, across a field, it was a notable tribute to the penetrative power of my shrill young voice. "What are you doing to that poor child?" he wailed from the courtyard below; "I thought he was being *murdered*." It was difficult to explain through the window the precise reason for the tearful caterwauling but he duly retreated, suitably embarrassed. I suppose that ultimately I tired and may even, once the crowd of spectators had dispersed, have provided the necessary sample. That I have forgotton, but I have always remembered the gratifying sensation caused by The Great Scream; it was, in a way, my first public performance.

Geoffrey Household, T.D.
Author, distinguished Territorial and wartime soldier.

A child can be ashamed for the most ridiculous reasons and any enterprising teenager unashamed when he ought to be. I will leave the latter occasions alone, for I cannot seriously regret actions which would only be considered crimes by a schoolmaster trained in Victorian morality, but I keenly remember one incident charming to the adult but of utter humiliation to the child.

I must have been seven, fully able to read and write and, apparently, to spot differences of style, but I still believed firmly in fairies. When in trouble I would communicate with these mysterious friends by leaving little notes tucked away in the lower fronds of a large potted fern which stood in a corner of the dining room. It was no wonder that I believed, since my notes were invariably answered and in rhyme.

Now, like most little boys in the early 1900s I was dragged by my mother – out of pity for my future partners – to a weekly dancing class where besides waltzes and polkas I was trained in the tiresome drill of the Lancers and Sir Roger de Coverley. There I lost my heart to a pair of red stockings. She was a few years older than I and not, I think, particularly good-looking. It was the red stockings which did the damage.

But, alas, I was already engaged to a jolly little girl who shared our morning walks – a procession of ourselves, two prams containing family babies and two nannies. They were easily left behind while we explored the life of the lanes and hedgerows, and we agreed that when we grew up we should be married.

This presented me with a very private problem of honour which could only be solved by the fairies. So I slipped a note into the fern to explain that I had promised to marry Agnes but was in love with Christine and her red stockings. Eagerly I looked next morning for a reply. It was there and rather longer than usual. It told me that I should not bother about such commitments at my age. Though it did not moralise it was slightly different in tone from the fairies' customary gossamer style, so I looked more closely than ever before at the delicate handwriting and realised that it was my father's fancifully disguised. I forgave my dear and poetical parent who would always enter as a playfellow into any childish fantasy, but I was utterly ashamed of my own gullibility and that I had laid myself open to such a rape of my privacy. For days I was silent while my spirit blushed and blushed.

His Honour Judge Humphries.
A Circuit Judge.

At the elementary school which I attended in Barrow-in-Furness (then a 'deprived' area), the teachers, no doubt with the best of intentions, asked each child to write down what it had eaten at mid-day at home. This happened several times. Eventually one of the teachers spoke to my mother (who in fact fed her family generously) asking why each mid-day I only had 'a cup of Oxo', which was what I always wrote down at school. My mother was appalled, explained the varied, nourishing diet of the last few days and satisfied the teacher that her children were not being deprived. Inevitably, I was called upon to explain. At *that* stage I told the truth: I could not spell words like 'Cauliflower au gratin' or 'Quiche Lorraine'; but I could easily spell 'a cup of Oxo'.

**H. Montgomery Hyde, M.A. Oxon., D.Lit. Belfast, F.R., His.S.,
F.R.S.L., M.R.I.A.
Author, barrister, biographer and criminologist.**

The summer of the year 1928 was a happy time for me and also an
adventurous one. I had just won an open scholarship to Magdalen College,
Oxford, and I planned to go up to Oxford in the autumn. Meanwhile, since
I had not taken German as a subject at school, I enrolled for a holiday
course in this language at the University of Munich. This began towards the
end of August and lasted throughout September. The Bavarian capital was
and still is, despite its bombing in the war, an attractive city, architecturally
and culturally, and I loved it, especially its opera and concerts, which were
given in the exquisite baroque theatre in the old Royal Residence.

In Munich I found an excellent pension, which had been recommended
to me before I left home. It was in the Schellingstrasse, one of the small
streets off the Ludwigstrasse, thus being centrally and conveniently placed
for the university and the other points of interest. All I paid for a room and
full board was five marks a day, the equivalent now of 25p in Britain. The
other inmates were students or post-graduates reading for advanced
degrees, among them several Americans as well as Oxford men, so that it
was a congenial little society we had in the Pension Molsen-Hostrup. In the
evenings most of us used to foregather in the Hofbräuhaus, the old Court
brewery, on the other side of the Maximilianstrasse, next door to the
Munich Theatre. There we talked mostly about books and only a little
about politics. We knew that the German Chancellor was a Christian
Democrat, Hermann Müller, who headed a coalition which included the
National Socialist Party. But this small party had only 12 seats out of a
total of 491 in the *Reichstag*. The leader of the Nazis, as they called
themselves, was a small-time politician named Adolf Hitler in what was
generally regarded as the lunatic fringe of Bavarian politics at that period.
We were much more interested in the English writer Margaret Kennedy and
her best-selling novel *The Constant Nymph,* now largely forgotten, which
had shocked many people on its first appearance and had just been
translated into German. We would argue interminably about its merits and
its approach to the fight for freedom of the arts from the customs and
beliefs of the day.

The strong beer in the Hofbräuhaus was served in litre tankards made of

a grey stone-like substance embossed with the Bavarian crown and the initials HB in blue. One evening one of the others bet me five marks I would not drain a full tankard at a single gulp. (A litre equals 1¾ pints.) I succeeded in doing it without feeling any ill effects, much to the amazement of my companions. Another of those present then bet me ten marks that I would not steal the tankard and take it back with me to the pension. I immediately responded to this challenge and seizing the tankard I ran off down the stairs to the street pursued by several barmen and shouts of *"Räuber! Räuber!"* – drawing attention to my theft of the precious tankard.

I crossed the Maximilianstrasse, passed the Royal Residence, and reached the Ludwigstrasse still pursued by the barmen. However, my tough training at Sedbergh school, where I spent five years, had made me quite a fast runner and I eventually managed to shake off my pursuers by turning into one of the side streets off the Ludwigstrasse to reach the pension uncaught if not undetected.

I brought the tankard with me to Oxford, where I had Oscar Wilde's old rooms in Magdalen. It occupied a conspicuous place in the middle of the mantelpiece over the fireplace in these famous rooms, and in the photograph of them which I reproduced in my biography of Oscar Wilde in 1975 the tankard can be plainly seen. When World War II came and I joined up in the army, I stored the tankard along with my furniture and other possessions in a warehouse in London where it mysteriously disappeared, although all my other possessions were intact when I recovered them at the end of the war. I have often wondered what happened to the tankard. Maybe I was not the last to steal this interesting relic of my student days.

Lord Ironside.
A Governor of Tonbridge School.

The image of Mr Chips at school has now been displaced by Master Chip, and computers, always thought to be high-speed morons, are gaining a little more intelligence and can even talk to each other.

Two bright new ultra slim micro-computers were chatting to each other in the Upper Sixth recently about their diets and this is what I heard.

"I go for fish and chips" said Logica to Silica.

"That's silly. If you want to slim, why eat chips?"

"I don't" said Logica, "but I am getting so forgetful that I have chips with everything in case I lose my memory."

When I was attending the Annual Summer Prize Giving at a mixed school some years ago in Kent where the standard of dress, as everywhere nowadays was unisex, all the Governors had the opportunity of meeting parents and prize-winners at tea afterwards. The Chairman of the Governors was doing his best to chat everybody up and went up to one young man and gave him his congratulations on winning the maths prize. The fond parent standing close by immediately intervened.

"Oh no, she's my daughter".

Apologetically he said, "Oh I am frightfully sorry sir. For a moment I thought it was Jimmy".

"That's all right, I'm her mother".

Sir Geoffrey Jackson, K.C.M.G.
H.M. Ambassador to Uruguay, 1969-72.
(Kidnapped and held by terrorists for 8 months in 1971.)
Broadcaster and author.

The first 'mischief' I remember is almost my first memory too. It was certainly 'out of school', because I had not yet started school with my brothers. So much of my time was spent playing alone in the garden – quite a big one, on the edge of the fields.

One morning, after a hearty breakfast, my mother wrapped me up well and turned me loose on the lawn, warning me not to get into mischief; the day before I had found a thrush's nest, and broken a beautiful blue egg taking it to her. Behind the rhododendrons I had also found a gap in the hedge, so I decided to explore the meadow beyond. It was a glorious winter morning. The field sparkled with hoar-frost, the sky was blue, and the farmer's big Shire-horses breathed plumes of steam – there were no diesel-tractors then.

In spite of the sun, soon my hands and feet felt cold. But across towards the farm-house there was more steam, rising from what to me was a veritable mountain. Obviously I had to climb it, right to the top. When I sat down it was pleasantly soft and warm. So I started to wriggle and burrow. I became more and more comfortable.

When a frantic young mother found me and woke me up, I was blissfully cocooned up to my neck in fragrant horse-manure. It seemed unfair when she insisted on giving me a bath, also that she scolded me so. But long afterwards she told me that she had been quite amused, and rather proud of me!

Lord Jacques.
Chairman of the Co-operative Union Ltd. Lord-in-Waiting, 1974–77.
A Deputy Speaker, House of Lords.

I was appointed Secretary of a Co-operative Society at 21 years of age and looked even younger. Shortly after appointment, I had to make a declaration witnessed by a Justice of the Peace. There was a wholesale greengrocer who was a J.P. near where I lodged so I thought I would get him to witness it. I called on him after lunch one day and was told he would see me in a few minutes. After half-an-hour he appeared from his office; apologised profusely, saying he had forgotten I was waiting and said "never mind lad, here is a nice apple" and gave me a big rosy apple. I then presented the document to be signed. He said "Oh! the Secretary must come himself, he cannot send an office boy to get this done". I said "I am the Secretary". He replied "Oh! my God what have I done now". We became quite good friends.

Martin Jarvis.
Actor of stage and screen.

I lived in South Norwood, in South London, as a child, and every Sunday I had to attend Sunday School at St John's Church. The religious

178

instruction was given by Father Bailey. At about 2.30 every Sunday afternoon my mother would say "Martin, it's time for Sunday School". And off I would have to go, reluctantly up the hill to the Church, clutching my collection money in my irreligious hand.

Sunday School was boring though, and it wasn't long before I decided that if I set off at the right time my parents wouldn't actually know if I never went to the Church.

So what I used to do was to walk up Auckland Road, go right past the Church and along to Westow Street, where those twin palaces of fantasy stood – the Century Cinema and the Granada Cinema. Using my collection money plus my sixpence pocket money (ninepence altogether) I would scuttle inside one or other of the cinemas and lose myself in the Sunday feature fantasies of Bob Hope in 'The Lemon-Drop Kid', James Stewart in 'No Highway' or John Gregson in 'Angels One-Five'. Not so spiritual as Father Bailey's Sunday School but a great deal more uplifting. I saw Biblical epics too, like 'The Robe' and 'The Ten Commandments'; so when my mother and father asked me what I had learned at Sunday School that afternoon I was able to describe Moses parting the Red Sea with a particularly graphic accuracy.

Of course it couldn't last. My come-uppance came when my mother bumped into Father Bailey one day and he said "I'm sorry we haven't seen young Martin at Sunday School for so long."

After that it was no more Sunday afternoon fantasies for me, no more pocket money, and a lot of religious instruction. From Father Bailey – not from Cecil B De Mille!

Peter Jay.
Chairman, Nat. Council for Vol. Org.; Dir. Economist Intelligence Unit.
H.M. Ambassador to U.S., 1977–79.

I have probably 'blotted out' the memory of the truly shameful moments of my childhood. But the incident which sticks most embarrassingly in my mind involved my great grandmother, a mischievous uncle and a lavatory.

During the war, at the age of about six, I was evacuated for a while to my great grandmother's house at St Helens in the Isle of Wight. The old lady was, I think, 94, but decidedly 'spry' as my more youthful grandmother used to describe her.

Also evacuated was my uncle, a wicked 13 year old, now a revered senior schoolmaster. One afternoon he took it into his head to instruct me in the greatest possible detail in the peculiarities of the lock on the door of my great grandmother's downstairs WC.

It was one of those old-fashioned rotating latches, which could only be operated from the inside. In the '3 o'clock' position the door was unlocked and the word 'Vacant' appeared on the outer side of the door. In the '9 o'clock' position the door was locked and the word 'engaged' appeared outside.

My uncle explained to me that it was possible, with some delicacy, to lodge the latch somewhere between the '10 o'clock' and '11 o'clock' positions. He further speculated that if, with the lock in this position, one were then to slam the door from the outside, the latch would then fall to the '9 o'clock' position, thus leaving the door locked with no-one on the inside to open it and no means of opening it from the outside!

On what I now recognise as the principle of 'mischief thou art afoot; now let it work' my uncle, having sown the seed of wickedness in my mind, then beat a tactical retreat from the scene. But such wisdom had not yet troubled my younger mind.

I was further intrigued by the fact that, although this lavatory had a ground level window, it had underneath it a deep drop into a basement 'area', which was in turn guarded by a high spiked iron railing on the garden side. It was therefore the work of a moment to put my uncle's plan into practice, everything working with all too clockwork-like precision.

The adrenalin of mischief in the doing was soon replaced by highly deflationary clouds of guilt, apprehension and the need for concealment. I seized upon my governess' suggestion that the time had come for a walk across the 'duvver' with unwonted enthusiasm.

Imagine, therefore, what coals of fire were heaped upon my head – and what indignation I felt against my angel-faced uncle who had instigated the whole affair – when on my return from the walk I discovered that my great

180

grandmother – in full length grey lace like a character in Great Expectations – had, on discovering the locked door to the empty room, ascended the spiked fence, climbed down to the basement 'area', climbed up to the lavatory window, crawled in through it head first and unlocked the door! For days afterwards she muttered about the mystery of the locked door; and for days afterwards I imagined I kept a poe-face.

Now at almost half her then age I suspect that she knew exactly what had happened, in which case she certainly knew also the most effective form of retribution – day after day nursing the viper of unconfessed guilt!

Barbara Jefford.
Star of stage and screen.

In the early Thirties my father and mother and I lived in one big wing of a large house on the outskirts of Newton Abbot in Devonshire.

The house stood on a hill, and its extensive grounds included flower and vegetable gardens (I had my own little 'patch'), what seemed to me then to be vast expanses of lawns, in which daffodils bloomed in clumps in Spring, and shrubberies with Rhododendrons: the latter were ideal play-places for a small girl – to whom they were forests. I can remember dressing up in an old green petticoat of my mother's, making ivy-wreathes for my hair and spending hours pretending to be, no, *being* a wood-nymph – no doubt much to the amusement of the various tradesmen coming up the drive from the main road: they would be encountered by a 'sprite' offering bunches of wild flowers, singing and dancing! As far as I can remember though, they treated these performances with admirable seriousness.

The grounds of our house adjoined those of a similar one which was a School, and two things were forbidden to me: one was that I must never go through the gates at the end of the drive and onto the main road and the other was never, *never* to go into the next-door garden. The temptation to do the latter was irresistible – it was also quite easy, because there was a hole in the hedge.

One morning, dressed in a bright scarlet coat (I suppose I must have been about four years old), I got through to the forbidden garden, stood in it for a few minutes and then, flushed with triumph, pushed back through the hedge to home ground.

My mother must have seen all this from an upstairs window – red is not a good colour to wear when you're doing something secret – and, when I came in, asked me if I had been doing something naughty. When I replied "No" (acting like mad) I was told that God could see everything – God at an upstairs window! – and that in addition to breaking a rule I had lied and Daddy would have to be told. My father was a Clerk at Lloyds Bank and used to walk to and from work – he would be back at lunch time.

Something had to be done to put myself right with God and Daddy, I thought. Weeding! I'd noticed a lot of new ones springing up in my father's garden, and so (secure in the knowledge that weeding was a *good* thing to do) I pulled them all up and put them neatly on the path. The weeds turned out to be bean-plants, and, when shown the good work my Mama was very cross indeed. Now what to do? Up to my bedroom to collect my Micky Mouse purse – with, I expect about two shillings savings in it – then out, down the drive and through the forbidden gates to walk to the town, buy new beans, plant them and, so, put everything right before Daddy came home: the beans would, of course, have grown again by then.

I suppose I had run about twenty-five panicky yards when I met my father on his way home. The whole story was tearfully poured out and, after the shock of seeing this distracted small girl rushing towards him and delivering the familiar lecture about *never* going onto the main road, he kissed me, mopped up the tears and I was hoisted onto the dear shoulder and carried home with all my sins forgiven!

The Lord Jenkins of Putney (Hugh Jenkins).
Member of Parliament, 1964–79. Minister for the Arts, 1974–76.

Enfield Grammar School used to put on an annual Gilbert and Sullivan production. Having done chorus and minor roles in the Mikado and the Gondoliers, I was, having a strong treble voice, cast as Phyllis in Iolanthe. It was 1923 and I was getting on for sixteen years old.

In an all-boys school, playing a girl was always a bit tricky and I decided the only thing to do with Phyllis was to send up the whole idea of girlishness by fluttering and simpering about the stage like a demented fairy. I thought

I was over-doing it to a ludicrous degree and was astonished to be hailed by the Enfield Gazette and Observer as the 'success of the evening'. I have never had such a good notice since.

The fall occurred the following evening. My voice broke on a top note and, try as I would, only the most ghastly sounds emerged for the rest of a disastrous performance. Fluttering and simpering were out of the question, when nothing but a dreadful cracked baritone came out. I walked and spoke through the rest of the show in an agony of embarrassment and received a sympathetic clap at the end, but I have never since attempted to play a role on any stage. I decided from then on any words I said in public would be my own and I would certainly not try to sing them. However, I was left with a sympathy for performers which I never lost.

Richard Jenkyns.
Fellow of All Souls, Oxon, 1972–81. Fellow in Classics, Lady Margaret Hall since 1981. Author.

My earliest memory by far is of being in my cot in the bedroom at the top of the stairs while my mother and the au pair could be heard rushing about anxiously below looking for something – some favourite rag or toy animal – which I required before I would consent to go quietly to sleep. My memory is one of enormous satisfaction at the exercise of power, at the knowledge that I was in authority up there in bed and could put other people to trouble (that was an important part of the pleasure) simply to gratify my own desires. In later life I have never found it difficult to believe in original sin.

In my second term at prep. school I went through a conversion experience. During my first term I had been a rather well-behaved little boy, but now there suddenly dawned upon me with the force of revelation the realisation that it was Bad to be Good and Good to be Bad (when I got to university and started studying philosophy I had trouble with this principle, but for the time being it served well enough). The catalyst for my conversion was the discovery that by bouncing up and down very vigorously indeed on my iron-framed bed it could be made to glide at a pretty decent speed across the lino to the other side of the dormitory. This was of course Very Wrong; but I knew with the certainty of pure faith that it was something that a boy had to do.

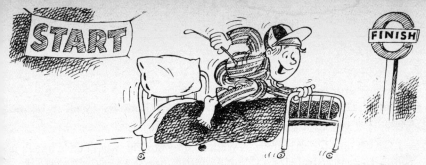

The other reason why it was necessary to be bad was that talking after lights-out was strictly agaist the rules. Since I had so much interesting and amusing information to communicate, it would have been intolerable to have deprived my fellows of the advantages of my conversation. Twice at least I was beaten for this offence; it did me a great deal of good – if, that is, it is a good thing that I have been talking too much ever since.

Later I went on to a public school, and in due course I was made a prefect. Turning teenagers into prefects can be a bad idea, since it may make them boringly respectable. When I left school, one of my masters wrote, "He is very mature for his age. No doubt he will get younger at university." When I went to visit him a couple of years ago, I reminded him of his words. "And was my prophecy correct?" he asked. I told him that it was.

Paul Jennings.
Author.

When I was 4½ and we were hanging about waiting for some meal, table laid etc., it suddenly struck me that it would be interesting, scientifically interesting to give my sister (2½) a teaspoonful of sugar with mustard on the underside of the spoon. I didn't want to *hurt* her, I just wanted to see what would happen.

Well, of course, she yelled the place down, and I wasn't at that meal. I knew all the aunts, in whose house this happened, were right to go on at me; I knew somewhere deep down that I'd known she would scream. It just seemed an interesting thing to do at that time.

Later, I put some mustard under a spoonful of sugar (admittedly not *quite* so much as before, but not a negligible amount) and consumed it in public, saying "Look, *I* don't scream", or words to that effect. I need hardly say that this did not go down well.

I just accepted this as evidence that no one shared my interest in this branch of science.

184

Charles Elliott Jervis, O.B.E.
Editor-in-Chief, Press Association, 1954–65. Founder member of the Press Council.

I HAVE blue blood in me. . . . Well, let me put it this way, I have (and am willing to demonstrate for a suitable contribution to Help the Aged) a blue spot of ink on the front of my left thigh and it has been there for 71 years! Every time, in a bath or while changing undergarments, I view this scar, there comes to mind the picture of a pretty little blonde who sat beside me during my first year at school. And I keep wondering if she, too, has a blue spot on her leg.

How, or why, a class of infants should have been issued with pens and inkwells at such a tender age is beyond me, but it was so. And I have the scar to prove it.

It was in no romantic ceremonial of swearing eternal devotion that my leg was injected with ink from a razor-sharp nib. It was a vicious stab from the pen of my desk companion. My immediate response was to emulate the incision on her leg. And did she scream? Blue murder. Blue spot. We were separated then and there and never met again.

I make known these dark secrets with some trepidation. Will publication be followed by a request from the Liverpool Education Authority for a return of its property, to wit, a pen nib? Will I be sued for astronomic damages by little Miss Goldilocks alleging that the blue scar ruined her chances of marriage with a belted Earl? My only defence could be that she was given an indelible proof of aristocratic lineage.

In these much more broadminded and enlightened days I am prepared to undertake a theatrical tour and appear on TV exhibiting my thigh. And, less exhausting, in the days of my decrepitude a competition could be instituted offering prizes for guessing to a millimetre the precise site of my blue spot.

To say nothing of a gigantic search to find the lady and of a dual  appearance on TV, bare-thighed, performing a soft-shoe shuffle and singing, "If you were the only girl in the world". The possibilities are endless.

Jill Johnson.
Actress.

I have always been passionately fond of horseracing and once when there was a Meeting at my home town I decided to play truant and go to it. My form mistress was away sick and as her substitute was unfamiliar with the class it seemed a golden opportunity. I became somewhat apprehensive as I reached the course fearing I might bump into a parent of one of my schoolfriends. However the only person I recognised, in a secluded spot behind the paddock, locked in the arms of a sailor, was my form mistress. She certainly saw me but the subject was never mentioned when we both returned to school the following morning.

Wilfred Josephs, D.Mus.
Composer of Operas, stage and screen music.

As a teenager I smoked heavily, although I don't smoke at all now, enough to need a cigarette first thing in the morning and last thing at night when I was lying in bed reading, despite the horror of my father who (I suppose rightly) didn't like the idea of my smoking in bed.

Week after week, month after month, I endured the nagging of my very middle-aged parents and this produced the same sort of reaction that I get from my own children now: the pitiful look of boredom when being told off for the umpteenth time. The generation gap. In desperation I set out to counteract this injunction on smoking in bed.

I found myself a cube-shaped cigar box, at the bottom of which I glued a tobacco tin. I also inserted a bamboo cigarette holder that pointed upwards. The cigarette holder had about 5 ft of heavy bore rubber tubing attached to it through a hole in the side of the box and at the other end of the tubing was a second bamboo cigarette holder, which made a mouthpiece for me. On top of this there were elastic bands holding the lid in such a way that it could be opened with a string. When you pulled the string, the box closed, whether the cigarette was lit or not! I used to sit in bed hoping my father would come in to tell me off for smoking in bed, when I would say I am *not* smoking in bed. The cigarette was miles away from the bed and there was no possible way it could set fire to the bed. What's more if I wanted to put the cigarette out I could just pull the string, closing the lid and the cigarette would go out.

The pitiful look of contempt from my father, and the thought he had produced a lunatic son, which he probably had, was worth all the effort of making the apparatus!

Frank Judd.
Director, V.S.O., Chairman, Centre for World Development Education, Minister of State, Foreign and Commonwealth Office, 1976–79.

My grandmother was a courageous and wonderful old soul. The widow of a Scottish missionary, she had come through a tough life – two of her children dead before the age of five in India and two sons killed in the army – with her character and humour unimpaired. Finding herself coming to live in a left-orientated family, her loyalty and wicked sense of fun combined to persuade me, aged two in Coronation Year, to clap my hands and cry "Good King George, good King George" for what seemed like ages at a time.

My father was no republican as the family three-line whips for the sovereign's Christmas Day broadcast well testified. He was nonetheless a firm Labour voter and deeply worried by the advent of Fascism. Provoked, as was no doubt the intention, he responded in kind and set about getting me to yell "Up the Reds!"

So there I was in my push chair outside the village newsagent while my grandmother bought her 'News Chronicle'. "Good King George, good King George" I cooed to the delight of the affluent shoppers who assembled in an admiring ring.

As my grandmother emerged from the shop to witness this reassuring picture of patriotic enthusiasm, I let out a cheerful whoop: "Up the Reds!" In that village, where I still live, I have been regarded as a potential subversive ever since.

P. J. Kavanagh.
Poet and novelist.

I once went to a school I disliked very much. My previous school had been run by jolly nuns who made much of one, but here there were masters who seemed permanently in a rage. It was 1940 and I was nine years old.

At the end of my first term the positions in form were pinned to the classroom noticeboard for Parents' Day. When I looked at these for the first time, with my father, I saw I was bottom in everything. To my surprise my father was disgusted with me. Surely, I thought, he could see there must be something wrong with the school.

During the next term our town was often bombed. We slept in the cellar of the apartment-house with the occupants of the other flats. I enjoyed the queer, old cellar-smell that made me think of smugglers and caves.

One night an air-raid warden shouted down through the pavement grating that we had better get out, the house next door was on fire.

So we walked in our night things through the fire-bright town to a darker, safer part, where our friends could give us shelter. The walk I knew well; it took us past my school. I prayed that it had been bombed but there seemed little chance. As we approached it, the streets were comparatively dark. Then we turned a corner and there it was, crackling away like a bonfire. I felt no surprise. It was what I had prayed for. Nor did I feel guilty that my prayers had directed a bomb so well. I was merely pleased that I would not have to go to the place next day, or even for a few days after that.

As it turned out, I never went there again.

Louis Kentner.
Concert pianist.

When I was still a young boy and a student at the then Royal Academy in Budapest, I was called upon to appear at a pupils' concert, to play Beethoven's 'Moonlight' Sonata. I was scheduled to open the concert.

This did not please my father, a very ambitious man who thought that the place in the programme which I was given was not good enough and might not benefit my future career as a concert pianist. On my father's

instigation I disappeared in a lavatory just as the concert was due to start. A great fuss ensued; I was searched for everywhere and when I was discovered in my hiding place my professor naturally assumed that I was sick with concert nerves, not a rare occurrence on these occasions. I heard with relief someone shouting "Alright, let the organist take the first number" and I instantly emerged, feeling very guilty. But the little crowd of people who had gathered outside my 'shelter' was extremely sympathetic when I came out. One old lady said, "Poor boy, he looks quite pale and shaken."

I never told the story till years later and then only cautiously. I do not remember what my performance was like.

Tony Kershaw.
Management Consultant.

'Jesuit wings' are two long strips of black cloth which hang from the shoulders of the sleeveless cassock worn by Jesuit teachers. It was the practice among errant spirits to engage a certain ageing and eccentric priest in conversation whilst another pupil secretly knotted his 'wings' together. Sometimes one would have a chance to loop the knotted 'wings' over a convenient door-handle. The game was a ritual in that the old priest always checked his 'wings' before moving off and carefully untied the knot.

I was persuaded one day to play the trick on a new young Jesuit – six feet tall and 14 stone of muscular Christianity. He was cornered in conversation by my fellow conspirators and I performed the deed – looping his knotted 'wings' over the valve of a radiator. The group dispersed, the young priest moved briskly away and brought 4 feet of cast-iron radiator crashing to the floor. Fortunately no-one was hurt in the incident but I retain painful memories of the consequent retribution.

The Earl of Kintore.
Engineer; Delegate, Council of Europe and Western European Union, 1954–64.

I remember a misdemeanor of my childhood which had spectacular results.

My parents were giving a 'smart' lunch party in our Scottish mansion. We kids were excluded. The meals were carried up a steep narrow stair from the pantry below to the dining room above.

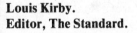

We managed to apply a liberal dressing of soft soap to the stairs, between courses and when the unfortunate footman (Fred to us) carried down the tray, he and the broken china arrived in a spectacular heap at the bottom. A stupid trick, as my father later impressed on my seat of learning.

Louis Kirby.
Editor, The Standard.

At grammar school we habitually subjected Wingy, the science master, to a dreadful third-form war-game which was a cross between Carry On and Colditz.

It began simply by solemnly assembling in the form-room whenever the timetable said 'laboratory' – and vice versa – then, when Wingy would discover our whereabouts, filing into the correct place one by one, as slowly and as noisily as possible.

When Wingy had worked out the patterns of our little ploy, we switched tactics and started a new game; and so the campaign continued, with the stakes becoming higher each time. But it abruptly ended when I came up with the idea of climbing into the first-floor form-room in a daring daylight break-in. What was more, to demonstrate to doubters that it could be done, I offered to be the first guinea pig.

So Demonstration Day found me waiting *outside* the school until the science lesson had begun. On the pre-arranged signal (a ball of paper tossed out of the specially-opened window) I shinned up the drainpipe aided by

190

tough old ivy, slipped over the sill and dropped to the floor inside. (Meanwhile Wingy's attention was being dramatically distracted by one of my accomplices involving himself in an earnest and complicated sortie around the blackboard under cover of a pseudo search for knowledge.)

Next I had to reach my desk, using a stomach crawl recently learnt at cadet corps; and I was intent on this, head well down, when I noticed two things simultaneously that alerted me that something was not quite right.

First, the bustle in the classroom had unaccountably dissolved into a deathly silence. Second, there were two highly-polished black shoes barring my path, and they could belong to only one person. It was the Headmaster, paying us an unwelcome visit.

He bent down briskly, tapped me on the head, rapped out "Stomach crawl . . . continue!" and (helpfully holding open the door) guided me out of the room, along the corridor, bumping down the stairs on my aching stomach, and all the way to his study.

Where I summarily received the fiercest caning of my life.

Hugh Klare, C.B.E.
Writer on Crime and Penology. Member of Parole Board, 1972–74.
A Governor, British Institute of Human Rights, 1974–80.

I was born in a small town 30 miles south of Vienna, surrounded by gentle green hills. The factory which gave employment to nearly all its 10,000 inhabitants was tucked away out of sight. It was a company town, with comfortable houses and excellent schools. But there were two architectural aberrations: one of its churches was inappropriately built as a miniature replica of the famous *Karlskirche* in Vienna, and the theatre tried hard to look like a small copy of the Opera house there.

Whether it was because the town was really rather pretty or, more likely, because the company was generous to them, the fact was that the theatre attracted well-known artists. One was the tenor Leo Slezak, then – this was in the early 1920s – a household name. Slezak stayed with my parents. In his honour a garden party had been laid on. There was champagne and wild strawberries (delicious, cheap and abundant in those days). Assorted local dignitaries strolled about. I was made to put on my white sailor suit.

Feeling foolish and with half an hour to spare, I made myself scarce. Our house was on the edge of the town. Ten minutes away, there was a farm, with animals of every size and shape. Far more interesting than a tenor. Engrossed, I wandered about looking. Or rather not looking. For I stumbled over a stone and was deposited smartly into the middle of a fresh and steaming midden.

I jumped up, horrified. Had that beastly suit got dirty? No, I seemed to have been lucky. Hardly a stain in sight. Relieved I ran back. Slowing up as I got near to our garden, I could make out my mother in animated conversation with Slezak. As nonchalantly as I could, I made my way through the guests. I did notice some rather curious looks as I passed people. But nothing prepared me for the effect my approach had on my mother and her companion. Although they had been facing another way, they both swivelled round as if pulled by a magnet. They sniffed. An amazed look spread over their faces. "Where *have* you been?" asked my mother, giving me a searching look. I felt myself going red. "Er – umh", I stammered, "Well, I . . .", and then I dried up. "It's quite simple, my dear," said Slezak to my mother and gave me a wink, "we've caught him *in fragrante delicto*."

Wyn Knowles.
Editor, 'Woman's Hour', BBC, since 1971; producer 'Mrs Dale's Diary'; writer of radio talks and documentaries.

I was never naughty at school; before school perhaps. When really cross I would say: "Let's play bears" and take a large bite out of my sister, until one day I bit myself by mistake. But at school I was shy, anxious and good. Well no, not *really* good. I remember a nun telling me: "You're not naughty and not good, just wobbling like a jelly in the middle." If I'd been really naughty, she said, there'd be some hope for me. I might repent and become a prefect or even a saint. I worried about this – how to please the nuns by being naughty? Yet they never seemed pleased with the sinners. I would listen deeply shocked to the lectures they handed out to them. But while I took them to heart, they seemed to have little or no effect on the culprits. Could they really be saints in the making?

My school memories are not funny, even today. They are poignant.

Being sent to find out the time from the clock outside the classroom when I couldn't tell the time and wouldn't admit to it. I had to try and make up a plausible answer – agony. I suffered from the sin of Pride – the worst in the Catholic book.

The shame of wetting my knickers when I was a big girl of seven and being found out. Why? I somehow could not explain that I was unable to lock the lavatory door and keep out some tormenting small boys.

And then there was the day of my First Communion when all the school walked in procession round the church, the seven First Communicants in the forefront. We were distinguished from the other white-clad girls because our veils were held on by wreaths of artificial flowers instead of merely fixed with hair-grips. But the uneven number seven posed a problem. The symmetry of the procession would be spoilt by an odd couple, one wearing a wreath and one without, so mine was taken off. "God will see you wearing a much more beautiful one than all the others," I was told. But you see I was not a *really* good little girl so I grieved all the way through the service.

David Kossoff.
Actor, raconteur, writer of bible stories.

It was my first paid employment. I was seven. We lived on the borders of Hoxton and Islington, near a canal bridge. The trams once over the bridge would go either straight on, past my mother's draper's shop, or to the left, along the canal. The man in charge of the lever which changed the tram line points was called Wally and every evening two-penn'orth of chips were brought to him. By me, for twopence a week.

The chip shop was about a quarter of a mile and the chips, hot, with vinegar and salt added, a most tempting package. When I was first taken on I was most careful not to touch the goods. Then, when I got to know the work I would help myself to one or two chips. Who would miss one or two chips? And two-penn'orth was a lot of chips in those days. Even five or six chips wouldn't be missed. Ten even. A dozen.

Wally was my friend. He liked me and was interested in all my doings. He was big and weatherbeaten and missed nothing. Everybody knew him and he was always there. A friend. And I was stealing from him. Well, not stealing exactly. What, a few chips? Some nights not such a few.

From Wally, not a word. He would open the carefully closed-again package and sniff the contents with great pleasure.

"Luvly, I'm ready for 'em. You're a good boy. Many waitin'?" Always the same words.

So we went on, I nicked his chips every night, till one night I was not well and my sister filled in for me, delivering a pristine untampered, heavier pack.

Wally weighed it in his hand and made no comment. I returned to my duty and to my pilferage. On the next end-of-week payday Wally gave me my twopence wages. Plus another twopence.

"It's not a rise, Davy".

"What is it then?"

"It's for you to buy yourself a package of chips to have all to yourself. Then you won't have to take any of mine. See you tomorrow." See you tomorrow. He was not sacking me. He was still my friend. I cried myself to sleep that night, full of the truly enormous shame that only a seven-year-old knows. And I never stole another chip.

Sir Hector Laing.
Chairman, United Biscuits.

When I finally passed my School Certificate after several unsuccessful attempts, my headmaster summoned me to give me the good news. "Laing," he said, "I'm delighted to tell you that you have at last passed your School Certificate". "Oh Jesus," I involuntarily exclaimed. "Very good choice," said the headmaster, and that was how I got to Jesus College, Cambridge.

Michael Langdon.
Principal Bass, Royal Opera House 1950–78.
Now, Director, National Opera Studio.

Many years ago, when working as a clerk at the Wolverhampton & District Building Society, I convinced an even more junior member of the staff that I was an expert at opening safes (even hinting at a career in crime on the side). He challenged me to prove it.

It so happened that the Building Society possessed a large outer door to the Strong Room, with a very stiff unlocking lever. I knew that the boy would not be able to turn this lever unaided, and so I crept down to the Strong Room, after 'borrowing' the key to this outer door, and unlocked it, leaving the lever in the closed position.

I then took the lad down with me, with many secretive glances and whispered instructions to be quiet, and asked him to check that the door was, indeed, locked. After straining at the lever for what seemed an eternity he agreed that the door was secure. "Now let's see what you can do?" he commanded.

I took out a small penknife and fiddled around inside the keyhole, meanwhile pressing my ear to the door and adopting a very professional air. Unfortunately, I was so keen to observe the expression on his face when I finally announced that I had 'unlocked' this great door by means of a small penknife, that in glancing back over my shoulder at him I lost my grip on the knife. I turned back in horror, just in time to see it slip through the keyhole, and, with a succession of horrifying 'clinks' and 'clunks' make its way down into the interior mechanism of the door.

With a silent prayer I grasped the lever and attempted to turn it into the unlocked position, but it was firmly jammed. "See!" hissed my little friend, "You *can't* do it, can you?" The truth of the matter was that I had, of course, well and truly 'done it'. After confessing to the boss, who, for some incredible reason, did not sack me on the spot, two men from Chubb's had to be brought in to dismantle the door – a task that took a day and a half.

Do you wonder that whenever I see someone on television casually slip a door latch with a plastic credit card that I feel that I went wrong somewhere?

Evelyn Laye, C.B.E.
Star of the musical stage and screen.

At seven years of age, I used to go to church regularly each Sunday – to look at the choirboys.

Richard Leech.
Qualified doctor, but now actor of stage and screen.

I first trod the boards at the age of four. It was in my Mother's drawing-room, and the production was *Alice in Wonderland,* an all star spectacular designed to raise at least £50 for the Children's League of Pity. Most of the cast are now bishops and stockbrokers, or married to them. Tiger-lily is the wife of a poet, one of the pansies is Professor of Gynaecology, and the King's Herald, also a doctor, did heroic work for the Navy in an open boat with ten volunteers, researching shock and exposure. I was the White Rabbit and my Mum, who was director, designer and wardrobe mistress as well as the back legs of the horse, did me proud with a splendid costume which framed my cherubic features with two floppy ears lined with pink velvet. It was, I suppose, what would now be called a catsuit – a woolly one-piece into which I had to be sewn for the performance. "Oh my ears and whiskers, I shall be late!" I piped.

I remember diving down the rabbit burrow. It was made of an artificial grass rug – the kind you often see on butcher's slabs when the shop is shut – draped over a child's hoop. I remember my waistcoat cut from black and white checked crêpe paper, and I remember my gold watch on its chain. I remember Alice. She was a Big Girl, almost grown up, and had beautiful long golden hair. But the thing I remember most vividly is being sewn into the suit again some time after the performance for a guest appearance at a fancy dress ball.

I have never been troubled by shyness. I am not the shrinking violet type. I've always been an extrovert show-off and I blush to record that at children's gatherings I was invariably the life and soul, as well as the liver and lights of the party. My personal appearance as the White Rabbit was no exception.

The King's Herald was there too. He was an extrovert also and we egged each other on to more and more hideous exploits of noisy exhibition. Awash with lemonade, jellies and iced buns, I suddenly realised that I needed to relieve my bladder urgently. I found the loo and whizzed in, dancing from toe to toe and holding my breath while I felt in panic for my flies. Then – horror of horrors – I discovered that my beautiful velvet lined costume was a fly-less straight jacket.

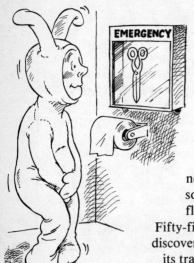

Scarlet-faced and in agony I picked at the seams, but it was unrippable. I had a nanny somewhere, but I calculated that to go searching for her would take too long, and indeed even my calculations took too long, for as I agonised, so Nature inexorably insisted on fulfilment and my catsuit was filled full.

Extroversion has its compensations. It is usually accompanied by optimism. What with the intense relief and the highly absorbent quality of the fabric I soon persuaded myself that I had really nothing to worry about. I returned to the party and soon the King's Herald and I were rolling round the floor like puppies in a kennel.

Fifty-five years and a bit later I still can't forgive him. He discovered my sodden secret and stopping the party dead in its tracks with a screech to split eardrums, proclaimed my shame to the world, while I was picked from the floor by an outraged nanny and whisked from the room.

There's little doubt my Mother's amateur theatricals inspired me with a lifelong addiction to the stage. I wonder if the damp experience of that fancy dress ball was responsible for the King's Herald going to sea to research into 'shock and exposure'.

Prudence Leith.
Company director, Cookery Editor, the Guardian; part-time Member, British Railways Board.

My brother David and I, when we were 10 and 8, had a great game. We would hide behind the garden wall and, as cars drove down the road, we would douse them with water from one of those old-fashioned fruit tree sprayers that you operated like a giant flit-gun. Most cars in the South African summer, before the days of air-conditioning, had all the windows open, and sometimes, which was marvellous, the target would be an open tourer or sports car.

By the time the occupants of the car recovered from the shock, and slowed down, gasping, they would be half-way down the road, the shower would be over, and they never came back to investigate.

One day, we had a bonanza. A wedding convoy led by the bride and groom in an open Rolls Royce, processed slowly down the road. We were merciless. First we soaked the bride, her groom, and the chauffeur, then set about the guests. None of the cars stopped, because, after all, they were in a procession and on their way to the reception.

But we had reckoned without the wit of the – presumably – best man and ushers, who were in the last car. They had ample time, with the ducking and weaving going on in front of them, to realise what was happening.

They stopped at our gate. Like terrified rabbits we just sat there, next to the bucket, incriminating spray in David's hands, waiting for judgement. And it came with a vengeance. One of the young men held me still while the other sprayed me from top to toe at point-blank range. Then they did the same to David, and finally up-ended him in the bucket of water. They didn't say a word. Just got back in their car and drove off after our victims.

Jan Le Witt.
Painter and Poet. Fellow of International P.E.N.
Member Executive Council European Society of Culture, Venice.

Adam and I lived in the same apartment house and, inseparable as we were, we walked each morning reluctantly to school.

Outside the school boundary we found life enjoyable and carefree, it was all fun and games. The tricks we jointly conceived were to be sure never derivative. We had the ambition of being original and inventive; sawing off the hind legs of a teacher's chair and fixing it with sellotape was commonplace stuff. We set our targets much higher than that. Moreover, everything we conceived was thoroughly rehearsed, there was no haphazard improvisation as far as we were concerned.

One day Adam, conniving Adam, came up with a stunning idea which we both at once endorsed. A purse was to be filled with pebbles, an assortment of flat stones masquerading as coins, the bulging purse was to be tied to a length of thread and placed appropriately in the middle of the pavement, a tempting bait – so we thought – for some unsuspecting passer-by.

Adam's role was to take up a strategic position and at the given signal

198

(twice 'pst') I would give the
thread with the purse in tow a sharp pull so
as to make it disappear in the nick of time, should anyone approaching
try to grab it.

A middle-aged lady with noble features wearing a marine blue coat
was the first to oblige. Automatically she bent down to pick up the
purse – a pavement after all is no place for such objects. As she stretched
out her arm in Tantalus fashion she slipped and fell on her knees.

To our everlasting shame we both, the perpetrators, lacked the
presence of mind to come to the lady's aid and take her home as she was
limping and appeared in pain. We were truly sorry for what had happened,
and were no longer delighted at the ruse we prepared for unsuspecting
innocence. Some grown-up showing compassion helped the lady into a
taxicab whilst Adam and I, overcome by remorse and fearing retribution,
took shelter in a dim corner by the dustbin yard.

At our school there was a lovely-looking girl, with blue eyes set in a
graceful oval face. I took an immediate liking to her and, whenever we
met face to face, my pulsebeat quickened and my heart went up and
down. Still at that tender age I was nevertheless in love with her and, as
Baudelaire put it:'what is so annoying about Love is that it is a crime
which one cannot do without an accomplice.'

My fondness for her was such that up till then I did not hesitate to
confide my innermost secrets to her but now, following the disgrace and
my cowardly behaviour towards the lady who – I learnt from a reliable
source – happened to be the mother of my blue-eyed girl friend, the very
object of my love, I felt thoroughly ashamed. Quite ostentatiously she
was now ignoring me, and I suffered agonies every time she turned her
back on me.

One day in the wake of her disapproving look she spelled it out: "So you are the one who conceived that awful prank, it was you who fooled my mother, do you realise that she is still in pain?''

Years passed. It seems that our own pranks are nothing compared with the tricks fate is capable of playing. Who would have thought that the lady whom I fooled, brought down to her knees, would one day embrace me warmly as her son-in-law, pardon me, and spare me the task of sending my conscience to the cleaners. . .

Maurice Lindsay, C.B.E., T.D., D. Litt.
Poet; Director, The Scottish Civic Trust.

Our Latin Master, a domine of the old school who wore a peaked starched collar and glinted the strictest of discipline through narrow, gold-rimmed spectacles, was not a man you could let down your guard with. To disturb what we regarded as his over-emphasis on an invariable daily order, we hit upon two ploys. One was to mishang at decidedly improbable angles the faded sepia reproductions of ancient Roman heroes on the walls of the classroom. The domine took no notice, so we had to think of something more dramatic.

A plot was hatched. We bought several pairs of kippers and allowed them to ripen in somebody's coal cellar. We then arrived early one morning in the classroom and wedged them firmly and squelchingly behind the central heating system.

As the poet Burns puts it, 'The best laid schemes of mice and men gang aft agley.' When in due course the classroom filled with an appalling aroma of decay, the master appeared not to notice. Almost sick with the hot stench of rotting kipper, however, we had no choice but to stuff our handkerchiefs over our noses and make a show of paying attention.

Eventually, the releasing bell rang. ''Wait a moment boys,'' glinted the Latin Master. ''In view of the all-too-obvious fact that some slight and at present unexplained unpleasantness of the atmosphere has disturbed your powers of concentration, you will all report back here at 4 o'clock in the afternoon. By then, no doubt, the janitor will have discovered and removed the cause of the . . . er . . . trouble, and you will once again be able to concentrate. Dismiss!''

It was a long time before I could face up to another kipper at the breakfast table.

Moira Lister.
Star of stage and screen.

When I was four years old my two sisters were in boarding school at the Convent of Notre Dâme. I was very jealous that they should be in such a lovely school and I was too little to join them.

However, one weekend I was allowed to visit them and spend the night in their dorm. With great excitement I helped Mummy to pack a tuck box for them and off we went. After a great day, we decided on a midnight picnic in the dorm. The tuck box was excitedly depleted by little grabbing hands from the other girls but I was given the tin of golden syrup and told to go down the other end of the dorm to the girl who had the opener. Very proud to be given such responsibility, I ran down, got the tin opened and very carefully holding my arm well out to the side, walked back. In my excitement I had not noticed the tin was upside down. A row of twelve beds had a rich yellow ribbon of glistening gooey golden syrup right across their blankets. So my Convent visit came to a very sticky end.

Julian Lloyd Webber.
World renowned solo cellist.

I remember I was about nine years old. It was summer and holiday preparations were under way. Often a time for rampant squabbles, but on this occasion there was a seething silence. My parents were insisting that I should take the cello and I was insisting that I should not, on the entirely reasonable grounds that daily cello practice could not be considered a proper holiday. Besides, we were going to the country, a village in Norfolk where I knew there would be many more interesting things to do and a boy cannot be expected to practise all the time. However, reason did not prevail. I had run out of arguments and the matter was closed. I retreated to plan my next move.

Running away was definitely out. That would merely postpone our departure and I had tormented visions of myself locked in a room with the cello while everyone else was having fun. It occurred to me to break the cello strings but since they were instantly replaceable it was not a very practical solution. But the bow . . . I certainly could not practise without the bow. What a marvellous idea! But there were difficulties attached to it, not least in convincing my parents that there had been a Terrible Accident. Not only that, I loved the cello, I loved playing the cello and this course of action did seem a touch extreme, but I could think of no other way which would be quite so certain or, I feared, so final. I picked up the bow and looked at it. It would be a terrible pity. I sat down, still holding it, trying to will myself into snapping it. I began to feel a delicious sense of naughtiness creeping over me, becoming more and more exciting, eating away at my resistance until I had almost forgotten the reason. I just had to do it. I cracked the bow across my knee. The noise was not as loud as I had expected, just enough to temper my glee with horror. Not only had I committed the act, now I had to get away with it. Without allowing myself time to ponder the enormity of it too deeply, I rushed to my mother, broken bow in hand.

"Look what's happened. I didn't realise it was there and I sat on it."

There was silence for a moment and I knew that really I was as shocked as she was but I could see in her face that she couldn't imagine my doing something quite so dreadful on purpose and, although perhaps reluctantly, that she believed me.

My enjoyment of the holiday was tinged only very slightly with shame and that disappeared as soon as the bow returned from the repairers with hardly a sign of its unfortunate mishap. I still have it. In fact I still use it from time to time but I never take it on holiday.

Sylvia, Lady Loch.
A story by her late husband, George Henry Compton, Third Baron Loch.

When I was a boy, my father was Lord-in-Waiting to King George V. The King and my father were also great friends, having a close link in their almost fanatical love of shooting. On a number of occasions, the Monarch came down to my home in Suffolk when shooting in the area, and on one occasion Queen Mary came too and had tea with my mother.

I ought to add at this point that when I was born, the King had very graciously consented to be my godfather.

During Queen Mary's visit to our house, she suddenly expressed the wish to go up to the nursery and see the godchild. The Nanny was busy with one of my sisters when the door opened and, without warning, the Queen and my mother stood on the threshold.

I, who was too young even to remember all this, was apparently firmly ensconced in one corner, sitting cross-legged and avidly studying the wall.

The Queen came up to me and tapped me on the shoulder. Apparently, I did not stir but continued to stare in front of me. "How are you, my little man?" the old Queen enquired in her imperious voice. Nanny's ears were burning with embarrassment as apparently her charge made no

reply. After the question had been repeated at least three times, I am told I looked at Queen Mary with more than a little hint of irritation, and holding my finger to my lips said "Shhh! I'm a hare — pretending to have babies."

Years later, around the age of fourteen, I was a page at the court, in attendance with my father at one of the levées that were held from time to time. The first time this happened, Queen Mary singled me out from everyone else in attendance and said, "Young man! I hope you're a little more comfortable than the last time I saw you?"

I must have flushed to the roots of my hair, because of course I had been ribbed so much by the family, I knew exactly what she was talking about. I mumbled a reply.

It is only now as I see our own Queen, Elizabeth II, with her wonderful memory for people and events, carrying out her marvellous job in this country, that I fully appreciate what a remarkable person old Queen

Mary must have been, and what an incredible gift she and her successors had and still have. Or is it simply that through the years and years of self-discipline and inner strength, one can school oneself to remember the tiniest details about other people?

Sir Douglas Lovelock, K.C.B.
First Church Commissioner; Formerly Chairman, H.M. Customs and Excise.

A new and rather officious Sergeant was drilling the cadet corps at my school. We all enjoyed clicking our heels and stamping when the squad turned but he would have none of this. "I'm going to turn my back", he said "and I don't even want to be able to hear you when you about turn."

After a few minutes he pronounced himself fully satisfied. No wonder! While his back was turned, the squad had walked off the parade ground and was back in the warmth of the school building.

Sue MacGregor.
Presenter, B.B.C. 'Woman's Hour'.

When I was about four or five my mother fondly imagined that forbidding me more than a couple of sweets a week would be good for my character – and for my teeth. We lived in Scotland at the time, in Elgin, and my best friend was Lorna Thomson from down the road. Her mother kept the sweetie ration in her bedroom and soon discovered that Lorna and I were helping ourselves (this was not long after the War and sweeties were indeed rationed so this was Not On). One day Lorna said "Mummy may we go and play in your bedroom?" "Yes," said Mrs Thomson, "but you are not to eat the sweets".

Ten minutes or so afterwards two small girls with bulging cheeks arrived downstairs and Mrs T. snapped, "What did I say about the sweets?" Whereupon came the retort, "We are not eating them, we are

204

just sucking them and then putting them back".

Lord Mancroft.
Chairman, The British Greyhound Racing Board.

In the Thirties, I was a not very serious-minded undergraduate at Oxford. One night, quite late, some friends and I ran foul of the Junior Proctor out on his police rounds.

We were caught and fined. I felt that my own fine (for I was unjustly thought to be the ringleader) was too severe and I determined to be revenged on the Junior Proctor.

He was a Balliol man. A few nights later we obtained a very small pig from a local farmer, covered it with grease and with painstaking cunning introduced it, under cover of darkness, into the Senior Common room of Balliol where the dons were enjoying their Port. The spectacle of the dons trying to waylay the pig was enjoyable.

We were never discovered.

Some 20 years later, my friend Lord Fairfax was addressing the House of Lords about an amendment to the Landlord and Tenant Bill, of which he disapproved. The chaos resulting from the proposed clause, he explained, would be only equal to that obtaining in the Senior Common Room of Balliol College after Lord Mancroft had succeeded in his task of introducing therein that small but well-greased pig.

From the opposite benches, Lord Lyndsey of Birker arose in wrath. "Oh, so it was that blighter Mancroft, was it? Let me get at him."

It should be realised that at the time of the greased pig saga, Lord Lyndsey was Master of Balliol.

Norris McWhirter, C.B.E.
Author, publisher, broadcaster; Director, Guinness Superlatives Ltd.

If I live into the next century it will be rather fun to recall casually my last meeting with Rudyard Kipling.

On a family holiday in Guernsey my father, who was the first man to be editor of three Fleet Street newspapers, took my mother and my two brothers to the Old Government House Hotel in St Peter Port. My twin Ross, and I were 8 at the time and on the high-spirited side. Unknown to us in the room below ours was the great author of the Jungle Books; Stalky & Co; Kim; the Just So Stories and Puck of Pook's Hill, who was also the cousin of Stanley Baldwin, five times Prime Minister. We used to devote at least an hour a day to 'fighting'. This day it took the form of cold water and tooth mugs. One badly-aimed shot precipitated a mug full of cold water over the edge of the room's balcony. Sitting on the balcony below, reading his newspaper, was the great man. Suddenly from skyward there descended a douche of water, which besplattered both him and his newspaper. An emissary from the management laid an immediate complaint to my father, who understandably was furious.

That night at dinner we were ordered to make an apology for our conduct to Rudyard Kipling, who was sitting alone having his dinner. I have the clearest recollection of how two well-scrubbed little boys advanced in some trepidation to repeat our carefully drafted and rehearsed apology. Mr. Kipling wore gold-rimmed spectacles, which glinted in the light, and had rather bushy eyebrows. He may have tried to look forebidding, but did not succeed, because he could barely contain his amusement at seeing two curly-topped, solemn little boys who were as alike as two peas in a pod. His twinkly dark brown eyes gave him away, but we managed to maintain our genuine expression of contrition. We were duly forgiven for what in law was technically an assault committed by two people who were under the age of culpability.

Alan Melville.
Revue writer and author.

Shortly before Christmas each year in my home town – Berwick-upon-Tweed – there was held a Children's Fancy Dress Ball in the Corn Exchange. It caused immense excitement, rivalry and ill-feeling among both the youthful participants and their parents. Especially the mothers, who began secret preparations early in the autumn in the hope that their offspring and no-one else's would make off with the First Prize (usually a two-pound box of Cadbury's Assorted Chocolates). After some years of kitting us out as Red Indian Chiefs (very popular), Pirate Kings (fairly popular) and Beau Brummells (*hated*), my own mother and the mother of my temporary best friend, Douglas Henderson, decided on originality rather than ostentation. They also hit on an idea which was simple and much cheaper than knocking up another Beau Brummell outfit.

At that time there was a popular advertisement on all the hoardings plugging Halls' Distemper; it consisted of two characters in spotless white painters' overalls carrying between them on their shoulders a lengthy plank bearing the simple inscription HALLS DISTEMPER. It seemed a sure-fire winner; my father was in the timber importing business, so there was no trouble about the plank; our mothers got out their treadle sewing-machines and run up the overalls in next to no time. My colleague and I (we were both around eight) set out for the Corn Exchange carrying the plank in the approved manner and with high hopes of making off with the first prize and later in the evening dividing the chocolates between us, me trying to get the hard centres and palming anything that looked like ginger on my co-entrant. By the time we'd walked all the way down the High Street and reached the Corn Exchange the plank had got very heavy indeed, and the idiot at its other end seemed to me to be remarkably clumsy about steering it round corners. When we got to the entrance to the revels, we had a blazing row and I hit him with the plank. Quite hard; he had to be given first aid in a side room and then taken home in a cab. This made me angrier than ever; to enter a Fancy Dress contest as the two characters advertising Halls' Distemper and find yourself performing solo, lugging the beastly plank round and round the ballroom floor on your own while the judges were trying to work out what you were supposed to represent . . . it's not conducive to confidence in winning. Nor did I; the chocolates were won, if I remember rightly, by a particularly horrid ginger-haired boy called Stanley Ballard who went as, of all things, the White Rabbit in 'Alice'. This, of course, made me angrier than ever and I refused to carry the plank home; my mother had to lug it all the way back up the High Street, my father having made it clear that it was only on loan and had to be returned. When my mother reported the afternoon's events to the old man, I was put face downwards over the usual chair and given a thrashing. It seemed to me most unfair; I dropped Douglas Henderson like a hot potato and took up with a girl called Dorothy Craig. Mainly, I must admit, because she had a hamster.

Bernard Miles—Lord Miles of Blackfriars.
Actor, director and writer. Founder and Managing Governor of the
Mermaid Theatre.

In the mid-1930s, I toured with the famous radio comedian Eric
Barker. In Birmingham, we found digs with a Mrs Pellew
– a nice double bed-sitter for 35/- per week – we had to
buy our own food, but she would cook it. A deal was
struck, but as she left the room, she turned in the doorway
and said:

"There is only one thing. If you have occasion
to use the chamber-pot, please
don't put it back under the bed,
as the steam rusts the springs."
We did as we had been told, and
the springs remained intact.

Edward Milne.
Author and lecturer; M.P. for Blyth, 1960–74.

This story concerns our twin daughters, Rita and Kathleen.

Rita was in the garden when a neighbour passed and said, "Hullo, who
are you?" "I'm Rita," she said. "How do I know you are Rita?" To
which Rita replied, "I know because Kathleen's in the bathroom."

Major-General The Viscount Monckton of Brenchley, C.B., O.B.E.,
M.C., D.L.
Soldier and farmer. President, British Association Sovereign Military
Order of Malta.

My first term at Harrow as a boy of thirteen was spent in a house called
The Grove, under a famous housemaster, Mr C. G. Pope.

I had always been keen on horses and whilst at school I used to have the
odd postal bet. In those days letters from bookmakers were not marked
'Private' and had their names on the outside.

In due course I was sent for by the housemaster and told to stop betting.

Stupidly, I got hold of the envelope, put a note in it saying "Mind your own business" and dropped it in the postbox. Next morning I was sent for and given a rocket, and as a punishment was told to produce every morning by 8 o'clock a list of the horses I would bet on in each race, with a theoretical stake of 5 shillings. At the end of each week I had to make a summary.

At the end of term I was sent for and told to add up the losses I had incurred and quickly learned my lesson, that betting was a mug's game.

The Hon. Ewen E. S. Montagu, C.B.E., Q.C., D.L.
Judge, Chairman of Middlesex Sessions, 1956–69. The Judge Advocate of the Fleet, 1945–73. Author (The Man Who Never Was).

During the time which included the First World War my mother and father had a very large country house, near Southampton, where they entertained a lot. When an American Admiral brought his flagship to that port for a boiler-clean my parents gave a large formal dinner-party for him – and we youngsters were, resentfully, banished for the evening.

After the staff had served dessert I locked the inner doors of the dining room, having already locked all the many doors and windows from the garden to the house and, with explanations, locked up the staff so that no bells could be answered. I then turned off the main switch in the semi-basement.

The remainder of us, gathered at the dining room keyhole, heard father say: "Don't worry, they are just switching from one generator to the other at Southampton, it often happens nowadays, it'll go on again in a minute". When the lights still hadn't gone on again a couple of minutes later, through the keyhole my father was heard to say, "No, it's Ewen" (when there was any mischief, I was always immediately blamed, usually rightly).

The party then tried to leave the room; all doors were immovable. Shouts for me to unlock them; no response, except for a chorus of ribald songs. Bells were rung, no response. Father says, "We'll just go out into the garden and then in by the sitting room door". Exeunt all into the garden; no entry into the locked sitting room. A march round the house trying all doors and windows; finally a drop into a semi-basement and in through a larder window which we had missed – all in formal evening dress!

When the Admiral left, he said with obvious sincerity, how much he had enjoyed the evening and added, "I never knew that English country-house life was like that!'' Fortunately his obvious enjoyment mitigated the penalty!

Lee Montague.
Film and T.V. actor.

There was no question but that I had to see the famous Moscow Dynamo football team – I just had to. They were on their first much-publicised visit to the shores of their allies after the end of the war ("Which war Daddy?" "The Second World War, son!") and were due to play a couple of matches. One of them was to be at Stamford Bridge. There was one problem though. I was due to attend school at the same time. (In those days there was no such thing as evening matches – if you see what I mean.) I racked my brains for a way out of my dilemma. I knew that to argue with my parents or headmaster that this was an Anglo-Russian Cultural Event would hardly cut any ice! But, although a future career as an actor had not entered my head, the seeds had obviously been sown – and on the day of the football match, they were duly harvested!

The morning after the match, I was to be seen limping into school – not your Richard III gait but rather a gentle limp stolen, I suspect, from a much-loved cinema actor of that time – one Herbert Marshall.

"You were absent yesterday afternoon."

"Yes Sir."

"Why?"

I related the sorry tale. How, while returning to my home in the lunch hour, I had tripped and fallen while running for a bus. How I had been assisted by a friendly passer-by and how, having reached home, blood pouring from the wound, it was bandaged but I was advised to rest for the remainder of the day. And while telling the story, I gently raised my trouser leg and showed – from calf to knee – the gory mess. It was but a brief glimpse that Mr Wright had of the blood-soaked bandage.

"This is no way to get our Matric is it? Be careful in future."

And I limped away – recalling what a wonderful match it had been – and reminding myself to buy another bottle of Heinz Tomato Ketchup.

210

Brian Moore.
I.T.V. football commentator and presenter.

It was my first night as a choirboy. I was eight years old and practice at
Benenden in Kent was on Wednesday nights. I have to admit that I had been
lured by the money – a penny for each service on Sunday, tuppence for
practice and a half-day outing each year to Hastings.

Each Wednesday the village boys got their voices in trim with a crafty
drag behind the largest gravestone. And, as a new boy, it was my turn to
take the money and buy the cigarettes.

The village shop, run by Mr Baldwin, sold everything
from bicycles and groceries to cigarettes, sweets and
razor blades. And, behind a screen, Mr Baldwin
became the local barber.
"Ten Woodbines for Mr Moore, please," I piped
up. There was a crash behind the screen as the
clippers and combs went flying – and my enraged
Father stormed into view. One haircut every three
months – and it had to be now!
In forty seconds, in front of an admiring audience,
he gave me the verbal hiding of my life and I
vowed never to deceive my Dad again. It took
me another forty years to give up smoking.

Lord Morris.
Conservative member, House of Lords. Chairman, Pencotech Limited.

On a summer's evening in 1953, instead of doing my evening prep, I
tuned in to the 9 o'clock news. To my unalloyed delight there was
announced an event affecting the epicentre of every schoolboy's existence
– sweets were to come off ration as of midnight that night.

It so happened we had just been issued with our supply of sweet coupons.
Discreet disclosure of this news to a few carefully selected friends (upon
sanction of death should my news prove false), delivered to me their full
supply of now worthless coupons. Inevitably there existed in the better
scholastic establishments a lively market in sweet coupons. The price
remained steady year by year, tending to rise in the winter months and

towards the end of coupon issues when trading became heavy. Some smart selling well below market between 9.30 and lights out and the reading of newspapers the following morning, realised the handsome profit of £2.3s.6d and some extremely disgruntled investors who drew little comfort from being reminded of the legal maxim 'caveat emptor'. Needless to say, some unprincipled sneak shopped me to the Headmaster. Whilst admiring my business acumen, he was quite unmoved by the arguments:

(a) That taking advantage of information affecting the market was the very stuff of the Stock Exchange and

(b) that many of his charges had learned an invaluable lesson for later life, namely never to buy below market other than with extreme care.

The Headmaster, Dom Wilfred Passmore, O.S.B., posted a notice on the school noticeboard saying, "All those boys foolish and greedy enough to buy worthless sweet coupons from Morris I, and who wish their money refunded, should attend a creditors' meeting in Classroom IV at 7 p.m. tonight." The Headmaster took the opportunity of lecturing all on Stock Exchange practice and on the thin line to be drawn between fair trading and fraud. The outcome was that I enjoyed not one sou of my short-gotten gains, lost one hour of precious free time and one poor boy, who had deliberately overstated his claim, got thrashed within an inch of his life!

Peggy Mount.
Actress, National Theatre player.

I was a bridesmaid. We were rather poor. My mum bought me a pale blue crêpe de chine dress, with a panel down the front centre, hand embroidered below the neckline, black patent strap shoes, white socks and a straw hat trimmed with forget-me-nots and white gloves. After the wedding, outside the church, my ten-year-old sweetheart, Reggie, said, "I've got a boat Peg, come on!" He had an orange box, with an old mackintosh tied round it! We got into it at the deep end of the swimming pool. Fortunately, I could swim. My pale blue crêpe de chine dress shrank. My shoes fell off, my hat floated away. I could not understand why I got such a b . . . . y good hiding!

212

Richard Murdoch.
Actor of stage and screen.

I cannot claim that this happened to me but a boy was expelled from school for cribbing. The father went to see the Headmaster to seek an explanation. The Headmaster explained that in one paper the son's answers had been word for word the same as the boy sitting next to him. "But the other boy might have been cribbing from my son,"said the father. "I don't think so", said the Headmaster. "There was one difficult question and your son's neighbour had written 'I know nothing about this subject'. Your son had written 'Neither do I.'"

Michael Noakes, P.P.R.O.I., R.P.
Portraitist of the royal family and other distinguished people.

"Boy!" said the Head Master, "I have no objection to your writing home and telling your parents that there have been some cases of influenza at Downside."

In spite of that reassurance, his eyes glinted through the tremendously thick spectacle-lenses. I wilted.

"However, I am puzzled that you feel that Jenkins, Pratt and Fitzroy together constitute an epidemic on the scale that you implied in your letter. I suggest that in future you avoid giving such free rein to your sense of the dramatic. You may go."

I mumbled a rather pink apology and turned to the door.

"One moment," commanded The Bear. "I might add that the reason that your father contacted me was not because he was particularly impressed with your lurid description of a decimated School population. He was more concerned with our apparent inability here to instill into you a grasp of elementary spelling. I should like you to take note that when you next have occasion to write to your parents to inform them that 'the boys are going down like flies', the word is not spelt 'f-l-y-s'."

Charles Osborne.
Literature director, Arts Council of Great Britain; author and journalist.

We lived in Brisbane, and during my school-days, whenever my parents were away, I was left in the care of my Yorkshire grandmother. I must have been about thirteen when we had the embarrassing ginger-ale disaster. Grandma retired to bed early, but always left a snack and a soft drink in my room for when I came home late from the movies or wherever. Our house was one of those Queensland colonial bungalows, with a wide verandah around three sides. The loo, as with most of those old houses, was outside: in our case that meant crossing the verandah, going down steps to the back of the house, and to a w.c. inconveniently placed under the house itself. One night I came home very late from a party, having told grandma I was going to the 'flicks'. A tropical thunderstorm was in progress, and I was thoroughly drenched after running home from the tram-stop several blocks away.

I was in my room, having undressed and dried myself, and I was about to climb into bed when I realized I was bursting for a pee. Oh God, did I really have to dress again and make a dash for it through the rain? My eye fell on the bottle of ginger-ale grandma had left for me. Opening my bedroom window slightly, I emptied its contents without letting too much rain into the room, then peed into the bottle and hid it in the wardrobe, intending to get rid of it the following morning.

Of course I forgot, and when, the following evening, I came home in time for dinner, grandma had a fascinating tale to tell. "I'm glad you didn't drink your ginger-ale last night, love", she began. I remembered. "W-why, gran, what do you mean?"

"Well, I found it in your wardrobe when I was putting your clothes away after you, today. So I put the bottle back in the fridge, and at lunch-time I thought I'd pour myself a glass. But it was flat, and it tasted funny, there was certainly *something* wrong with it. So I put the top back on the bottle and, after lunch, I took it back to Johnson's (the corner shop), and complained to Mrs Johnson about it. So she had a taste of it too, and she said, "Mrs Osborne, that does taste queer. Let's see what my husband thinks." So Mr Johnson came out, and he tasted it, and he said, "Mrs Osborne, that's not ginger beer, that's urine."

How did he know, I wondered.

"They were very apologetic, love, and they gave me the money back. Mr Johnson said he was going to send it back to the factory and complain

strongly about it. Fancy one of the workers playing a nasty joke like that.''

Well, I hadn't been caught, and my main feeling was one of relief, coupled with a certain satisfaction at the thought of the three of them all sipping away like connoisseurs. I hope no one at the soft drink factory got the sack. I've told the story many times, and occasionally someone remarks in reply that it's a folk-tale that they've heard before. Maybe, but, if so, then I may well be the folk who started it, because it certainly happened as I've described it, on a rainy night in Brisbane in 1940.

Juliet Pannett, P.S., F.R.S.A.
Portrait painter. Freelance artist to The Times, Daily Telegraph and Radio Times.

I did a portrait of Field Marshal Lord Slim. When I showed it to him he said,''You have made me look CROSS – but I know I do! Once, when I was in Burma, a Press Photographer followed me round and kept NOT taking a photograph.'' At last he said,''Would you please smile, Sir?'' and I said ''I am smiling!''

I drew Lord Mountbatten at the Ministry of Defence in 1960. While I was drawing he told me an amusing story from the War years. He wanted Churchill to see and test some pieces of Mulberry Harbour, so he took them round to No. 10. The valet said he couldn't possibly see Mr Churchill as he was in his bath. ''JUST where I want him to be,'' said Lord Mountbatten and went into the bathroom and gave Winston the bits to try out in the bath.

Anthony Parker.
Producer/director, Thames Television.

I was seven, and along with my friends Ian, Trevor and Gerald we made up a gang whose headquarters was a den in a double hedgerow of the local Barleymow playing fields.

One day we played 'Doctors and Nurses' with Joan, a sweet-six-year old and her more mature friend Mavis, a delightful seven-year-old blonde with an attractive stutter. A man called Hughes passed by going fishing and we fled in haste our separate ways.

I was lying in bed at 8 o'clock that evening, when I became aware of a knock at my parents' front door. I lay there midst increasing guilt and trepidation as I heard my father – a God-fearing son of a blacksmith/preacher – open the door to Mavis's mother – a nervous woman whose own stutter was less endearing than her daughter's – and who requested the return of Mavis's knickers.

A visit to Ian's and Trevor's houses had failed to reveal their whereabouts but Gerald – always a reliable witness – swore, accurately it transpired, that they were in Tony Parker's blue school raincoat pocket! My father duly handed them over to Mavis's mum with a promise that the wretched Tony would deliver his apologies in person on the morrow.

My memory of my own stuttered apology delivered as promised remains with me to this day – but so too do the happy hours the gang spent in our den!

When I was nearly nine my Grandmother, who was a great age, died in our house. My brother, Leslie, who was fourteen, was left to cope with callers while my parents went out to make the necessary arrangements. I was sent out to play Cowboys and Indians with the gang, Trevor, Ian, Gerald and Mavis's brother, Frank, who also had a stutter.

During the game I was 'shot' and we got on to the subject of being dead. I boasted I had a dead Grandmother in our house, but the gang didn't believe me and dared me to show her to them.

We trouped over to our house – of Leslie there was no sign – he had got scared and was apparently sitting on the fence at the far end of the garden frightened to go indoors. I led the gang into the room – Grandma lay there on the bed with a lace cover over her face.

Frank wouldn't believe she was dead and the others said she was just asleep, so I put one knee on the bed in order to remove the lace cover. In doing so I disturbed the balance of the bed and a strange gasping noise issued from my late grandmother.

We all fled to the safety of the playing fields to discuss our frightening experience.

That night, as I lay fretfully awake, unable to shake off the memory of that awful moment in the room below, I heard a knock at our door. My father was greeted, on opening the door, with Frank's mother saying,

"Your Tony has shown our little Frank your poor dead mother, and he's been sick three times, and can't sleep!" She added that Frank said that the rest of the gang had also been there and no doubt their parents would be having problems too! Indeed they were. The whole gang, myself included, took several weeks before a peaceful night's sleep became the norm again.

Poor Leslie got the blame from my parents for not remaining bravely at his post!

Harry Patterson, alias Jack Higgins.
Author (The Eagle Has Landed).

In 1945 just after the war ended there was still a tramcar service in Leeds where I was at school. The tramdrivers and clippies went on strike because they wanted to force the bosses to sack all the women employed during the war. As the strike was unpopular, the authorities decided to break it and soon blacklegs by the score were queuing up to run the trams – students and large numbers of servicemen on leave. I took a day off school and joined the queue hoping to be a clippie, but there were too many of us so I switched to the queue for would-be drivers. I was all of fifteen, swore blind that I was eighteen and the clerk at the desk was too tired to argue. I was shown how to drive a tram along with three other people, drove one for a quarter of a mile under the supervision of an inspector and was passed fit to drive. I managed the circular route once, the most youthful and incompetent tram driver ever to operate in Leeds. Just past Oakwood on the track, I was coasting at full speed, tried to brake at the sight of a tram stalled in front of me, failed and smashed into the back. The entire floor came up around me and the tram tilted to one side on its bogey. They sent for another inspector to bring it in, swaying precariously. I filled in an accident report in my schoolboy hand, received fifteen shillings as a day's pay and was kicked out. When I got back to school the head sent for me. It turned out that he had been a passenger on the upper deck of my tram, had recognised me instantly. "Incompetent as usual, Patterson," he said and promptly gave me six of the best. Years later, I met Jimmy Saville at a function and discovered that like me, he too had been a tramdriver for a day in that strike and had suffered the same sort of accident.

Jan Pieńkowski.
Designer and illustrator.

My first encounter with the British way of life was in the infamous winter of 1946. Having been taught about Britain's temperate climate I was sent to a boarding school on the Welsh border, which dispelled many of my illusions.

The school undoubtedly had advantages – I learned to speak English reasonably, mainly in self-defence.

It was not exactly a baptism of fire – the dormitory windows were always open and enough snow occasionally drifted on to the window-sills to have snowball fights.

Lights-out was at eight o'clock and, since we did not go to sleep for an hour or two we used to amuse ourselves in various traditional ways. One of the boys was very gifted in the art of story-telling, usually ending with a cliff-hanger. Alas, I could only understand small portions of these exciting tales, which was another incentive to learn the language. Other entertainments were usually at somebody else's expense.

The most unfortunate episode, which makes me blush to this day, involved me in the role of ring-leader. One of the boys was keen on angling and had a quantity of very strong twine. This gave me my great idea. We waited till our chosen victim was asleep and stealthily cobbled up his sheets all round the edge like a sack. Although there were, I seem to recall, four boys doing the job it still seemed to take a very long time. When the work was complete a jug of icy water, which had not yet had the chance to freeze, was poured on the unfortunate lad who woke up to a double shock. He struggled to get out of his cold, wet envelope and did a sort of dance like a pantomime ghost causing great entertainment and delight. Boys from the neighbouring dorm came in to see what was going on, unfortunately so did the housemaster.

I cannot remember my punishment: I am sure it was inadequate.

Lucinda Green (Lucinda Prior-Palmer).
Three-day Event Rider. World Champion, 1982. Five times winner of Badminton, twice at Burghley.

Never very brave about having injections from the doctor, as a child I was even worse. At about the age of six my final diphtheria jab was due

218

and because the last one had left me wailing for the best part of the following night, no one told me when the doctor was due to turn up and give me the ultimate dose.

One dreadful afternoon I saw his car parked outside the front door at the same time as I heard my father calling around the garden for me. I ran to the cow-shed and hid. My father saw me and so I made a bee-line for the boiler room in the house and locked myself in – to little avail, as the spare key was soon found and I could hear it turning in the lock from the far side of the door. I scrambled up to above head-height and jumped out of the tiny little window. Back into the house, I raced up the stairs and shut myself in the bathroom, where there was no key, but a bolt on *my* side. One by one, Father, Mother and Nanny came to try and talk me out. By then I was a sobbing mess, but determined not to surrender my backside to that needle.

What seemed like an age later, the doctor's car was heard to drive away. I let myself out in utter disgrace, but not before my father's head had appeared at the top of a 25' ladder in the bathroom window. He was angry.

I don't think I have ever finished my course of diphtheria injections.

The Hon. Terence Prittie, M.B.E.
Author, journalist and broadcaster.

One would like to think one never did anything bad. But –

At the age of five, I was small but strong. My father took a poor view of me, so when a number of guests came in for a drink, it was my elder brother who was brought in and paraded in front of them. Duly, I was sent for. My father lay in wait behind the door and squirted me in the face with a soda-siphon.

Well-meant, no doubt, but I howled and all the guests were on my side. My father said "All right. He can take a whang at my chin". He crouched and proffered it, and I gave it all I had got. He stood up, and slowly extracted a tooth.

Everyone but myself laughed. It was an unfilial act.

Dr. Magnus Pyke, O.B.E., C.Chem., F.R.C.S., F.Inst.Biol., F.I.F.S.T., F.R.S.E.
Research scientist, writer, broadcaster and lately Secretary, British Association for the Advancement of Science.

There may be people who retain vividly into their old age memories of their childhood and the naughty things they did then. I am not one of these. I remember the various phases of my childhood quite well. For instance, I recall being pushed around London W2 in one of those old-fashioned prams with my younger sister at the other end. It was raining and, both parts of the hood being up, we were enclosed in a rather dark but cosy travelling capsule. Suddenly, the pram, in negotiating a rather high curb, keeled over on to its side and my baby sister and I were abruptly muddled up together. The year must have been about 1912, so that this mild adventure has been embedded in my memory for seventy years. And since it does not involve naughtiness, it is not properly eligible for this book. In the main, I suppose, my childhood was uneventful and my behaviour, for the most part, innocuous.

Nor am I really justified in recalling the occasion when I was about ten and had insisted that I could replace a pane of glass in a door half way up the stairs leading to a curious little platform at the back of our house called 'the leads'. I obtained the glass and the putty but the job was more difficult than I had anticipated. There came the call to tea; I ignored it. The light of early evening began to fail; I worked on. It grew dark; I brought out a desk lamp on a long flex and stood it on a stool. Still I laboured. At last the job was done. I stepped back to admire my handiwork. The lamp tottered, overbalanced and quite slowly fell and broke the pane of glass I had just so laboriously installed. But no, that was not naughtiness; clumsiness perhaps, but not naughtiness. What an intolerably earnest-minded child I must have been.

Here, then, is my last try. The year is 1932, fifty years ago. I am now a student, studying for a degree in agricultural chemistry at McGill University in Canada. To achieve this, a student was required to clamber from his freshman year to his sophomore year, then to the status of junior and finally to his, or her, senior year. At each stage, it was necessary to pass a number of obligatory subjects such as, in my case, chemistry, as well as a number of optional ones. Among the latter, I selected apiculture, that is to say, beekeeping. Why, you may ask, did I choose beekeeping, when I am not fond of bees and bees, sighting me some distance away doing them no harm, will fly straight across to sting me? The answer is that I had obtained inside information that the instructor in apiculture was an enthusiast, constantly discouraged by the sparsity of those who opted for his subject, who was known always to pass anyone who was prepared to enrol with him. Looking back on the incident over half a century, I still think it was naughty of me – prudent, perhaps, but naughty – to take advantage of him in this way. And, please don't ask me to hive your swarm; I know as little about bees now as I knew then.

Natasha Pyne.
Actress, stage and screen.

When I was eight years old, I had my appendix out. In those days it meant about ten days' stay in hospital. I was in a children's ward and in the next bed to mine was a boy of about the same age as myself, who had one arm in plaster and a leg in traction and so was completely bed-bound.

One night, about 11pm, he was in great need to spend a penny. At the time, the nurse must have had the same problem, as she was nowhere to be seen, so I crawled out of bed. (By this time I was a bit bent over, recovering from my operation, so I was rather shuffly!) I went to the cupboard where the portable toilet bottles were kept!

I gave my needy friend the object, then popped off to dig out a sweet from my locker. I then returned to collect the 'bottle' from the next bed, took it, slipped, knocked his traction set-up, the bottle flew out of my hands, contents spilt all over the young lad, whilst I slid on my bottom across the floor into the middle of the ward.

As I ground to a halt my 'friend' was howling, I was crying and most of the other inmates had woken up and were joining in!

The nurse ran in, saw what had happened to the traction, and I sobbed out what I had done. Instead of helping, I'd completely soaked my neighbour, his bed had to be changed and his traction re-arranged.

After a good telling-off, a few days later we were all laughing about it a great deal, even my much abused next-door mate who definitely came off worst!

We parted good friends, but it didn't cure me of being a bit too eager to mind other people's business!

The Right Rev. Derek Rawcliffe.
Bishop of Glasgow and Galloway.

I have always had a weakness for fiddling with things to see what will happen when you press this or pull that. This has led to various embarrassing incidents, of which I relate two.

Years ago, when I was on leave in England from the South Pacific, I visited a retired bishop who had been kind to me when I was preparing to go abroad as a missionary. He went off to the kitchen to make some tea and I was left in his sitting room. He had an electric clock, whose spindle in the middle of the face was spinning at an enormous rate. Having never seen one of these before, I wondered what would happen if I touched the spinning spindle. I resisted the temptation to touch it for some time, but still my host had not returned and finally my hand reached out and touched the spinning piece of metal. It stopped spinning and would not start again. What could I do to restart it? Nothing worked, and the tea came. I said nothing, my host didn't notice that the clock had stopped, and eventually I went home.

Then conscience began to work. Had I messed the clock up? Would my friend be at some expense to have it put right? I went to an electrical dealer to get an answer, but he could tell me nothing certain. Finally I realised that there was nothing for it but to write a very embarrassing letter and confess what I had done.

A very understanding reply came a few days later, and the news that the clock had picked up on its own twelve hours later when the time had come round to the same hour again.

The other incident I relate happened only a few years ago, when some friends in London offered their house for my wife and me to stay in. They were going to be away for the first night, and my wife too was joining me there the next day, so I was alone there for one night. I collected the key from the neighbour across the street and settled down there. In the morning I had a bath. Hanging down from the ceiling beside the bath was a cord with a push button. What was it? A light switch? Or what? I couldn't resist pressing it to find out. Immediately one of the large electric bells in the kitchen started to ring loudly. I tried pressing the button again (or thought I had) but nothing happened. What could I do? I had to stop that bell or the neighbours might call the police, and would they believe that I was in the house legitimately?

I went down to the kitchen as quickly as I could and tried there to stop the bell. Perched on top of table and chair I tried to disconnect the thing, but no good. It just went on and on. I held the clapper away from the bell for a bit of silence while I thought. Then I had to let go and the bell went on as loudly as ever. What could I do? Finally I stuffed a handkerchief between the clapper and the bell and got it firmly wedged and left it.

It was still there later in the day when I collected my wife and when our friends returned home. I had once again to do the embarrassing thing and tell them of my curiosity over the push-button and my inability to stop the bell. They told me all I had to do was to push the button a second time. I said I had tried that – but obviously I hadn't tried hard enough, for when I pushed it this time the bell – with handkerchief now removed – stopped at once.

I don't suppose I shall learn from incidents like that, but curiosity will get the better of me again and lead to further embarrassing incidents.

Anthony Read.
Author and screenwriter.

In the wartime winter of 1944, my mother and I spent Christmas with my Aunt Rita and cousin Bev. In spite of rationing and shortages, we had all managed to save enough special things to make Christmas enjoyable, sometimes at considerable sacrifice.

On Christmas morning, Bev and I inevitably awoke early. We examined and compared presents, delighted that Father Christmas had not forgotten us. Then we turned to our mothers' presents. Among them we found a pot marked 'vanishing cream', but to our great disappointment found it did not work. No matter how much of the stuff we rubbed into our hands and faces, we remained solidly and obviously visible. Not even a finger disappeared. When the cream was all gone, we turned to other things.

Being thoughtful little boys, we decided to take our mothers a cup of tea when it was late enough to wake them. We managed it very well, and were received with cries of delight when we appeared in the bedroom with the tray.

"That's very good," Aunt Rita praised us. "Now there's just one other thing you can do. As it's Christmas, we have something special for our early morning tea. On the mantelpiece downstairs you'll find a little bottle . . ."

"Oh, no," we broke in quickly. "There's no little bottle there."

"Yes, yes," she persisted. "A little brown bottle. I've been saving it specially for today. Just go and bring it please."

We swayed gently, and tried to look innocent.

"What little bottle?" we asked – and spoiled the impression completely by hiccuping loudly.

It's a pity the vanishing cream didn't work. It would have been very useful during the next few minutes. Oddly enough, since then I've never been able to understand the pleasure of lacing a cup of tea with whisky, even on Christmas morning . . .

Ian Richardson.
Actor.

Someone once remarked that a weed is only a flower in the wrong place, and my major misdeed bore much the same character. It was, in fact, a deed of disinterested virtue.

It was at the time of the birth of my sister, and I was about four years old. I was considerably in the dark as to what was about to happen (the facts of life were not deemed to be subjects of discussion in Scottish homes of the period) but I had managed to glean that by some magical process there was going to be a baby arriving. I had looked hopefully out of the door and along the street for some time in the hopes of seeing it

arrive. I had heard someone mention the word 'delivery', so I supposed it would come in a van, but there was only the milkman and the coalman and after a while I gave up loitering round the door and went inside. My mother didn't seem to be about.

There was, however, considerable activity upstairs. I was almost knocked over by one of our neighbours, a large and comfortable woman who normally moved with a dropsical shuffle, who came hurtling down the stairs in the direction of the kitchen from which issued a considerable amount of steam.

My father appeared at the door of the living room, and hovered uncertainly at the door. He looked funny. Uncomfortable. After a minute or two he went back in again as if he didn't know why he had come out. I followed him in. "Is the baby coming?" I asked. He looked at me as if he had forgotten who I was and didn't know if it was worth the effort to try and remember. "I didn't see the van," I continued, "Maybe, as babies aren't very big, it'll come on a bicycle." My father gave a kind of strangled gurgle and made for the door again. "I'm going for a walk," he said. I knew Dad's walks. They usually ended at a pub, and I got left outside with a packet of crisps, so I volunteered my company, but he didn't seem too keen. "You just stay here", he said, "haud your whisht and be helpful." I held my whisht and he was gone. Then I sat down and thought about being helpful. I was often asked to be helpful, but usually the method of my helpfulness was indicated. "Ian, you be helpful and carry the messages." "Ian, you be helpful and dry the dishes." "Ian, you be helpful and run round to Grannie's . . ." I had been given no pointer this time.

I ran through all the things I was usually asked to do, but none of them seemed to be required at the moment. I tried to think of anything I had heard my mother say she wanted done, and after a few minutes of deep concentration it came to me like divine revelation. I leapt to my feet and went and got a brush. It wasn't quite the right kind, but it would have to do. I went into the living room and got busy.

It was hard work, and I didn't seem to have got the technique quite right. After a bit, I went and got a bucket of water.

Time passes quickly when one is absorbed, and I think absorbed is probably the right word for it. The room was also rather absorbed. I had just about finished when the door opened and my father appeared at the door. An indescribable expression came over his face; a mixture of pain and disbelief, as of one who has just swallowed a whole pickled egg by mistake. He was, perhaps fortunately, speechless. He just gazed. The carpet had got a bit wet when I tried to remove some of the far-flung side-effects of my labour and its cheerful pattern now resembled the great Grimpen Mire; the papered walls were liberally decorated with sable handprints; the three-piece suite was decidedly piebald, and the air was thick with an acrid smell and many floating particles. In the middle of all this he saw a totally black child, smiling angelically through his once blond fringe. "Has the baby come?" I said. He didn't answer, but there was a wail from upstairs which sounded promising. "Look," I said, proudly, but I hope with a touch of humility, "I've swept the chimney!"

Sir Ralph Richardson.
Actor.

"You are a very naughty boy", my two aunts told me when, aged nine, I stood on the platform of Newcastle station. "You should not have brought that mouse, your grandmother will never allow it."

"In that case," I replied, "I shall take the next train back to Brighton."

My grandmother had a big house in Newcastle and had summoned me from Brighton to visit her. We had never met, my parents had separated and I was a far away offspring. I was sent on the journey alone, but took my mouse with me for company. In doubt, my aunts, who had been sent to meet me, conveyed me to the house. My grandmother was considered to be very strong willed; she was the daughter of Elizabeth Fry, who had defied prison governors in her time. When we met she was charming to me and was delighted to see my mouse. I spent a happy week with her.

She died ten years later, and in her will she remembered me with a legacy of five hundred pounds. Then I thought I was a millionaire and lived happily ever after.

Lady Ryder of Warsaw, C.M.G., O.B.E.
Social worker and founder, The Sue Ryder Foundation.

I remember being a weekly boarder at my first school. One day, on hearing that parents of would-be pupils were to be shown around, I behaved very mischievously and, with another girl, stuffed several pillowcases and laid these out on one of the four beds in our room. The 'body' we then covered with a sheet on which we placed flowers and a prayer book. There was a loud collective gasp as the mistress opened the door and the visitors saw the touching scene before them. I was hiding behind the door in the loo opposite. Naturally, and properly, I was later sent for and received a severe warning. We were both made to pay from one to threepence from our pocket money for each article used to stuff the 'body', and this meant borrowing. It took us two terms – or more – to pay our fines!

Sir Donald Sargent, K.B.E., C.B.
Retired Senior Civil Servant.
Chairman, Civil Service Retirement Fellowship, 1968–1974.

When I was at Cambridge a certain lecturer always lectured at the unpopular hour of 9 a.m. Not surprisingly, he was much afflicted by late-comers. One morning he lost his patience and expostulated, "It really is too bad. Every morning I get here punctually at nine, having gone without my breakfast, if necessary, to do it and people drift in at five past, ten past and a quarter past nine. It isn't good enough. I expect you to do something about it."

Something was done; next morning he arrived to find on his desk, bacon and eggs and a pot of coffee, with appropriate cutlery.

Lord Seebohm.
President of Age Concern.
Chairman, Barclays Bank International, 1965–1972.

In 1921, when I was at the Dragon School, I had an urge to knit myself a scarf. In order to collect enough wool I gradually unpicked the binding on the ends of the blankets in our dormitory until I had a sizeable ball of red wool. With the help of two penholders, I had completed about 18 inches when I foolishly left it under my pillow. Most of my knitting was done at night in the light summer evenings. On returning after breakfast, my life's work had gone!

I forgot all about it until Speech Day. There must have been two hundred people at the prize-giving presided over by the Headmaster, 'Hum' Lynam, assisted by a Bishop. After all the normal prizes had been presented 'Hum' said, "And now we have a very special prize for knitting which is awarded to Frederic Seebohm if he will come up and collect it." I was duly presented with my unfinished scarf accompanied by the jeers of the crowd and my face was as red as the wool. However, I comforted myself by knowing that the alternative would have been six of the best from 'Tortoise', the Housemaster who had a wicked wrist with a cane!

Michael Segal.
Actor, stage and screen.

I have always been one for a gag – for a laugh – and comedy business.

My older brother was playing Richard III. I was still at school and they needed to cast a messenger so I auditioned for the part. Being very nervous, my first attempt was rather quiet so I heard whispers of "He's not loud enough – he won't be heard." So I said, "Can I have another go?" So next time I really shouted it aloud. I got the part. They forgot to tell me that the part involved being slapped round the face by Richard III – my brother.

I went home full of enthusiasm and thought, "What can I really make of this part?" Then it came to me quite clearly.

I got some dried peas and at rehearsal I put them in my mouth and of course this all required quite a technique, to speak the lines with my mouth full. I rushed on and in a garbled fashion pronounced the words,

"My lord, the army of the Duke of Buckingham . . ." At this King Richard says "Out oh you owls, nothing but songs of death. Take *that*, until thou bringst me better news." Whereupon he slapped me across the face. I spat out the peas. It sounded and looked as though he had knocked out all my teeth. Everybody fell about, including poor Richard III. There wasn't much rehearsal that night!

Mark Shivas.
Film and T.V. producer.

Most of us came to school by bus or bike, but one of our number had been given a Morris Minor by his dad. I think the dad could have been an estate agent: certainly lots of us Whitgift boys become estate agents and stockbrokers in their fathers' footsteps.

This little grey car was a great liberation for us all and it not only took us to places outside London we'd never been to before, but it allowed us extra games within the Croydon area.

One of the biggest movie palaces in the country, the Davis Theatre, was a mile down the road from our school. In those days, a line of people outside a cinema was a common sight. Our invention no doubt came from a residual cinematic memory. The Morris Minor would roar up to the front of the Davis, and, as far as we could contrive, scream to a halt in front of an astonished crowd. Leaving the engine running, two of us would leap out in heavy raincoats with menacing looks on our faces and run across to the third friend who had been planted in the middle of the queue. He would be dragged away by the armpits, his heels dragging on the pavements. As he shouted for help, he was bundled into the car. The car would then roar away down the road. The kick was to see how many, or how few, of the cinema-goers started towards us in a feeble effort to stop this daylight kidnap. At the time, it was as close to making our own movies as we could get.

The Rev. Canon Dr. Stephen S. Smalley.
The Precentor of Coventry Cathedral.

An afternoon towards the end of March 1937. Home from the last day
of my Prep. school term, I was snugly ensconced in the bathroom,
scouring with the absorption of some diminutive Pilate or Lady Macbeth
the grimy accretions of eleven weeks' education from my six-year-old
hands. Suddenly an incandescent volcano erupted through the door,
scattering broadcast the animal sculptures in delicate grey lather with
which I had painstakingly adorned the edges of the washbasin. It was my
mother, wildly brandishing my opened school report. She was almost
incoherent with rage.

"What have you been doing? What have you been up to? How could
you? How dare you? Wait till your father sees this!"

"What's the matter, Mummy?" I faltered, from a leaden stomach.
"What does it say?"

"Look!", she spluttered, puce in the face. "Just *look* at this!" With
difficulty, I followed the direction of her shaking forefinger, to read the
damning indictment:

"*Conduct*: Stephen is given to losing his temper."

Harold Snoad.
Producer and director, BBC Television.

In 1941 at the age of seven I was taken by my parents to the London
Palladium as a special treat. It was a variety show consisting of the usual
varied acts.

One particular act was very impressive and involved a swarthy-looking
Spaniard doing various dare-devil
antics on a high wire. As always on
these occasions he had kept the
most spectacular trick to last.
This consisted of walking slowly
across the high wire with his
head held right back holding
a dagger in his mouth by the
handle. On the tip of the

dagger was balanced the tip of a long heavy sword which he had already demonstrated was both very sharp and pointed.

The angle of his head during this trick was such that one false move would have meant that the sword would have come crashing down and embedded itself in the man's wind pipe.

The packed Palladium had fallen into total silence apart from a roll on the snare drum as he made his precarious way painfully slowly along the thin wire.

He was now at the centre and even the drum roll had stopped as he stood first on one shaking leg and then the other before *kneeling* on the wire. You could have heard a pin drop as the hair on the napes of three thousand necks stood up.

I chose this moment to say in an extremely loud voice heard by virtually everyone in the theatre, "If the Germans came now would they stop him doing that?"

Godfrey Talbot, M.V.O., O.B.E.
Author, broadcaster, B.B.C. commentator accredited to Buckingham Palace.

I was not a demonstrative child but I remember being fascinated – and puzzled – by words and the use which people made of them in public. Maybe that was some foundation for an adult career in the business of speaking and writing. I don't know. What I do know is that, as a small boy in a devoted but disciplined Yorkshire Nonconformist family, I very occasionally burst out from the encompassing Northern brusqueness and what father called the 'companionable silence' of our old-fashioned Sabbaths.

Thus, a friend and I stole into our then-empty Chapel, after Sunday School next door, to play at 'having a service'. He sat in a pew, whilst I mounted the pulpit. From up there I began delivering a mock-sermon, whose hero was a chap called Abraham Aniseed (which was the best we'd made of our local preacher's frequent reference to 'Abram and his seed, forever').

But the chapel wasn't *quite* empty. The caretaker was about – as I suddenly found when he raced up the pulpit stairs and boxed my sacrilegious ears. I got a second walloping at home, later, after our Minister had asked why the white ledges of his pulpit had dark streaks all over them.

They were *my* streaks, from hands difficult to clean. For I had done a more dreadful deed the day before. Workmen had been asphalting the road near our house, and I pinched some lumps of still-malleable bitumen which they had been boiling. 'Gas-tar', we called it. It was nice for modelling, almost as good as Plasticine, though it did make your paws mucky.

Anyhow, I had the idea to fashion some 'pretend Pomfret-cakes' (Pontefract Cakes were round, flat jujubes of jet-black colour, nice and very chewy liquorice lozenges – favourite children's sweets). I made six, most carefully, and put them in a chocolate box. To complete the joke, I offered one to the little girl next door, who gladly popped the thing into her mouth and began to bite and suck. Before I had time to tell her it was pure gas-tar, the damage was done and the child was spitting ebony down her pinafore.

Roused by the girl's screams as she tried to claw the nauseous black glue from teeth and gums, the mother came tearing out to see what was the matter. She felled *me* with not only a look but with the back of her hand, and, with the madly incongruous shout of "You know she only likes wine gums!", she bore her offspring off – first to the kitchen sink and then to the doctor's. I was in disgrace abounding.

The Viscount Thurso, J.P.
Farmer; (90 cows and 2 bulls).

When I was about 5 years old, Lloyd George came to tea and I was duly brought in by Nanny to meet the famous man. As he patted me on the head he asked, "Well, my little man, and what are you going to be when you grow up?"

"I am going to be a farmer", I replied.

"Ah," said the Liberal leader, pricking up his ears, "and what sort of a farm are you going to have?"

I looked him in the eye and solemnly replied, "I am going to have 19 bulls and 1 cow."

Even Lloyd George found this a bit hard to comment on.

Richard Todd.
Actor.

On my first day at my Prep School, for some reason or other I arrived late, and was told to go off at once and announce myself to the form mistress, Miss Copleston.

I duly went off and knocked at the door indicated, without the vaguest idea what to do next. At seven years of age I was not too well-practiced in such things.

I was bidden to enter and found myself confronted by a room full of boys already at their desks.

Quaking with uncertainty I faced the mistress and blurted out the first thing that came to my head: "Please, Miss Cobblestones, I'm Todd." It says much for the disciplined relationship that she had already established with her little charges that there was not even a snigger from the others, nor did she seem to have noticed my blunder. She simply said, "Yes, I know. We were expecting you," and led me to my desk.

J. C. Trewin, O.B.E., F.R.S.L., M.A.(Hon.).
Writer, threatre critic and historian, literary editor, The Observer, 1943–48.

The road I took to school when I was twelve was the steepest hill in the district. When staying with my aunt near its top, I would run down it daily at a pace that I am sure could have outmatched Sebastian Coe. One morning, being very late indeed, I scorched down the pavement so fast that I probably left a red-hot trail. Just at the bottom a younger boy whom I hardly knew, but who was in the Prep, was emerging from the door of his house. Cannoning into him, I knocked him flat. The last I saw was a body stretched out on the pavement. I realised then that the victim must be dead. Should I give myself up or get to school in time? I chose to get to school, and that was the beginning of three months or so during which I expected the police at any moment. I did not dare to inquire at the Prep. I did not look at a paper. I would go home by wildly circuitous routes and back lanes, taking as long as half an hour to cover what normally would be a few minutes' walk. For a while I contemplated a false beard or moustache but bravely put the idea aside. If I were seized, that would be that. Days and weeks passed; remarkably the police did not arrive; with my parents I had by now moved to another address.

Though in the conscience-laden midnights I was apt to see myself as a murderer, the first horror very gradually wore off. About a dozen years later, I suppose, I happened to meet the corpse in the middle of the town. "Ages since we've met," it said cheerfully. "Are you all right?" I asked, still incredulous. "Never been better," it said. Well . . . after more than sixty years, I wonder sometimes what really happened.

Charles Vance.
Actor, director, theatrical producer and publisher.

I suppose I was about 12; certainly it was at that insufferable age when one's arrogance about one's abilities was not to be questioned . . . and certainly not by a mere games master!

It was in the early weeks of my second summer term at boarding school and having made the under-15 rugby team the previous two terms, as far as I was concerned it was a matter of formality that I would be selected for the equivalent cricket team.

It was less a love of the sport for its own sake than the prospect of playing away every other weekend and so escape from 'prison' that motivated my desperate concern to be selected.

On Thursday the team list went up on the school board . . . and I was not on it. I brooded all night in the dorm and on Friday formulated my plans to avenge this gross slight on my unquestioned talents. By Friday night I'd worked it out. Each week, on Saturday morning during prep, the cricket bags for the travelling team were packed by matron and the games master and left in the Senior Common Room to be picked up by the team before boarding the school bus to travel to the school where the match would be played.

I contrived, God knoweth how, to get out of prep an hour early and, having previously laid my plans, collected eleven pairs of rugger shorts from the sports locker and substituted them for the eleven pairs of white cricket flannels which matron had packed. These were hidden in a locker and I disappeared from view. The cricket team would now travel to play an important away match without long trousers and only rugger shorts to cover their embarrassment!

Revenge is sweet and I relished the coming afternoon when I would think on my form colleagues covered in shame . . . how nasty little boys

234

can be!

My sweet revenge was short lived! Just before noon I was summoned to the form master's study to say that somebody minor (the name now thankfully eludes me) had been stricken with one of those perpetual ailments of schoolboys and that I was now on the cricket team which was already boarding the bus. The bags had already been packed aboard; the rest of the team was awaiting me and so I was hoisted by my own petard.

Yes, that very afternoon I was obliged to play a cricket match against a leading public school wearing a white shirt and a pair of navy blue rugger shorts. I of course suffered more than the rest of the team; they at least were in ignorance of our forthcoming embarrassment. . . . I spent a long bus journey knowing what was coming.

Lord Wallace of Coslany, F.R.S.A., F.Inst.M., J.P., D.L., K.St.J.
Labour party spokesman and whip, House of Lords, since 1979.

When I was a choirboy at St James Church, Cheltenham, we had an initiation procedure for new boys which consisted of waylaying the victim after choir practice and pushing him down into the church coal hole.

One night we had a newcomer to 'welcome' and eventually a figure passed by in the dark. Accordingly, we dashed forward and pushed him down the coal hole. Unfortunately for us it turned out to be the Choirmaster, Dr Wingate, the organist and music teacher at Cheltenham College.

As a result of our mistake, we were docked our choir pay of 2/6d due normally every six months.

Doreen Wallace.
Novelist.

I was not much of a prankster at school; I think pranks come from boredom and I wasn't bored, though I had ten years of boarding school.

One thing I did in the holidays which misfired: I built a very good dam

in the beck which poured down the fellside and past our back door.
Came the winter rains and our kitchen floor was flooded: but it wasn't a
joke, it was a lesson in basic engineering.

At school I parodied a verse of Omar and left it on the piano of an
over-sized music teacher:

"Ah love, could thou and I with fat conspire
To grasp this sorry mound of flesh entire,
Would we not chop off fifty pounds, and then
Re-mould it nearer to the heart's desire?"

That wasn't funny either, it was nasty and as
it deserved, no notice was taken of it.

I was an only child – my brothers were a
dog, a lame drake and a billy-goat which
regularly knocked me down; my sister was
a ferret which sat round my neck
like a fur collar. Life was
far too interesting to need
pepping-up with jokery. It
is only now, in my
extreme old age, that I
am bored.

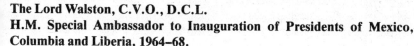

The Lord Walston, C.V.O., D.C.L.
**H.M. Special Ambassador to Inauguration of Presidents of Mexico,
Columbia and Liberia, 1964–68.**

I was an enormously shy boy and for all my childhood embarrassment
was more or less permanent. One occasion stands out.

As a very new boy at school I was asked to tea by the headmaster's
wife. There were a few other boys including some senior ones, and a
smattering of grownup guests. I sat on the edge of a spindley chair
feeling acutely uncomfortable. My discomfort was greatly increased
when one of the stretchers on the chair holding the legs firm broke, and
the chair started to wobble dangerously. I was far too shy to point this
out so I sat for the rest of tea holding the legs together with one hand and
nibbling my sandwich with the other.

Some thirty years later I remembered the occasion. I was travelling in Bolivia and had to spend the night in a remote provincial town 10,000 feet up in the Andes. There was a solitary Englishman and his wife living there and he kindly asked me out to his house to spend the evening. For me it was a pleasant occasion and for him a very special one since he had not seen a fellow countryman for many years. He produced a bottle of the local alcohol, and kept on replenishing my glass as well as his. At that time I did not realise that alcohol goes to one's head far more rapidly at high altitudes: and after my fourth or fifth drink I realised I was very drunk. At that moment his wife came in to announce supper. I was able to stagger into the dining room, but once more had to eat with only one hand while I clung on the the chair with the other one to stop myself falling off. After gulping down large chunks of bread and a bowl of hot soup my balance slightly returned, and I was able to use both hands. But I was just as acutely embarrassed then as I had been at the school tea party.

Lord Whaddon.
Member, Council of Management, COSIRA, Director, Cambridge Chemical Company.

At six years of age I was fascinated by steam engines. My mind was completely absorbed thinking of the operation of the valves as I changed into pyjamas and climbed into bed. I was still concentrating on the question as I drifted off to sleep. It was then that my mother burst into the bedroom to point out that it was 1.30 in the afternoon and I was due at school in half an hour!

David Wickes.
Independent film producer and director.

It was a wet Saturday in Leamington Spa. I was a spotty boy of fourteen, and my best friend Michael had just rushed round to my house with dreadful news. The beautiful 18-year-old girl with whom both of us were secretly and desperately in love was getting married that very afternoon — to a decrepit old man of twenty-three.

Our depression knew no depths. How could this stunning creature throw herself away when, in just a few years, one of *us* would be available?

It made no sense. After a couple of swigs from my father's brandy bottle, we manfully resolved to attend the wedding. In person.

Leaning our bikes on the church railings, we crept unsteadily up into the gallery, just in time to see our dream girl float away for ever in a shimmer of white lace. We hid until the church was safely empty, then tiptoed miserably down the stairs toward the great doors. They were locked! We pounded and yelled, but it was no use. Everyone had gone home. So there we stood – two lovelorn boys with squeaky voices in a gothic church.

We might have found some way out if Michael hadn't chosen that moment to produce the rest of my father's brandy. Soon we were fantasising about knights of old being locked in churches to meditate before a battle. 'Vigil' my friend called it. In half an hour, we were lying full length on the pews, watching in horror as the rafters spun and lurched crazily above us. Then everything went blank.

It was dark when I woke up, and it felt as if someone had parked a truck on my head. Michael lay on the floor of the church, gulping air like a stranded goldfish, while I stumbled around for what seemed like a fortnight, looking for the vestry toilet in the blackness. By dawn, we were shivering side by side on the altar steps, waiting for some avenging angel to deliver the coup de grace.

It was the verger who delivered us, by unlocking the doors for early communion. "Hey!" he bellowed as we staggered past him into the blinding sunlight, "What were you two doing in the church?" All I could manage was one word. "Vigil," I croaked. Then I fell off my bike.

I forget how we were punished. It didn't seem to matter much, even at the time. After all, first love is painful enough on its own. But first hangovers are far, far worse.

Lord Wolfenden, C.B.E.
Oxford and England hockey player. Headmaster Uppingham School, 1934–44. Headmaster Shrewsbury School, 1944–50. Vice-Chancellor, Reading University, 1950–63. Director and Principal Librarian, British Museum, 1969–73.

When I was sixteen I was deeply in love with the middle one of my Headmaster's three daughters. So at the right time of the year I audaciously composed a Valentine for her. The problem was how to get it delivered with appropriate secrecy.

Then I had an idea. The fives-courts were very near to the Headmaster's house. At the open end of the courts there was a low wall over which spectators leaned and on which we parked our coats before we played. The girls often came and watched, especially when their father was playing. I could easily slip the precious missive into my jacket pocket, and surely I could then find some way of accidentally getting it into her hand only a few inches away without her knowing whence it came.

But the plan went wrong. The girls duly came to watch. Their father and I and the other two players duly folded our jackets and hitched them over the wall. At the end of the game I nonchalantly recovered my jacket, put my hand in the pocket – and there was nothing there. Agony, rage and despair. It must have slipped out somehow in the folding process.

Worse was to come. The Headmaster was local President of the PUGPUPs (Pick Up Glass, Pick Up Paper) fanatically devoted to keeping streets and open places tidy. Walking back to his house he saw fluttering across the lawn a piece of paper, which he triumphantly pursued, picked up and read.

What he said to his daughter I never knew. What he said to me I shall never forget. Summoned to his study next morning, heart beating fast, I was told to sit down. "This is your handwriting, isn't it?" Yes, I was pretty sure it was. "Now look here, old chap, two things. First, if you must carry confidential documents about with you, see that you keep them safe in your pocket and don't leave them blowing about on my

239

lawn. Secondly, you can't expect your headmaster to act as your messenger boy. Here you are, take it and get it to her yourself." Legitimised by my headmaster's command, I secretively mounted the impressive front steps of his house and popped the thing, discreetly veiled in an envelope addressed to his middle daughter, into the letter-box.

We have been very happily married for more than fifty years.

Baroness Wootton of Abinger, C.H.
Deputy Speaker, House of Lords, 1968. Hon. Fellow, Girton College, Cambridge and Bedford College, London. Hon. Doctor of 11 British Universities and Columbia University, N.Y.

I remember two incidents from my childhood. When asked (age about ten) what I should do when grown up, my reply was, "I shall be an organising female with a briefcase". I am.

I had two older brothers, but no sisters. I constantly played them off against one another.

We had a nanny whom I adored (I did not get on with my mother); but periodically, if I had done anything wrong, she would become totally unapproachable for a day or two, and I felt that this was the end of the world. Well do I remember the day that I said to myself, "This won't last for ever," which of course it didn't. That discovery was a milestone on the road to maturity.

Alexander Young.
Tenor of international repute.

I was fortunate enough to sing for Sir Thomas Beecham on a number of occasions. Anyone who worked with him was almost bound to experience some example of his dry humour.

I had been engaged to sing Mozart's Requiem with Sir Thomas at the Royal Festival Hall, and he had decided to precede this with a short Freemasons Cantata by the same composer, which is rarely heard. There had been some trouble about obtaining the music, because at the time the work was out of print, so that neither vocal scores, nor orchestral parts were obtainable. Sir Thomas possessed two of his own full scores, and the baritone and myself copied out our parts from one of these. The librarian of the Royal Philharmonic Orchestra, a Mr Brownfoot, had engaged a team of music copyists to copy out the orchestral parts, and on the morning of the concert, they were still employed in this task.

So it was, on this particular morning, Sir Thomas shuffled into the concert hall, looking as though he was not in the best of moods. A sharp rap of his baton on the desk, and the orchestra started off, only to be stopped two or three bars later. "What's this piffling noise?" shouted Sir Thomas. "Please Sir Thomas," said Mr Brownfoot, who was standing at the back, "we are just finishing writing out the parts." There was a short pause, while Brownfoot rustled around the desks with more MS parts, and then we were off again, only to be brought to a stop after a few more bars. This time the complaint was slightly different — "Brownfoot, where's the trumpet part?" Another slight pause followed, while Brownfoot edged his way through the orchestra to the foot of Beecham's rostrum, and rather quietly, in a voice redolent of pained surprise he replied:

"Please Sir Thomas it isn't scored for trumpet," to which the never-to-be-outdone baronet retorted: "Well, damn well go and write a part!"

With the now-familiar twinkle in the eye, off we went again and both rehearsal and concert went with the customary Beecham swing!